# Haynes
# Restoration Manual

# MG Midget & Austin-Healey Sprite

Lindsay Porter

First published by G. T. Foulis, 1984
Reprinted 1985, 1986, 1987, 1989,
1990, 1992 & 1993
Second (revised and expanded
edition) 1995
Reprinted (with new cover and
minor text amendments) by Haynes
Publishing as *MG Midget & Austin-
Healey Sprite Restoration Manual*,
1998, 2000 (twice), 2002, 2004,
2007, 2009 and 2010

A catalogue record for this book is
available from the British Library

ISBN 978 1 85960 614 8

Library of Congress catalog card
No. 95-77385

Haynes Publishing,
Sparkford, Yeovil, Somerset
BA22 7JJ, UK

Tel: 01963 442030
Fax: 01963 440001
Int. tel: +44 1963 442030
Int. fax: +44 1963 440001
E-mail: sales@haynes.co.uk
Website: www.haynes.co.uk

Printed in the USA

**Jurisdictions which have strict
emission control laws may
consider any modification to a
vehicle to be an infringement of
those laws. You are advised to
check with the appropriate body or
authority whether your proposed
modification complies fully with
the law. The publishers accept no
liability in this regard.**

**While every effort is taken to
ensure the accuracy of the
information given in this book, no
liability can be accepted by the
author or publishers for any loss,
damage or injury caused by errors
in, or omissions from, the
information given.**

**Other Haynes Publishing titles of
interest to MG enthusiasts:**

*MGB Car Service and Repair
Manual* (0111)

*MG Midget & Austin-Healey Sprite
Car Service and Repair Manual*
(0265)

*MGB – Restoration Manual (2nd
Edition)* by Lindsay Porter (H607)

*MGB – The Illustrated History (2nd
Edition)* by Jonathan Wood &
Lionel Burrell (F948 now out of
print)

*Haynes Classic Makes Series:
MG: Britain's Favourite Sports Car
(2nd Edition)*
by Malcolm Green (H4129)

# Contents

# Foreword by Roche Bentley

Lindsay Porter's excellent MGB – A Guide to Purchase and D.I.Y. Restoration was the MG Owners' Club best seller in 1982/3 with over four thousand copies sold to Club members alone. Now the Club's Sprite and Midget members can consider undertaking repairs and restorations of their cars with expert help from this highly accomplished author.

Until recently, the Sprites and Midgets enjoyed the ownership of the young hearted who wished for economical open topped sports car motoring in a car relatively cheap and easy to maintain. Now, as the models become rarer, many of the owners have found that they cannot replace them with any other car

which can give so much pleasure for so little cost and that's why present day Sprite and Midget owners are so keen to maintain their cars in good condition for as long as possible. Anyone contemplating the purchase and maintenance of a Sprite or Midget should certainly read this book carefully and any owner wishing to restore a model to first class condition will find this book invaluable.

The MG Owners' Club, currently serving forty thousand members, has an extremely large following of Sprite and Midget owners. Our task in helping these members in maintaining their cars in good condition and at reasonable cost is greatly assisted by this book.

Roche Bentley
Club Secretary, MG Owners' Club,
Swavesey, Cambridge.

# Using this book

The layout of this book has been designed to be both attractive and easy to follow during practical work on your car. However, to obtain maximum benefit from the book, it is important to note the following points:

1) Apart from the introductory pages, this book is split into two parts: chapters 1 to 7 dealing with history, buying and practical procedures; appendices 1 to 9 providing supplementary information. Each chapter/ appendix may be sub-divided into sections and even sub-sections. Section headings are in italic type between horizontal lines and sub- section headings are similar, but without horizontal lines.

2) Photograph captions are an integral part of the text (except those in chapters 1 and 2) – therefore the photographs and their captions are arranged to "read" in exactly the same way as the normal text. In other words they run down each column and the columns run

from left to right of the page.

Each photograph caption carries an alpha-numerical identity, relating it to a specific section. The letters before the caption number are simply the initial letters of key words in the relevant section heading, whilst the caption number shows the position of the particular photograph in the section's picture sequence. Thus photograph/ caption "DR22" is the 22nd photograph in the section headed "Door Repairs".

3) Figures – illustrations which are not photographs – are numbered consecutively throughout the book. Figure captions do not form any part of the text. Therefore Figure 5 is simply the 5th figure in the book.

4) All references to the left or right of the vehicle are from the point of view of somebody standing behind the car looking forwards.

5) Because this book majors upon restoration, regular maintenance procedures and

normal mechanical repairs of all the car's components, are beyond its scope. It is therefore strongly recommended that the Haynes *MG Midget and A-H Sprite Owner's Workshop Manual* should be used as a companion volume.

6) We know it's a boring subject, especially when you really want to get on with a job – but your safety, through the use of correct workshop procedures, must ALWAYS be your foremost consideration. It is essential that you read, and UNDERSTAND, appendix 1 before undertaking any of the practical tasks detailed in this book.

7) Whilst great care is taken to ensure that the information in this book is as accurate as possible, the author, editor or publisher cannot accept any liability for loss, damage or injury caused by errors in, or omissions from, the information given.

# Introduction & Acknowledgements

It is highly ironic that, as this book is being written, exactly the same conditions exist as those in the mid-1950s which led to the introduction of the Austin-Healey 'Frogeye' Sprite. Then, there was no small, inexpensive sports car on the market, a gap which was spotted by the motoring industry baron Leonard Lord and filled with the aid of the Healey Company. Today, there is no comparable car around, and only the vaguest promises being made by Austin Rover, the descendants of the old British Motor Corporation, that one could, at some time in the future, be introduced.

There may not be any new Sprites or Midgets around, but surely the next best thing for the enthusiast would be to recreate one as good as new. And that's what this book is all about; it's a guide covering every stage in the purchase and restoration of a Midget or Sprite so that if the work is carried out properly, you should end up with something even better than a new car — a Midget or Sprite

with something of the restorer's own individuality built into it.

You'll be maintaining one of the dwindling numbers of the last of the real sports cars; the Abingdon MGs and the Healey Sprites. The fine traditions embodied in every one of them can, now, only be upheld by the restorer — which is why there is a chapter on the history and the heritage that lies behind the cars — and it is hoped that every owner, whether carrying out a minor repair or a full-blown rebuild, will remember to include in his 'tool kit' something of the proud spirit of Healey of Warwick where the cars were first designed and of M.G.'s Abingdon where all the Sprites and Midgets were built.

Once again, my wife Shan has been unstintingly generous in the time she has given in helping with the preparation of this book, in spite of her own writing commitments. Diane Hayton, too, put in a lot of work at short notice and produced some superbly typed copy. Dave Jones, Ray Walker and Mel Jarvis all carried out work on Sprites and

Midgets in my bodyshop, The Classic Restoration Centre, and were as conscientious and enthusiastic over preparing the shots for this book as they are about their work. James Thacker, Sprite and Midget racer, provided help and advice regarding tuning and a number of owners were generous with their time in allowing their cars to be photographed for this book and for the two *Super Profiles* that preceeded it. Thanks too, to Roche Bentley of the MGOC for his kind words of encouragement and for writing the foreword to this book.

John Williams, *Practical Classics* and *The Automobile* photographer, put in some sterling work in the darkroom and produced hundreds of super prints while Paul Skilleter, too, helped my own darkroom contributions. Paul also took some of the shots used in the 'Buying' section of this book.

Peter Osborne at SIP (Industrial Products) Ltd and also The Welding Centre of Glasgow have been extremely helpful in terms of technical advice and information and in their supply of the high quality equipment which has been used in the workshop side of the preparation of this book.

In the end, though, the greatest amount of help came from my friends Jed Watts and Grahame Sykes at Spridgebits. They have a personal as well as a vested interest in everything to do with Midgets and Sprites and it's perfectly true to say that what those two don't know about these cars isn't worth knowing. What is more, I know from the days when I was simply a customer of theirs that this friendly, helpful approach is part and parcel of their whole business attitude.

Once again, as I said upon completing the *MGB Guide to Purchase and Restoration*, one of the best things to come out of writing these books is that you make so many good friends! My grateful thanks are due, and gladly given, to them all.

# 1 Heritage

## From Whence They Came . . .

It is the marketing man's dream to catch, or invent a trend and then exploit it. Expendable items, ranging from pop-up toasters to politicians, receive the full treatment from the media people who try to create a personality, an individual appeal for their product and think nothing of spending millions to achieve it. Therefore how ironic it is that those objects and people with the greatest character have usually acquired this quality naturally.

One such character is the 'Spridget'. Originally conceived as a humble sports car costing little to produce, the car immediately established itself as a firm favourite with such a strong personality that it is still much easier to think of the 'Spridget', the Frogeye in particular, as a smiling, bright-eyed, fun-loving friend rather than as a mechanical object.

And yet there is no doubt that the creators of Midgets and Sprites never set out to style a car with these characteristics. The traditions from which the car was born included, in addition to the respected Austin and Morris background, the awesome sporting reputations of M.G. at Abingdon and even more influentially, Healey of Warwick. The car was designed to appeal to the person in the cockpit, not to the onlooker; successive generations of club level motor sport enthusiasts have proved the Spridget's dynamic qualities time and again on the circuit, whilst owners have always been able to hold their heads up with pride when comparing the handling and road manners of their cars with those of the prettier opposition.

The main credit for the creation of this combination of character with verve and light-heartedness with tenacious handling, must lie with the Healey concern, based at Warwick, just south of Birmingham. Donald Healey had built up a reputation for himself as one of those peculiarly British businessmen who run the show in an autocratic but inspiring way. He was born in 1898 in the village of Perranporth, Cornwall: a land of fishing, tin mines and winter mists. His father, however, had other interests and, well before the days of the Great War, the roar of his Panhard Levassor could be heard as it fought the steep gradients of the area. Donald's father's interest in cars sowed seeds in Donald for a life of things mechanical and, after leaving school, Donald Healey became an apprentice at the Sopwith Aviation Company. There, he learned to fly and during the war joined the Royal Flying Corps. After the end of hostilities, Donald Healey opened a small garage in his home town and in a short period of time began to combine his knowledge of motor cars with the sharply honed skills of the trained flyer by involving himself in motor sport. In less than a decade of working upwards through the ranks of rallying, Donald Healey reached the very pinnacle when, in 1931, he won the Monte Carlo Rally outright driving an impressive 4.5-litre Invicta: the first British driver to do so.

After more rallying, and a period of experimental work with Riley, Donald Healey joined the Triumph Motor Company where he was placed in charge of design and experimental work. He was able to campaign in motor sport although, of course, his choice of make was somewhat restricted!

By 1937, the year of his last Monte, Donald Healey had become Triumph's Technical Director and by 1939 he was General Manager. He later moved to Humber where he teamed up with two men who were to have an especially strong influence on the Healey cars to come: Ben Bowden would design the first bodies on to the back of sheets of wartime wallpaper, whilst 'Sammy' Sampietro designed the car's formidable and complex suspension arrangements.

By 1945, and after Triumph had turned down Healey's ideas for a new car, production of the first Healey car's chassis components began at the Westland Garage in Hereford. The Healey contacts at Riley were utilised and a Riley engine was procured and then the Triumph connection proved its worth when a former Triumph employee offered part of his concrete mixer factory at The Cape, Warwick, as a site for assembly. In the summer of 1945, 'production' of the first car was underway!

The car was an open tourer and was called the "Westland". It was rapidly followed by the production of a saloon version known as the "Elliot" (the name of the body manufacturers). Both models used Riley mechanical components throughout their production life and, because of their lightweight magnesium alloy bodies and slippery wind tunnel-created shapes, were both capable of well over the magic 'ton'.

Naturally, Healeys were rallied from the very earliest days. The marque's first event in 1948 was the famed Targa Florio, where an Elliot was driven, as in all the best stories,

by a private entrant, an aristocrat who had only taken delivery of the car a few days before the race. 98 cars began the race but after a punishing 600 miles around Sicily, only 30 cars remained, the Healey among them and finishing an heroic 13th overall and first in its class.

After that first Italian success story other pleasing results followed in the Mille Miglia, the Alpine Rally, at Spa and at Montlhery: all of them highly commendable achievements for what was basically a touring car. However, as the post-war months rolled by, a resurgence of interest in circuit racing became apparent although, unfortunately for Healey, the heavy-bodied Westlands and Elliots were not at all well suited to the track. The challenge of circuit racing *had* to be met by Donald Healey; not only was it in his nature to compete, but competition successes were vital to the reputation of his performance orientated cars. The answer came in the form of a car that was destined to become one of the great landmarks of motoring.

Whilst the first two Healeys had been attractive packages of performance and comfort, the Healey Silverstone was systematically developed as a car with a single function in life. The basic Healey chassis and mechanical layout were utilised, except that the engine was moved back 8 inches and the rear frame and petrol tank layout were modified. The body, open of course, was reduced to the bare, highly aerodynamic elements of a low slung centre fuselage (although the chassis forced the driver's position up into the slipstream) and cycle-type front and rear wings, exposing the highly expensive and strange looking trailing arm front suspension.

Before long the Silverstone, with its headlamps squinting out of the upright Healey radiator grille, became a familiar sight at tracks the world over. One of its first successes was, appropriately enough, at Silverstone where the team prize was snatched from under the noses of the new and formidable

Jaguar XK120s when one of the latter team's cars retired. In the same period, the Silverstone was campaigned with some success in the usual European major rallies while the redoubtable Briggs Cunningham shipped the first Silverstone across the Atlantic and with an enormous 5.5-litre Cadillac engine under the bonnet, scored successes at Palm Beach and Watkins Glen.

In December 1949, the Nash-Healey was born, in concept at least, when Donald Healey met quite by chance, George Mason, President of the Nash Kelvinator Corporation on the *Queen Elizabeth*. As a result of the meeting, the Healey chassis was fitted with a full-width body—which included various Americanisations in its styling—and was powered by a 3.8-litre Nash engine. Not only did this give an increase in power to 125bhp, and thus even more appeal to the sporting owner, but, more importantly, opened the door to the American market much further than anything Healey had known before. Just as important, it gave the Healeys (for by now the Healey sons, Geoffrey and Brian were being eased into the team) an important lesson: it taught them that co-ordination with a much larger company was not only desirable but necessary if real expansion was to take place.

Motoring lore is full of romantic ideas and amazing coincidences—even if it contains few happy endings. One of the most well-loved tales concerns the sports car which Geoffrey Healey and the rest of the design team created as the first all-new Healey, to be known as the "Healey 100". The car's aggressive appeal has become a legend in itself, but the story behind the birth of the new car put the icing on the cake in a way which helped to make the car's launch a news item far beyond the realms of the motoring press. The first prototype of the Healey 100 was built just in time for the 1952 London Motor Show but so late was it that the car had to be slotted into a space behind a pillar. Nevertheless, the public took to the

car immediately and it rapidly became the star of the whole show with around 7 million dollars in orders being taken. Of course, this was simply too much for the old concrete mixer factory to cope with. However, a fairy godfather was around the corner in the form of Leonard Lord who saw the car at the show, admired it greatly and there and then agreed with Donald Healey to produce and market the car under a joint name. And so the Austin-Healey was born and, the very next day, the car appeared with its very own Austin-Healey badge. Or so the story goes.

In fact Lord was tough, abrasive and highly professional and Donald Healey far too experienced a campaigner to have found himself in need of such last minute assistance. The game is really given away when it is realised that the engine was an Austin Atlantic unit (the Riley engine having ceased production) and that the Healeys had been collaborating with Austin in the eighteen months or more during which time the Healey 100 had been developed. In fact the car was, in crude terms, a new Healey chassis and body powered by Austin components; the engine, gearbox, axle, suspension and brakes were all Austin units. The gearbox, designed for use with the weighty Austin Atlantic was modified by blanking off first gear and fitting a Laycock overdrive. The whole package was a light, well mannered but exciting 100mph sports car at well below the semi-bespoke prices of the earlier Healeys—but at the expense of loss of production at The Cape Works as Longbridge took over.

Development of the cars, and responsibility for racing, continued to be the province of Healey and 50 of the 100s, the racing 100s, were built at Warwick. Two years after the introduction of the 100, gearbox ratios were changed and first gear brought into use, giving a four speed 'box, while the 100M became available with most of the 100S's engine modifications but not, of course, with its lightweight racing body. In August 1956, the faithful 4-cylinder, 2600cc Austin A90

power plant was replaced by a developed version of the six-cylinder unit concurrently used in the Austin Westminster and known as the ''C-type'' engine. At the same time, general styling and cockpit comforts were improved and the car was made more weatherproof. Rear cockpit room was increased and provision made for two *very* occasional rear seats. One particular break from tradition was in the shape of the radiator grille where the wider, more aggressive grille was no longer recognisably descended from the traditional Warwick-shaped grille.

The car was not significantly faster than its predecessor, but was no longer powered by an engine at the end of its development tether, but by a much newer engine with a great deal of potential ahead of it. Also, the new ''six'' gave a great deal more smoothness and flexibility to what was a rather basic motor car.

Within two years of the announcement of the 100-Six, the Healey's position with regard to racing and rallying was drastically changed. The preparation of all works cars was centralised at BMC's Competition Department at Abingdon, and was thus based in but theoretically not a part of the M.G. factory. This followed a few relatively lean years for Healey when many major competition successes eluded the cars, mainly because of ill-luck which reached its nadir at Le Mans in 1955 when Lance Macklin's 100S was struck by Levegh's Mercedes near the pits area, the Mercedes cartwheeling into the crowd and killing eighty spectators. Healey cars continued to be vigorously campaigned and put up some notable achievements such as winning the Manufacturers' Team Prize in one of the toughest rallies of all, the Leige; a non-stop four day event covering the toughest mountain passes of Yugoslavia, Italy, Austria, France and Germany. Pat Moss and Ann Wisdom finished fourth behind Porsches and an Alfa. By 1959 the status of the Austin-Healey had changed in the eyes of BMC. No longer was it the recipient

of hand-me-down engines; now it was the *first* to be fitted with a new engine—the 2.9-litre ''C-type'' unit. It gained a new name, too. From 1959, until it ceased production, it was known as the ''Austin-Healey 3000'' and it was in that guise that it gained its greatest ever popularity and its greatest series of successes in international rallying.

A year earlier, however, an event had taken place which is of more significance to our story: the Austin-Healey Sprite had been launched. Although the Healey heritage had formed the greatest part of the Sprite's background, there were other powerful influences too, not least that of Austin themselves.

## The Austin Background

The first Austin was marketed in 1906 as the 25/30HP by Herbert Austin who had just branched out on his own after a period with the venerable Wolseley company. The Austin company achieved its first popular success in 1921 with the 12HP but, in 1922, came the car that single-handedly turned Austin into a major producer of motor cars: the Austin Seven. The Seven was an ultra-lightweight family car with an open body and spindly wheels and mudguards. Its side-valve engine and drive train were far more efficient and long-lasting than the cyclecars of the day and what was more, it was cheaper! Austin had hit upon a formula which was to receive the respect and affection of the British motoring public in a way which was unique and which provided motoring to large numbers of people who otherwise could never have afforded a motor car.

The car's qualities were a reflection of the general ethos of the Austin company: a car that was dependable, reliable and which would sell. Innovation was to be left to others. The recipe enabled Austin, with the Seven to the fore, to weather the great recession.

Those who could afford a small car were attracted by the simplicity of the Seven. The body, mounted upon an uncluttered A-frame chassis, was fitted only with a folding canvas top at first, but a saloon body was soon to follow. Modifications followed in succession until the car became a vastly improved version of the original, but still with the same concept of economy and reliability. Large numbers of variations were offered on the Seven theme both by the factory and by outside coachbuilders. Two of them, the Ulster and the Nippy, were the company's first sporting cars and gave rise to an enthusiasm for racing the little cars and their derivatives that still persists today.

During the Second World War, Austin production continued as large numbers of militarised versions of their civilian cars were built. Consequently, as the war drew to a close, Austin's finances were in a healthy state. By 1947, a new range of family saloons known as A40s was on the market, and in 1950, an open version built "outside" by Jensen Motors and called the A40 Sports was introduced. However, it was not what most people would have called "sporting" and was endowed with a top speed not much faster than the lumbering saloons from which it was developed. The new and expanding range, introduced by Austin's chief, Leonard Lord, was obviously short of a sportscar.

When, in 1952, Sid Enever's Abingdon design team were able to offer their new masters at Longbridge a replacement for the T-series cars capable of being put into production within twelve months, Len Lord turned the idea down flat. It was not simply that Abingdon and Longbridge personnel were strangers to one another; the collaboration between Healey and Austin was also standing in the way of funding for Abingdon's plans. The Austin-Healey 100 was to be favoured at the expense— temporarily—of the MGA, and the big Healey filled the gap in Austin's model range but a *small* sports car

was still something that was missing from the scene.

The new 'Austin Seven', the Austin A30 was introduced in 1951 and was an instant success. The Austin Drawing Office produced a fanciful spaceframed sporting version of the car but it was far removed from reality and even further from production. The A30 itself went from strength to strength however and evolved into the A35 in 1956. The car's most important qualities, apart from its frugality with petrol and its endearing shape, were its mechanical robustness, simplicity and general effectiveness. The engine was Austin's own post-war all new overhead valve unit, designed solely for the A30 but quickly transplanted into the Morris Minor after the Austin-Nuffield take-over. The 803cc engine was uprated to 948cc for use in both the A35 and Minor 1000 in 1959 (the bores being siamesed to make room for the extra capacity). In this form the engine possessed strength in abundance, a useful increase in power and low down torque. To make the most of the extra power at lower revs, the gearbox, also new in 1951, was given higher ratios and the gap between second and third was closed a little. The banjo rear axle gained a higher ratio with the advent of the A35/Minor 1000 but lost none of its robustness. The car's front suspension was unchanged throughout its production run and consisted of a bottom pressed steel wishbone and coil spring with an upper link doubling up as the shock absorber arm. The A30/A35 steering was by cam gears and the brakes were hydraulic at front and mechanically operated at rear. Bodywork was of unitary, chassisless construction and provided full 4-seater accommodation within a restricted space.

## Abingdon Influences

While Austin, and the A35 in particular, had the second-greatest

influence of all on the development and final form of the 'Frogeye' Sprite, the less direct influence of M.G. at Abingdon cannot be ignored. Quite apart from the fact that the Frogeyes were actually to be built at Abingdon, it must also be remembered that for many years, from the early 'fifties almost up until the closure of Abingdon in 1981, M.G.s had been the market leaders in small, open-topped sports cars. The name "M.G." derives from the fact that William Morris, later Lord Nuffield, owned retail garages known as The Morris Garages which were eventually put under separate management from the Morris car manufacturing side which was, of course, going from strength to strength. In 1922, the Morris Garages' General Manager died in tragic circumstances and the Sales Manager, a young man by the name of Cecil Kimber, was promoted to fill his shoes. Within a year the business, now known as the M.G. Car Company had begun to rebody 'Bullnose' Morris Oxfords with a more attractive, high class body. This sideline rapidly grew until five years on, in 1928, M.G. had their own separate stand at the Motor Show where they presented the large, fast and prestigious 18/80 Six and the tiny but virtually as quick M-type Midget of which well over 3000 were to be built on a four-year production run. The M-type Midget was based upon a modified Morris Minor chassis and was powered by a lightly tuned Minor 847cc overhead camshaft engine. By all accounts, placing the seats further back than those in the Minor made gear changing awkward: nevertheless, the tiny, boat-tailed sports car with cycle wings and radiator shell whose shape was strongly echoed in most later cars, made a tremendous impact. *The Autocar* wrote, prophetically, "The M.G. Midget will make history".

In fact it was the M-type's successor, the J-type, that was more of a trendsetter because, although it was a natural development from the M-type which had largely come about as a result of competition successes, the

J-type Midget put together the combination of excellent road behaviour and outstandingly good looks for the first time. It set the trend in sports cars for years to come and its concept was to be seen repeated in every small M.G. built until 1955.

This period saw M.G. Midgets develop through PA and PB form (1934-36) to the famous T-series which began with the TA (1936-39), the short-lived TB which did not outlast the outbreak of war in 1939, through the ever-growing production runs of the TC, TD and TF until the venerable and, by then, almost anachronistic range of cars was discontinued in 1955 having sold a total of over 50,000 and having grown in engine size to 1500cc. Cecil Kimber, after having built the company up, was dismissed in the early years of the war, reportedly for assuming more independence in the running of his own brainchild than his superiors were prepared to stomach.

The TD Midget had been the first to make inroads into the huge North American market and the TF had expanded the market. The new M.G. for 1955, the MGA, had to be good to satisfy that market, and it *was* good. It was *not* however, a Midget. The MGA was bigger, sleeker and faster than its predecessors and it was, of course, more expensive. This left a large gap in the market-place which others, sooner or later, were bound to fill.

## The Q-car Concept

Leonard Lord at Austin and Donald Healey had grown used to working together right from the start of the 1950s when the Austin-Healey 100 was first being developed at Warwick and later when the car was produced at Longbridge. The two men clearly held each other in some respect and it was as the result of one of their meetings in the winter of 1956 that the concept of the

original Sprite was born. As Geoffrey Healey writes in his book *More Healeys*, ''In his blunt down to earth manner, Len Lord then commented that what we needed was a small, low cost sports car to fill the gap left by the disappearance of the Austin Seven Nippy and Ulster models of pre-war fame. What he would really like to see, he said, was a bug. It is impossible to tell whether he was thinking aloud or deliberately giving DMH [Donald Healey] a broad hint of what we should do, but this conversation certainly set DMH thinking as he drove back from Longbridge.''

In 1956, Healey's body designer was Gerry Coker, who was to write many years later in a letter to the Austin Healey Owners' Club: ''For 1956 Mr. Healey wanted a cheap two-seater, 'that a chap could keep in his bike shed'. The original design had concealed headlamps and I liked to think of it as the poor kid's Ferrari. When I left the company in January of 1957 the bodyshell was finished and I thought it looked pretty good. Unfortunately, it did not appear in production as I had hoped though it seemed to enjoy production as the Frogeyed Sprite''

So the idea of a 'frogeyed' car (or 'bugeyed' as it became known in the 'States) seems to have come about because of the difficulty of mass producing a cheap car with folding headlamps rather than at the throwaway suggestion of Len Lord. The first two prototypes, factory coded Q1 and Q2 but affectionately nicknamed ''The Tiddlers'' by those who worked on them were in fact fitted with retracting headlamps whose lenses faced skywards when in the ''off'' position in the manner of certain modern Porsches. The cost of this system was increased enormously because of the complexity of providing a linkage that operated in conjunction with the one-piece, lift-open bonnet.

By the time Gerry Coker left the company the first bodyshells, built by Panel Craft, were complete and further design work was taken over by his successor Les Ireland. The attractive and well-proportioned body enclosed a structure that was

more revolutionary than the headlamps as far as use in a cheap car was concerned. The fact that unitary construction was used made the car unique; no sports car before it had been constructed in this way but the nature of the car's structure was even more impressive. Following D-type Jaguar practice, the floorpan, designed by Geoffrey Healey, consisted of a ''punt'' stiffened by sill, gearbox tunnel and front and rear bulkheads from the front of which 'chassis' legs protruded giving mountings for the engine, front suspension and steering rack. The rear bodywork lacked a bootlid because the rear panel, spot welded to the wings and boot floor beneath the number plate was a stressed panel and added strength to the rear end. At the rear, quarter-elliptic springs were fitted in the manner of the Mk I Jaguar. Boxes were built into the double-skinned rear bulkhead into which one end of each spring was held with long bolts. A reinforcing plate ran forwards to help to feed the spring loads into the rear of the floor. The rear axle was mounted upon the outer ends of the springs and radius arms were also attached by pivots to the axle and the body above the springs, and parallel to them, to help prevent torque reaction and sideways axle movements.

The cost of this exciting 'chassis' package was offset by the choice of mechanical components used in the car. The A35 engine was fitted, albeit after some tuning and development work had been carried out by Morris Engines at Coventry under Eddie Maher. As used in the Morris Minor, the engine was already more powerful because of the use of an SU carburettor, but for the Frogeye two 1 ⅛in SU HS1 carburettors with pancake air filters were used. Stronger valve springs, stellite-faced exhaust valves and copper-lead main bearings were added to the engine which now gave 43bhp at 5200rpm instead of the basic A35's 34bhp. In the event, the engines turned out to be Morris units because Austin found themselves too busy building up for the launch of the 1959 Mini. The gearbox was unchanged from its A35/Morris Minor 1000 specification and in practice gave the Sprite driver rather a large gap between second and third gear. The rear axle was a standard A35 unit and used the same differential ratio. The Austin mechanically-operated rear brakes were dispensed with and Minor-type rear brakes were utilised giving hydraulic operation all round. The handbrake was operated by a cable which activated a lever passing into the rear wheel cylinder itself. The only other modification to the axle was the addition of a welded vertical plate to which the springs and the radius arms were attached. Neither the A35 brake master cylinder, which operated only on the front brakes, nor the Minor master cylinder which was fitted awkwardly inside a chassis rail beneath the driver's feet, was suitable for the Sprite and so the MGA unit was fitted. This was a double-action master cylinder which also served the clutch and so, of necessity, a hydraulic clutch was fitted to the Sprite. The Standard 6 ¼ inch Borg and Beck clutch was used except that it was fitted with stronger springs.

Front brakes and front suspension were taken directly from the A35 except that the springs were given softer settings. To compensate for the softer springs, stiff shock absorber ratings were used giving the very safe, progressive if rather hard suspension for which the cars are famed. An attempt was made to use the A35's Cam Gears steering but its steering box, idler box and various linkages would have been enormously problematical to fit and would have given inferior performance to the chosen solution which was to utilise a Morris Minor steering rack. As Geoffrey Healey said in his book:

"We attempted to use the A35's steering gear but it quickly became obvious that little of the Austin stuff would suit. Instead, we took the Morris Minor rack and pinion and laid this in position. Once we had determined the correct

position and checked that the steering geometry was good through the various wheel movements, we had to get some special steering arms made up. Jack Merralls, our Warwick blacksmith, made us a pair in EN16 steel which were then heat treated by the local gasworks. These were then filed to the finished shape, drilled and fitted".

One other problem area which needed some of the Healey flair for innovation before it could be overcome was the rev. counter drive or rather the lack of one. Rev. counters were usually driven from the camshaft before the advent of electronic instruments, but the A-series Austin engine, designed for a range of family runabouts was not designed to accommodate such a drive and in any case, its fitting would have been a highly expensive affair. Instead Lucas, who supplied the cars' dynamos and Smiths, the manufacturers of the rev. counters, were charged with the task of devising a take-off from the rear of the belt driven dynamo.

John Thompson Motor Pressings of Ettingshall near Wolverhampton had been responsible for making the complex and incredibly sturdy 'Big' Healey chassis frames and they were employed to build the Sprite's floorpan in which most of the car's strength resided. Thompsons must have been pleased to get the work as they were short of it at that time but their eagerness led to them under-quoting which made them a loss at first.

The diehards at Thompsons were a little shaken by the appearance of this strange new phenomenon, the sports car floorpan. The author can well remember visiting the shop floor as a lad with his father who was (and still is) a Thompson employee and being shown a half-finished Sprite floorpan by a welder by the name of Jack. Jack disdainfully shook the floorpan like a wobble-board as if to say, "How the hell this is supposed to work, I'll never know!" But it did work. A greater marvel still was the production supply system.

John Thompsons' floorpan assemblies were shipped from Wolverhampton to Swindon where Pressed Steel welded on the bodies which they had fabricated. From there, the bare shells were transported to Cowley where they were painted and then they were taken to Abingdon for assembly. At around 150 miles, this "production line" must have been one of the longest and most unwieldy ever!

Incidentally, Longbridge, which would have seemed the natural home for an Austin was ruled out because there it was only possible to insert engines from beneath the A35 production line track, a feat which was impossible on the Sprite because of the nature of its construction. In any case, Longbridge was getting itself ready for Mini production and in the terms of that car's production figures, the Sprite would have been in the way. Consequently, versatile old Abingdon found itself with yet another non-M.G. to produce but at least from their point of view, it was a sports car and a fine one at that. And before long, Sid Enever and his Abingdon team were to leave their mark on the design of the Frogeye's successor.

## The Frogeye in Production

No one could have been expected to be quite as enthusiastic about the new car as were the BMC publicity department who announced in May 1958 that the appearance of the Frogeye "brings joy to the eyes of a connoisseur". The road tests that followed were quite remarkably kind to the car, *The Motor* claiming that the Sprite gave an "amazingly high" reading on "a pleasure-to-price ratio for cars". *Autosport* dubbed the car as, "Yet Another Spectacular Success", while the American *Sports Cars Illustrated* went on to say that, "On first look you feel as if you would like to pat it on the head—if it had one to pat" and, "It

pounces around in traffic like a playful kitten, goes when it's told and stops when it's bidden. Its steering is the sort of thing automobile writers dream about and seldom experience even on pure-bred racing machinery. Light withal, it gives a definite feeling of utter reliability, and only three days after the Austin Healey Sprite was introduced, a car appeared in Class H Production at Put-In Bay, Ohio''.

At £660 including tax in the U.K. and 1795 Dollars at East Coast POE, the Sprite had no competitor. The cheapest mass-production alternative was the MGA at £995 while the Triumph TR3 cost £1050. The Berkeley, available in 3 or 4-wheeler form at £650 had a great deal of character but was designed and built on a shoe-string, constructed in tiny numbers and became a byword for motoring unreliability (it was built so light so it's easy to push!), leaving the Sprite absolutely unchallenged at the price.

BMC pricing policy actually showed some deviousness. The Sprite's basic price did not include such ''ancillary equipment'' as a front bumper, adjustable passenger seat, heater or tachometer. In fact the number of cars supplied without ''extras'' and especially the tachometer and heater was very, very small indeed. It is just possible to hear an echo of the salesman's voice across the decades: ''Actually sir, you're fortunate that this car is already fitted with a heater, tachometer, front bumper and screenwasher. We can include the cost in the H.P. price, saving you from having to find £33.11s. 3d. later on . . .'' Some things never change!

In the first half-year of production, 8729 cars were built, while in 1959 the total shot up to 21,566. In 1960, the last full year of production, numbers dipped to 18,665 as the economy as a whole hiccuped. The 1959 figure was only ever exceeded twice in the following twenty years of combined Sprite/Midget production indicating the enormous appeal of the simple, original package.

The success of the original car could be seen in other ways too. Throughout its three years of production, virtually no significant production changes were made. Rear shock absorber/radius arm mountings were strengthened, the hood-to-windscreen fixing was changed to keep out water, wind and passing bugs, which the old hood admitted, and the steering wheel pattern was changed. If a different sort of Sprite was wanted, the only option was to have a standard one uprated.

A number of tuning firms offered tuning conversions on the Sprite, among the most successful of which was the Speedwell conversion. However, Healey themselves offered some of the most worthwhile conversions of all. *The Motor* tested a Warwick-tuned Sprite in early 1959, reporting that ''The result is a machine lifted out of the amusing runabout class into the ranks of serious sports cars''. This was a Stage 4 conversion and included a closer ratio gearbox, lower ratio rear axle, centre-lock wire wheels and disc brakes. The conversion raised maximum speed to over 91mph from a standard 82.9 while 0-50 came up more than 2 seconds faster at 11.6 seconds.

One other more widely available Healey-initiated option was the hardtop conversion. The new Weathershields sidescreens were tailored to fit the unassuming curves of the fibreglass hardtop which complemented the rounded shape of the car rather well. At the front, the hardtop was held down by two over-centre snap clips which were located in the windscreen hood fixing channel. Rear location was through the hood stay slots mounted at the cockpit sides while the rear screen was glass and the fibreglass was substantial and strong: both features in contrast to some of the cheaper competition. Two people, said *The Autocar*, could remove the top completely in two minutes and their road test indicated that the top was aerodynamically superior to the canvas hood giving better top-end acceleration figures, improved mpg

and no less than 5mph extra on top speed.

The Healey company at their Warwick headquarters never lost the early momentum of invention and innovation and they were constantly in the throes of new model development, some of it promoted by BMC most of it purely in-house and, seemingly, almost for the hell of it. One such project was the 'Super Sprite' which was begun as early as 1959. A dramatically more powerful 1100cc Coventry Climax engine was fitted (the same unit to be found in the then contemporary Lotus Elite) and a Les Ireland design of alloy body was fitted with the deep swage line sweeping from front to rear proclaiming its status as a Healey. The car was very much faster than the standard Sprite (a Brabham converted 1962 M.G. Midget with similar Climax engine had a theoretical maximum of around 112mph) and was fitted with disc brakes all round. Although the car must have seemed most exciting at the time, the response it drew from BMC was less than wholehearted—they even went so far as to issue a stern warning that ''outside'' engines were not to be used again!

## Metamorphosis

Undeterred, Healeys went on to produce a range of alternative Sprites which reached various stages of development. In the end, a variation on the theme was brought about on BMC's instigation that turned the car into the Mk II. The circumstances surrounding the lead up to the new car can be seen to enter the realms of high farce when it is realised that the Healeys were told to redevelop the car's front end while Sid Enever at Abingdon was told to get on with redesigning the rear end—and the two were specifically told not to communicate with one another! Of course, with only an hour's drive between the two concerns, each quickly found out what the other was doing and were able to collaborate. The Sprite's happy looking front end was revised at Warwick, at first by one which placed the headlamps in the wings but retained the characterful grille but later that too was changed. Abingdon squared-up the rear end in a way which was soon to be seen again on the MGB and a boot lid was added. The suspension system however, remained the same for the time being.

Of course, the M.G. involvement with the Sprite has never been over-emphasised but according to Wilson McComb, Abingdon worked on the first Sprite, known there as "The buzz-box" as early as 1957 and in that year a highly developed version of the 948cc unit had been developed by Abingdon for the Utah record attempt. After having built the Frogeyes, it was no surprise that Sid Enever at Abingdon was asked to head the design team given the task of working on the new car — or at least the rear end of the car. Had it not been for Enever and Healey getting together unofficially, the car could have been reminiscent of two unco-ordinated ends of a pantomine horse but as it was, the car came out very much of a piece. Incidentally, the MGB that was to follow the Sprite/Midget the following year also received rear end treatment that was *tres* Enever (even *tres* Pininfarina, some say, although there is no known substance to back the claim).

Mechanically, the Mk II Sprite/Midget was little different from its predecessor except that the altered cam, higher compression ratio pistons and larger valves gave a few more bhp to help cope with the increased weight. The carburettors, too, were larger and of a later type, losing those charming brass damper tops but the idiosyncratic tacho drive was retained at the rear of the dynamo.

The close-ratio gearbox which had been optional on the Mk I for a while now became standard while hoods, tonneaux and hardtops were all changed to suit the new rear-end shape. For some reason which

defies rational analysis the dashboard was changed in all sorts of small ways. The change to a modern type of switch is understandable but the reversal of some of the warning lamp positions can only lead one to assume that a poltergeist got to work on the drawings!

Although the new Sprite was introduced in May 1961 and the Midget a month later, neither lasted long before a major modification was introduced. The Minor-type 1098cc engine was fitted from October 1962 and mated to it was a greatly improved baulk-ring synchromesh gearbox which largely cured the problem of the model's synchro rubbishing itself within a relatively small mileage. At the same time an electronic tacho was fitted along with disc brakes and a host of other minor modifications, although the cars continued with the same Mark numbers.

The engine was soon found wanting; it was always a relatively rough-running unit when used in the lightly stressed BMC small saloons but when given a little extra tuning, the bottom end quickly suffered. These engines, given an 18CG prefix, were superseded in March 1964 with 18CC engines which had larger main bearings (now of a full 2 inches). These cars were known as "Sprite Mk III/Midget Mk II" as, after all, the whole engine had been closely scrutinised and largely redesigned. An even more dramatic change was the fitting of half-elliptic springs in place of the original Frogeye-type quarter-elliptics. It is even possible that the original designers of the car had contemplated this conversion, as the box section which was designed to sweep over the axle as far back as the rear panel at the outer edges of the Frogeye boot was perfectly placed and stressed to take brackets locating the ends of the new springs. Exciting in concept though the quarter-elliptic may have been, the new half-elliptics did away with most of the earlier cars' twitchings — caused by poor axle location — and gave a smoother ride because of the reduced spring

flexing of the new arrangement; and all with no loss of the car's already legendary road-holding power.

In other respects the cars were made to look more modern and became more comfortable to use. The old removable sidescreens were done away with, much to the disgust of the die-hards, and winding windows were installed which had the disadvantage of losing some elbow-room in the door space. Ventilation was improved by the addition of quarterlights and the hood was fixed to the new curved windscreen top by a pair of internal toggle clips rather than the more primitive method previously used. The dashboard layout was completely revised although it had the same switch and dial functions in all cases but the starter was now key-operated for the first time. The Sprite "lightning-flash" logo disappeared from the horn push to be replaced by an Austin logo on the Sprite, whilst the M.G. wore an MG in an octagon.

Interestingly, these were the only models of Sprites and Midgets to have colour keyed hoods so that red cars, for instance, had red hoods, but very few cars remain nowadays which are original in this respect.

Sprites and Midgets in this specification ran until October 1966 by which time they were looking decidedly sluggish in comparison with other cars of the day. The substitution of a 1275cc engine changed things dramatically. A higher final drive ratio meant that overall acceleration figures were only slightly better but top speed was over 10% higher while fuel consumption was actually better by quite a margin. At the same time, Sprite and Midget distinctions, such as they were, were becoming even more blurred. *Autocar* wrote, "It's harder than ever now to tell the Midget from the Sprite, as the chrome strip is no longer down the centre of the M.G. bonnet."

Other comments to come from the same April 1969 road test included " 'Safety Fast' has long been an M.G. slogan and the Midget is a car that is really worthy

of it . . . The little car feels ideally balanced . . .''

''A very comfortable seat provides excellent back and leg support.'' and, ''Its solid feeling, compact and free buzzing nature together with the gearbox which is a delight to snick around, tied with the utterly predictable handling, promised something which will not catch me out at an inconvenient moment.''

On the other side of the cons were, ''Its limitations [which] concern the very squashed but not cramped sitting position'' and, in a nutshell, the noise: the engine, the transmission and the flapping hood were all said to make life inside a Midget sound unnecessarily hectic.

The road test also considered the merits of the Triumph Spitfire Mk III alongside those of the Midget and ''CJH'' concluded at the end of his session, that, ''If the situation arose whereby one was to be mine, the two were side by side and I had one set of keys, the tyre dust would settle on the Spitfire as my Midget buzzed off.''

Two years after launching the 1275cc Mk IV Sprite/Mk III Midget, no more Sprites were shipped to the United States, only Midgets being exported there to take advantage of the undoubted esteem in which the M.G. name was held. In the same year of 1968, Midgets and British Sprites were changed to negative earth electrics, though still with dynamo and a few other relatively minor changes made including the substitution of a cross-flow radiator. In October 1969 a more major facelift took place: Rostyle wheels, black sills and, for a couple of months, black anodised windscreen surrounds were fitted. The rear bumper was now in two halves and a host of other trim changes took place, while mechanically very little altered. The changes were sufficient to prompt a model change so that Sprites became Mk IV, while Midgets one behind as always, were Mk III.

Although other minor changes took place in 1970, the next major change point came in January 1971 when the name Healey, so closely

associated with the cars since their beginnings in the mid-fifties was dropped in a manner so typical of BL at the time, with coarse disregard for the twin pillars of character and tradition which must lie somewhere near the heart of every car maker and especially sports car makers. Until June 1971, the Austins were known simply as Austin Sprites and were given a chassis number prefix ''AN'' instead of the previous ''HAN''. In June of that year, the Sprites were dropped altogether. It was perhaps a rational move because the Sprites and Midgets had become so indistinguishable, one from the other; but BL failed to note that buying a sports car is not in itself a rational activity and for each of the next three years, sales of the Midget dropped from a 1971 figure of 17,432 to a 1974 total of only 12,449, a fall of around 30%.

In the midst of this fall in sales, yet another face-lift took place when, in January 1972, the Frogeye style of round rear wheel arches which many felt complemented the general shape of the car so well, was reinstated in place of the squarer Abingdon initiated type. Mk II Rostyle wheels were also fitted and corporate styling rubber stamped its presence on such items as interior door handles, rocker switches and gear knobs. A Triumph steering rack was fitted giving gearing somewhat lower than previous Midgets and pressaging greater changes still to come. The car was slightly emasculated in another way too; the exhaust system no longer gave off a healthy M.G. crackle but instead burbled a muted drone through the extra silencer with which the car was now endowed. Clearly, there was insufficient length beneath the floor for this extra box so it was placed in a rather unsightly position across the car beneath the rear bumper. In spite of these quibbles, the Midget was still recognisably a not-very-distant relative of the Mk I and was arguably more attractive with its rounded rear wheel arches; it was certainly not controversial but all that was to change.

In October 1974, a new Midget appeared with more than just a face-lift — it had a body-lift, too! The old-timers who were disappointed when the sidescreens were dispensed with probably howled with rage at a Midget which rode higher than its predecessor (and handled a little worse in consequence), with enormous black plastic covered bumpers front and rear and even with a ''foreign'' engine and gearbox under the bonnet. The Triumph 1500 engine was pressed into service with the Midget, the decision having been made that at 1275cc the Austin A-series engine had reached the end of its stretchability and that it was difficult to tune it for American anti-smog laws without losing too much power. The Triumph unit, which had started, ironically, at the same 803cc capacity as the A-series engine (although Austin had introduced their engine in 1951 while Standard had waited until 1953 to introduce theirs), was also to be fitted to the Spitfire so that the costs of developing for export would be split between two models. There was an unarguable rationale about the gearbox change, too. It was basically a Marina unit and, while less crisp than the Sprite-type box, had the advantage of synchromesh on first.

But what did the buying public make of the mighty black covered bumpers front and rear which, though somehow less dominating than the MGB's bumpers nevertheless still covered over the traditional grille at the front and stuck out an awfully long way at the rear? Quite simply they liked them, or at least the cars to which they were attached; sales ceased their decline and climbed steadily back to a 1976 high of 17,121. Unfortunately, the respite was to prove all to temporary for the Midget. Sales from 1976 fell rapidly as both British and American governments fell in love with monetarism and caused massive rises in interest rates which made the cars highly expensive to buy on credit. In addition, BL were claiming that the cost of keeping up with

U.S. legislation was becoming prohibitive and the old Abingdon factory was becoming an anomaly within the car making division in that it was small, old-fashioned and too keen on autonomy for its own good. The writing was on the wall. In 1979, fewer than 10,000 units were produced and in November of that year, production ceased. Unsold cars lay around BL dealers' showrooms not for months, but for two or three years taking even longer to sell than the remaining MGBs which had also ceased production.

Strange though it may seem, at the other end of the car's 21 years, activity was on the increase as Frogeyes were becoming more and more sought after while their numbers ever diminished. Interest, too, was spreading to the later cars with popularity focusing on the latest 1275cc cars (the last of the "real" Midgets, as their owners like to think of them) and on the 1500s themselves which are recognised by their owners as the most comfortable and convenient way of Midgetting. Since the demise of the car, interest has increased at a phenomenal pace; after all, all the attributes of a classic in the making are there. The car was raced in its day (and still is with much success), it was designed and built by some of the most famous sports car people of all time and its attributes of fun with frugality and road behaviour that was "Safety Fast" make it very much a car for the 'eighties and beyond.

## Motorsport

With a pedigree that included Abingdon and Healey as forebears, it would hardly have been possible to have kept the Frogeyes off the track—even if anyone had wanted to. Only three days after the car was introduced to the 'States, a Sprite appeared in a Class H Production Race at Put-In Bay, Idaho, in what could only have been "Running-

In—Please Pass'' condition. With only 948cc on offer, Frogeyes never stood a chance of being competitive other than in their Class where they were very competitive indeed. This lack of horsepower was to handicap all the Sprites and Midgets throughout the ten years or so that Sprites and Midgets were campaigned as works cars, officially or otherwise.

All of the cars, right up to, but not including the 1500, have been great favourites in clubman's racing of various types where the private entrant is not overshadowed by works teams. The 1500 comes with too many built-in disadvantages to be considered as a track car: its body shell is too heavy because of the extra stiffness added to satisfy U.S. safety regulations; its ride level is too high to give satisfactory handling; and neither its engine nor its gearbox are inherently robust enough for the enormous stresses and strains of modern competitive racing. After all, a driver like James Thacker, who races an ex-Alec Poole, ex-works Midget, regularly produced lap times that are the equal of times put up by out and out racing cars of the 'fifties. This puts tremendous strain on cars but it is to the credit of the Spridget's basic engineering soundness that James' car is fitted with standard wheel hubs which stand up easily to the enormous cornering forces involved and that his engine carried him to success time and time again in both 1981 and 1982 without a rebuild save routine bearing shell and oil pump changes.

In fact, the ex-Alec Poole car had been used to wins, recording the only overall win of any significance at all by a Spridget when Alec drove it to success in the Kingsway Trophy Race at Phoenix Park, Dublin. In 1968, a Healey prepared Midget won the sports car category outright at Sebring, shortly before British Motor Holdings (to become BL) abolished Abingdon's racing activities.

Over the years, Sprite and Midget racing metamorphosed from the 1959 Targa Florio Sprite, virtually a production car with the mildest of engine tuning and A40 brakes, into the incredibly complex and sophisticated 1293cc fuel-injected cars which bore no resemblance whatever to the production Midgets. Class wins and great reliability were their speciality and a list of their major achievements is shown in an appendix. Readers interested in having a go at racing their Sprite or Midget will be relieved to learn that the M.G. Car Club operates a scheme whereby absolute beginners can have their first taste of race track driving without having to drive competitively against other drivers—they are given a time to race against, and so only have themselves to contend with. The M.G. Owners' Club also "goes racing" but, while being less race-orientated than the Car Club, at least has the virtue that their race times are slower and so should be easier for the first-timer. The addresses of both clubs are given in an appendix.

H1. The M.G. TF was the last in the line of original M.G. Midgets. The Abingdon management replaced it with the M.G.A., a somewhat larger sports car in a different mould, giving Leonard Lord the cue to bring out a small Austin or, as it turned out, an Austin-Healey.

H2. The immortal shape of the Mk I Sprite, cheerfully dubbed the 'Frogeye'. There was little sentimentality about the car's shape whilst it was actually being built, but nowadays it is regarded as heir apparent to the cult role of the T-series M.G.s.

H3. From above, the diminutive size of the Frogeye Sprite is particularly apparent. Once inside the car, it has a surprisingly large amount of leg room.

THE CAR THAT OFFERS SO MUCH · · · · FOR SO LITTLE · · · · ·

AUSTIN HEALEY

· · · SPORTS CAR PERFORMANCE · · · · · · · · ·

· · · · SMALL CAR ECONOMY

Sprite

H4. The original sales brochure was not slow to point out one of the most practical reasons for buying the new Sprite — "The designs of most of its major mechanical components have been proved in other B.M.C. models," it pointed out.

**H5.** The Austin-Healey Sprite Mk II looked an entirely different animal to the Mk I and most reaction to the new shape was favourable when it was first introduced. Beneath the skin, however, very little of the original car was altered. Floorpan and suspension, sills, bulkhead and most of the interior were unaltered as were, in essence, the car's mechanical components.

**H6.** One item that was changed was the carburettor/air cleaner set-up. The original S.U. HSI carbs were dropped in favour of HS2 $1\frac{1}{4}$in units, and the "brass-topped" dashpot chambers were replaced by the much more common plastic capped variety. These dashpots have been polished.

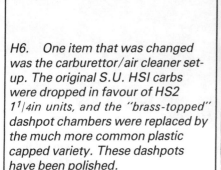

**H7.** Like all manufacturers, Abingdon produced a number of prototypes that never reached production. This transverse engined car with M.G.B. front-end styling, but Midget-style side lamps and windscreen supports, was apparently road tested — or so the wheel balancing weights would suggest. (Photo. B.L. Heritage.)

**H8.** The M.G.-designed rear end and Healey-designed front (compare the front wing line to that of a 'Big' Healey) remained unchanged throughout. By 1968, the year of this model, the Midget was of 1275cc.

H9.    In the 'States, the Midget Mk III still had square rear wheel arches. Note the principal differences over U.K. cars: number plate holder, sidemarker lamps and octagonal wheelnuts. The top of a U.S.-style dashboard is just visible. (Photo. B.L. Heritage.)

H10.    The U.K.-market Mk III Midget regained the round wheel arches of the original Frogeye Sprite. If you wonder why they never tried it before in conjunction with the later style front end . . .

H11.    . . . they did! Or, at least, the Healey Company did. Their redesigned front end prototype was fitted to a Mk I body and most people agree that the lighter appearance of the round rear wheel arch rather suits the car.

H12.    When the car was revamped to meet U.S. emission and safety rules in 1975, changes were far more dramatic. The front end was greatly altered by the addition of faired-in rubber-bumpers covering steel reinforcement of great weight.

H13. Under the bonnet, equally dramatic alterations were taking place. The Triumph 1500 engine's carburation and ignition fittings were reversed, compared with the A-series engine. Although larger, the engine, burdened with emission control equipment, was barely more powerful than the one it replaced, and it undoubtedly had a weaker bottom end.

H14. Although they have never been powerful enough to run away with any major trophies, 'Spridgets' have always been a good clubman's car: ideal for the relatively impecunious to 'have-a-go'. This more than slightly modified Midget is the property of the successful James Thacker. His car is sponsored by Spridgebits Ltd., the British Sprite and Midget specialists.

H15. U.S. cars were frequently 'customised' a little by the factory to give them extra appeal. This 'M.G. Midget Special' came with AM/FM Radio, chrome finish luggage rack, wheel trim rims and distinctive side-stripes as standard.

H16. Nowadays, it's difficult to find a Sprite or Midget owner who isn't a real enthusiast for his or her car. Although there is a sprinkling of Sprite owners in the British M.G. Owners Club, most M.G.O.C. and M.G. Car Club 'Spridget' owners are, not surprisingly, owners of M.G. Midgets. Austin-Healey enthusiasts are catered for by the Austin-Healey Car Club and it is at one of their meetings that this nature study was taken. (Photo: David Laugher.)

# 2 Buying

For a long time, Sprite and Midget owners have suffered from something of an inferiority complex: Frogeye Sprites were always seen as the little brothers of the "Big" Healey sports cars and the later Sprites and Midgets, all of them more closely associated with Abingdon, were considered to be smaller versions of the MGB range. However, Mk I Sprites and, more slowly, the later models are becoming recognised as sports cars which have got many first class attributes all of their own. In fact many of those attributes are features that the bigger sports cars that once left the Spridgets in their shadow do not have; Midgets and Sprites are frugal with fuel, their components are smaller and lighter and less expensive to replace, they are easy to handle and easy to park especially in town — in short they are the ideal sports cars for the 'eighties!

Rises in the cars' values are taking place steadily, with Frogeyes leading the way and the better of the later cars following on behind.

Unfortunately, less immaculate Sprites and Midgets have been held in low esteem for many years and this means that they have frequently been neglected and, even more frequently, fitted with non-standard parts, causing the would-be restorer problems to watch out for when buying a car. On the other hand, the cars' basic design is such that only the most completely rusted out examples are beyond rebuild while their mechanical components have been proven to be tough and reliable over many years and have also found use in literally millions of other cars made by B.M.C./B.L. so should be in plentiful supply for years to come.

This chapter aims to provide the prospective purchaser with a sequence of checks on a car under consideration which should be virtually foolproof in ensuring that a car is as good — or only as bad — as it seems. It should also provide the owner who is in the process of deciding whether to rebuild his or her car with the information necessary to make an estimate of the total amount of work — and thus expenditure required.

## Take Your Pick

First of all the prospective owner has to make a decision on which model of Sprite or Midget to buy. Although the same basic mechanical layout was placed within an essentially unchanged floorpan right the way through from 1958 to 1979, there is the very world of difference between the first Frogeye Sprite and the last of the Midgets.

It is possible to place the Sprite/Midget evolution into distinct eras which are generally, although not fully, reflected by the manufacturer's own model changes. Some idea of the changes that took place is given in Chapter One while the Appendices detail the technical and numerical background to the developments and should be used to check a car's originality in fine detail. Because of the structure common to the cars it is not unusual to find parts from later cars fitted to earlier models and, as a result, some earlier components such as the Mk I Sprite's carburettors and distributor and the Mk II Sprite's steering wheel, have become fairly uncommon. In some ways this makes originality, or at least access to the correct parts, almost as important as the car's condition when buying; poor bodywork can be repaired but some missing original parts cannot always be found—at any cost.

The first era covers, unsurprisingly, the 1958 to 1961 Frogeye Mk I. Gearboxes are about the weakest mechanical component of these cars but, as they were exactly the same as gearboxes used in Morris Minors and Austin A35s of the same time, parts are still available to rebuild them at home or have them rebuilt by a specialist. Engines, too, are virtually the same but beware—a Minor or A35 engine, even if adapted to Sprite specification will still have the wrong engine number. (See Appendix for details).

In spite of the relatively weak gearbox, even an 'original' Frogeye Sprite is still capable of everyday use provided that the owner is prepared to put up with a dire lack of creature comfort! The earlier Sprites with 'lift-the-dot' hood to screen fasteners do let in rather a lot of draught and water around the windscreen top, in fact all the soft-tops leak to some extent. Moreover, sidescreens tend to come loose and rattle and so do perspex windows. At its best, the heater is adequate while roadholding is a joy even by today's standards, especially if the little car is fitted with radial ply tyres. (Although it must be admitted that the thrills of sporting driving are greatly amplified by the noise, vibration and general excitement of driving an unrefined little car; a modern small saloon would probably handle even better but it would impart far less joy to the driver in doing so.)

In summary, the Frogeye is probably the world's most perfect

*"There's a surprising amount of room inside, even for tall people . . ."*

bundle of fun on four wheels. It's cheap and easy to run and maintain, a delight to drive, no more corrosion prone than any of its contemporaries and spares for mechanics and bodywork are in very plentiful supply. On the other hand, it can be a pain in the neck (and the ear, and the posterior) on a long drive or for boring, everyday use. But few owners, apart from the fanatical few who never use a soft-top and travel the length of the continent to go on holiday in their car, actually use a Frogeye for anything other than an occasional-use hobby car.

The second era covers the development of the Frogeye into the Mk II Sprite in May 1961 and the introduction of the Mk I Midget a month later. Basically the same engine (although with different camshaft, valves, pistons and carburettors) was fitted at first and the gearbox was the same, weaker, 'smooth casing' type although with higher intermediate ratios. The biggest change was in the bodywork which took on the more conventional shape which it was to retain until 1979. This model, complete with sidescreens on the door tops and the same quarter-elliptic rear suspension, was built until March 1964 BUT there was one other major production change which took place within the life of the Mk II Sprite/Mk I Midget which

was not reflected by the manufacturer's nomenclature.

In October 1962 a model which is now known unofficially as the "Mk II ½ Sprite/Mk 1 ½ Midget" was introduced with a 1098cc engine, in keeping with the simultaneous introduction of the engine to B.M.C.'s small saloon range. The new engine had crank sizes which were only just adequate for the lower powered saloon cars; for the Sprites and Midgets, the engine bottom end was most certainly a weak point. Very few "Mk II ½/Mk I ½" cars survive with the original engine but where they do exist, owners would be well advised to keep the revs down if they want to keep the original engine in one piece. On the other hand, a ribbed-casing gearbox with stronger synchromesh was fitted at the same time.

These 1961 to 1964 Sprites and Midgets, all with sidescreens and quarter-elliptic Frogeye-style rear springing are becoming sought after as interesting cars in their own right. Earlier 948cc cars with Mk I-style dynamos are the second rarest of all (20,450 Sprites and 16,080 Midgets were built) and are likely to become most collectable while 1098cc cars are still interesting and rather more stoppable, being fitted with disc brakes as standard and are *the* rarest of the models built (11,215 and 9601 respectively).

At this point it is worth digressing to point out the differences between an Austin-Healey Sprite and an M.G. Midget. It is common knowledge that at the start of production there was only a Sprite, the Mk I, or Frogeye, while at the end of production there was only the M.G. Midget 1500. But what happened in between? From 1961 to 1964, more Sprites were produced than Midgets and again in 1966 but in 1965 and in every year from 1967 to 1971, Midgets outpaced Sprites in production terms.

In those early years, a deliberate attempt was made to give Sprites and Midgets a separate identity at the lowest possible cost to the manufacturer. The M.G. cost, in June 1961, an extra £20.00 plus Purchase Tax and came equipped with chrome strips on the bodywork waist rail and down the centre of the bonnet, plain chrome hub caps (Sprite hub caps had a pressed "AH" motif), the grille had vertical slats instead of the Sprite's 'cheesegrater' style of grille and a central "M.G." grille badge. Inside the car, the M.G. dashboard was fitted with a padded roll across the top of the fascia and the steering wheel was coloured (Sprite wheels were black). Sprite seats were the same as those in the Frogeye while Midget seats had a horizontal panel across the top of the squab and the front of the cushion and the piping was in a contrasting colour. The Sprite dash retained the passenger's grab handle while it was deleted from the Midget and replaced by "M.G." inside an octagon with flashes either side.

None of this makes either car inherently any more desirable than the other, nor does it explain why Sprites outsold Midgets at the time, except that the customer was presumably prepared to save £20 plus tax and do without the fripperies. It does show, on the other hand, how originality can be so very important and so complex especially to the owner who wishes to show his or her car.

Interestingly, by 1966, when the Midget began to regularly outsell the Sprite, specification differences were minimal and the price difference of only £10 was less than 2% of the car's total price. The same limitations on "useability" which applied to the Mk I Sprite apply also to the Mk II Sprite/Mk I Midget, especially in respect of comfort (there isn't any!) and spares availability (plentiful). However, the Mk II/Mk I *does* have a proper boot which makes it so much easier to carry a little luggage or shopping without having to take a swallow-dive behind the rear seats to retrieve a missing parcel. Also, the later style of bodywork does mean that some body panels, especially front wings, are easier and cheaper to buy than Frogeye parts. But the reverse of that coin is that fewer parts are being specially re-manufactured for these cars at present; their current lowish values and scarcity in numbers make it uneconomic to do so. Therefore buying a Mk II/Mk I with original parts becomes more important than ever.

The weakness in the "Mk II ½/Mk I ½" engine means that it is relatively less important to check for bearing wear as it would have been when the cars were in current use and more important to check that the engine is still there — or at least, that the correct one is! It must have seemed a good idea in the late 'sixties — early 'seventies to fit a later, and stronger, second-hand engine to one of these cars with bottom-end trouble. Unfortunately, today's enthusiast would not agree! The correct 1098cc engine should begin with the prefix 10CG. Anything else, including the later 10CC prefix, and a replacement engine has been fitted.

The Mk III Sprite/Mk II Midget, introduced in March 1964, represented a conscious move on the part of the management away from the traditional image of the British sports car as something which was a functional piece of machinery operating successfully at the expense of driver and passenger comforts and towards a product which the average consumer would want to buy. The died-in-the-wool purist no doubt looked aghast at the Mk III/Mk II's wind-up windows, non-detachable windscreen and half-elliptic springing, but the consumers of the day looked at the new car, liked it and bought it in the second-largest numbers for any one production year in the cars' life. (The highest, incidentally, was in 1959 when only one model was on offer).

As far as today's enthusiast is concerned, the Mk III Sprite/Mk II Midget represents the most useable of the early Sprites and Midgets. Still with a 1098cc engine, the car can be driven remarkably economically, especially when carburettors are kept in tune and when valves are forming a good seal (burned exhaust valves are a minor problem with all A-series engines). For this model, however, the engine was considerably strengthened at the bottom end. Main bearings were increased to 2 inches in diameter and this eliminated the crank whip and short bearing life suffered by earlier engines. The engine output became marginally higher, too, as manifolds were improved and larger bore exhausts fitted.

The car's straight-line stability was improved by the half-elliptic springs (the old quarter-elliptics allowed the axle to move around a little) which also gave more spring travel and thus marginally greater comfort, although stiffer rear dampers left the rear suspension very hard by today's standards.

The wind-up windows and lock-up doors add significantly to the Spridgets' useability in modern circumstances (although the resultant loss of door pockets means that the usual personal debris has to be stuffed somewhere else) and the hood, which was changed to the MGB-type of the day, is marginally easier to fit than the earlier slot-into-windscreen type. Mechanically, these Sprites and Midgets are even easier to keep than any that have gone before with many components being found, once again, in the contemporary saloon models such as the ubiquitous Mini and 1100 range.

The next advance in the

evolution of the Spridget family was in the direction of greater performance. From October 1966 a completely redesigned and enlarged engine was fitted. Of 1275cc, the Sprites and Midgets were now possessed of quite respectable performance and more relaxed cruising ability; the rear axle ratio was raised to take advantage of the extra power available. Gearboxes were strengthened once again but, because first and reverse gear became straight-cut, they also became rather noisy. The soft-top was modified again and this time became one of the best on the market, being quick and easy to erect and lower from the passenger seat.

In 1968, the same Mk IV Sprite/Mk III Midget was improved again when an alternator was fitted as standard. At the same time, the car's interior became a little more 'corporate' as standard B.L. handles and levers were fitted.

In 1969, the Mk V Sprite/Mk IV Midget was launched by B.L. with no significant engineering alterations but with so many cosmetic and minor body changes that the general character of the car became altered. Lots of small changes were carried out which made the package seem far more up-to-date and which gives the car an aesthetic appeal that still seems to be appreciated today. Among the changes (detailed in the Appendix) were a split rear bumper and a quieter exhaust with laterally mounted auxiliary silencer, rubber insets in the over-riders, and inside the car, improved reclining seats and other trim and dash changes. From the point of view of pure convenience, there is no doubt that these cars were, and are, a small but significant advance on their predecessors.

A year later, a more important aesthetic change took place when part of the rear bodywork was modified. The rear wheel arches, constructed in the heavy, squared-off pattern similar to that used on the MGB, reverted back to the shape of those used a decade earlier on the Frogeye and became an elegant arch, following the flow of the rear wheel shape. Rostyle wheels were fitted too, in place of perforated disc wheels.

Shortly afterwards, in January 1971, the Healey name was dropped (the Sprite had not been exported for more than twelve months, anyway) and for six months was sold as the Austin Sprite. The very rarity of these cars could well make them worth something more than average in the long run.

Through the early 1970s, B.L. entered a race against time to meet the growing legal restrictions within the all-important U.S. market. Restrictions on exhaust emissions and on bodyshell stiffness all had to be met if the car was to continue to sell there and this gave B.L. a headache not only with the Midget but with the Spitfire, MGB and GT6, too. To reduce their problem, a decision was made to use the same engine for both Triumph Spitfire and the Midget. In 1300 form, the Spitfire and Midget were remarkably close in straight-line performance, so the fitting of the *same* engine to both cars did not seem such a heinous crime. Unfortunately for the M.G. purist, it was a *Triumph* engine that was chosen. Fortunately for the modern owner, engine supplies are in plentiful supply and gearbox supplies even more so, since the 1500 Midget's gearbox was stolen straight out of B.L.'s big selling Morris Marina.

For most people the most dramatic alterations to the Midget were to the bodywork. Its raised ride made the car look higher, handle worse but ride rather more comfortably. Its black front and rear bumpers were sensational at first, but are now accepted as a commonplace and give good resistance to car park collision damage, while inside the car, comfortable seats, carpets everywhere and most if not all mod-cons make the car an easy one to drive and own.

So which is the best Sprite or Midget to own? That depends on which Sprite or Midget you like, what you want to do with it and how much you can spend. Midget 1500s are the most predictable to price and will remain so as long as they continue to be regarded as a modern car. They are also probably the easiest to run and own, although late 1275s run them a close second. Frogeyes are probably next in the easy-to-keep stakes because they are so highly regarded as collector's cars and because they have already reached a value which makes it worthwhile to manufacture reproduction components for them.

948cc Mk IIs are probably the hardest to maintain in original condition although even they could be used as everyday cars provided that it is realised that most of the provisos mentioned earlier regarding the Frogeye's comfort and convenience apply also to these cars.

In short, each and every Spridget is a tribute to the Healey name that stood behind the original design and the M.G. name behind its development. It's useable, fun to own and, if needs be, eminently rebuildable. It's just important to buy carefully and make sure that you know just *what* you're buying by using the rest of this chapter with care.

## Where to Look

Over a third of a million Midgets and Sprites were built in total. Although they were never quite as popular in the 'States as the MGB (or, for that matter, the Spitfire and GT6) large numbers of them were exported there.

Consequently, British and American enthusiasts stand the greatest chance of finding the Sprite or Midget of their dreams reasonably easily, particularly if they live in or near one of the larger centres of population where a fair sprinkling of the later cars will be advertised in the local press. Others will simply have to reconcile themselves to having to look that bit harder and to be prepared to travel. A potentially potent source of cars

offered for sale for such people are the club magazines published in most western countries. (See Appendix for owner's club addresses).

The largest club, without a doubt, is the huge M.G. Owners' Club in Britain which carries pages of classified ads in its monthly magazine. The American MGB Association, in spite of its name, also represents Midget owners and its publication also carries a fair sprinkling of cars offered for sale.

Austin-Healey clubs cover most of the globe, it would seem, but their organisation is far less centralised.

The British clubs, split into various area groups, jointly produce a quarterly magazine called *Rev Counter* which, although it sounds like a vicars' census, actually includes details of all types of Healeys advertised for sale. The A-H Club of America also produces a regular newsletter.

In the more highly populated areas, the everyday car auctions, the ones that dealers use for buying and selling among themselves sometimes have Sprites and Midgets on offer. They tend to be later cars—the sort that a dealer would like to have in his showroom and older cars—the sort that dealers don't like to handle, no matter what their condition. Cars bought in this way are nearly always a lot less expensive than those bought through normal trade or private sources, but there is a snag. Time and the opportunity to check the car over before the auction are usually strictly limited (sometimes it is not even possible to open the car's doors!) and the car has to be paid for in cash but there is a period— usually 24 hours—within which the car can be returned for a refund should any undisclosed faults be found. It is essential to check through the auctioneer's terms and conditions before making a commitment and it is almost essential to make a 'dry-run'—visit an auction at least once without intending to buy anything. The ways of the auction world are unusual and take a little while to

become familiar with. If nothing else, it's one of the best forms of free entertainment around!

The 'quality' auction houses such as Sothebys have not yet really accepted the Spridgets, although the occasional extraordinary car has found its way through their doors. If your heart is set on a WSM Sprite a ''works'' racing car or one of the few remaining prototypes, it might be worth subscribing to Sothebys and receiving advance notice of auction dates and cars on offer but otherwise, forget it!

Another approach, and one which has been used with great success by the author, is to find the most popular medium for selling Sprites and Midgets in your area, be it the local press or the club magazine, or even the publications of a neighbouring area if you don't mind travelling, and place a series of advertisements stating ''M.G. Midget (or whatever) Wanted'' with some details of what is required. Unfortunately some newspapers— those in Paris being an example— refuse to accept such advertisements but the technique is quite common and often highly successful in the U.K. and has the added advantage that it relieves the hopeful purchaser of having to race to see the car before the ''competition'' gets there, and then of having to make a snap decision.

Another way of buying a car is through one of the recognised dealers in the cars. Dealers like Grahame Sykes and Jed Watts of Spridgebits Ltd in the U.K. and John Twist of University Motors Ltd in the U.S.A. usually have a wide selection of cars for sale and while these are usually a little more expensive than privately offered cars there are one or two distinct advantages in buying from the better specialist dealers. They know the cars literally inside out, are able to help you to track down just the car you might want and the better dealers, like the two mentioned above, have worked hard over a number of years to build up a good reputation and this is an asset which they cannot afford to throw away by ripping-off their customers.

Consequently cheap-jack repairs which an unscrupulous private individual or trader might carry out in order to sell a car are not worthwhile to those who value their reputation.

John Twist of University Motors, Michigan, U.S.A. writes, ''In the U.S.A. one of the best ways of finding an M.G. is through the local newspaper want ads. Other means include: bulletin boards in foreign car shops and parts outlets; various club publications; several of the major collector magazines such as *Hemmings Motor News; Cars and Parts; Road and Track*—these are monthly publications offering For Sale and Wanted columns. In addition there are two M.G. magazines now in print—*M.G. Magazine* which is obtainable from 2 Spencer Place, Scarsdale, NY 10583 and *Abingdon Classics*, from P.O. Box 233, Mulberry, Florida 33860.

''When a potential purchaser of an M.G. enters University Motors and wants an impression of the M.G. he wants to purchase we first look in the files (we have a cross-reference for chassis numbers) and can give an idea of any previous work carried out on it. (Other shops may be able to carry out this paperwork inspection, too.) It's important that if the seller says that the Midget or Sprite has recently been 'tuned' or 'rebuilt' (or some other such term meaning twenty different things) that the buyer call the shop where the work was performed and ask about the extent of the work completed and their impression of the car.''

## Making Sure

Checking over a prospective purchase not only can but *should* be very time consuming if the right car is to be bought rather than a glossed-over heap of trouble. What follows is an elimination sequence in three separate parts, each one taking longer and being more thorough than the last, this approach having the virtue of saving the purchaser both time and embarrassment. It is always easier to withdraw at an early stage than after an hour spent checking the car over with the aid of the owner's comments and mugs of coffee! Thus Stage A aims to eliminate the obvious 'nails' without having to probe too deeply, Stage B takes matters somewhat further for cars that pass the first stage while Stage C is the 'dirty hands' stage, the one you don't get into on a snowy February evening unless you are really serious!

## Tool Box

Old, warm clothes (if the ground is cold). An old mat or board if the ground is wet. A bright torch. A pair of ramps. A small hammer. A screwdriver or other probe. Copies of the following pages and a notepad. Pencil. A bottle, trolley or scissors jack. Axle stands.

## Safety

**Safety should be carefully considered and any necessary steps taken. In particular, do not rely on a handbrake holding a car on a slope or ramps. NEVER crawl under a car supported by a jack only.**

## Using the checklist

This checklist was designed by the author and is based upon his experience at his body shop, *The Classic Restoration Centre* and is compiled with the help of Spridgebits Ltd. It is designed to show step-by-step instructions for virtually all the checks to be made on a car offered for sale. After each check, the fault indicated is shown in brackets, e.g. the instructions: "Look along wings, door bottoms, wheel arches and sills from the front and rear of car" is followed by the fault, shown in brackets, as (Ripples indicate filler presence/crash damage. £££). The pound sterling signs require some explanation.

They are intended to give a guide to the cost of rectifying the fault if it exists. £ indicates that the cost is likely to be less than the cost of a new tyre, £££ stands for the cost of a new set of tyres, or more, while ££ means that the cost is likely to be between the two. The cost guide relates to the cost of the component/s only, other than in the case of bodywork—allow more if you have the work done for you.

When examining a car you are advised to take this book (or copies of the relevant buying checklists) and a notebook with you. As each item is checked a record can be kept in the notebook. You may wish to record a running cost total for necessary repairs as faults are discovered—this could be a useful bargaining tool at the end of your examination.

It is strongly recommended that the repair and restoration sections of this book and also *Haynes M.G. Midget and AH Sprite Owners' Workshop Manual* are examined so that the checker is fully familiar with every component being examined.

## Stage A — First Impressions

1. Is the car level all the way round? Are door pillar gaps even, or are they closed in? Does the bonnet fit badly (Frogeye) or are bonnet, bumper, grille even and level (post-Frogeye). (Down at one corner indicates weak springing. £ per spring. Or sagged suspension due to severe corrosion £££ + . Closed-up door gaps indicate severe corrosion £££ + . Badly fitting Frogeye bonnet indicates possible crash damage poorly repaired £££ + . Or simply a bonnet in need of adjustment. Out of line bonnet, bumper, grille on post-Frogeyes could indicate past crash damage £££ + .)
2. Look along wings, door bottoms, wheel arches and sills from the front and rear of the car.

(Ripples indicate filler presence or fibreglass panels £££.)
3. Check quality of chromework, especially bumpers. (Dents, dings and rust ££.)
4. Turn on all lights, indicators and reversing lights and check that they work. (Sidelights/marker lights rust in their sockets £ to ££. Rear licence/number plate lamps earthing/grounding problems plus other specific component problems.)
5. "Bounce" each corner of the car. (Worn shock absorbers allow the corners to feel springy and bounce up and down. Each damper—£.)
6. Check visually for rust—gain an overall impression at this stage. (From cosmetic, to dire! £ to £££ + —see following sections.)
7. Check for damage in rubber bumpers if fitted. (Rips and other damage ££.)
8. Examine general condition of interior at-a-glance. (Rips, dirt, parts missing ££ or £££.)
9. If a Frogeye is advertised as "unrestored", check wing top beading for presence of slight fluting which is often accidentally filled in during restoration. On all cars, check for presence of stress ribs pressed into the floor. Restored cars are often fitted with unoriginal flat steel floor. (Genuine cars may be worth much more £££.)
10. Check fit of curved part of rear chrome bumpers. (Accident damage. Possibly £££.)
11. Check hood for: fit around windows, rips and clarity of screen. (Hood replacement £££.)
12. Quality of paintwork. Does it shine when dry? Are there scratches beneath the shine? Is it chipped? (Neglect or poor-quality, cover-job respray £££.)
13. Does the seller/his surroundings look like those of an enthusiast? (Maintenance £££.)

## Stage B — Clean Hands!

If a car doesn't match up to

requirements after Stage A, don't be tempted—reject it! There are always more cars to be seen. Stage B decreases the risk of making a mistake without even getting your hands too dirty!

Check thoroughly for body corrosion in all the places shown below. Use a magnet to ensure that no filler is present—magnets will only stick to steel. Work carefully and methodically. Where a check-point applies to only one model of car, the model name appears right after the check-point number.

## Bodywork

1. Front apron, beneath grille. (Kerb thumping or other accident damage, corrosion, cheap repair ££.)
2. *Post-Frogeye.* Front wing headlamp area. (Corrosion, filler £££ if severe.)
3. *Post-Frogeye.* Lower front wing, just above sill line. (Corrosion, filler: £££ if severe because hidden corrosion indicated.)
4. *Frogeye.* Panel behind rear vertical faces of bonnet—seen with bonnet up. (Corrosion: £££ if severe because further corrosion indicated.)
5. *Post-Frogeye.* Vertical line a few inches back from front wheel arch. (Corrosion. Filler ££-£££.)
6. Door bottoms: *Frogeye,* check outer skin first. *Post-Frogeye,* check bottoms, outer skins, inner surfaces. (Corrosion, filler ££-£££. *Frogeye*—where available.)
7. Measure door fit along both front and rear vertical edges. (Open or closed at front could mean hinge pillar corrosion ££. *Quarter-elliptic cars,* rear door gap closed at bottom, open at top indicates severe corrosion in body structure. *Half-elliptic cars,* rear door gap closed at top, open at bottom indicates severe corrosion in body structure. All £££ + .)
8. Rear wheel arch. (Corrosion, filler ££-£££.)
9. Sills. Check for rust, rippling, poor fitting replacements. (Corrosion, filler, GRP replacements: ££-£££, depending

upon extent of adjacent corrosion. Poor fitting replacements: ££-£££, dependent upon amount of work involved.)
10. Open door. Lift up and down and note looseness. (Hinge wear £. Corroded hinge pillar ££-£££. Corroded door ££.)
11. *Frogeye.* Check the area along the length of the wing-top beading and along the beading below front and rear lamps. (Smooth finish along beading or misshapen beading suggests repair with filler or other substitute. Replacement of beading by removing wing—up to £££. Replacement of beading by soldering on £-££. Bubbling around beading. Cosmetic repairs £. Severe corrosion—up to £££.) *Post-Frogeye,* check the area along the length of the chrome strip. (Corrosion around trim clips. Unless severe, usually cosmetic £.)
12. *Quarter-elliptic cars,* check as carefully as possible including beneath dash, the bulkhead top beneath windscreen rubber. (Corrosion ££.)
13. Check rear apron and rear quarter panels at bases of rear wings. (Corrosion, filler ££.)
14. Look for cracking, buckling or other damage at the left side of the boot/trunk lid of later cars with automatic boot stay, where the support connects to the boot. (Fatigued steel requires welding, possibly plating and boot/trunk lid respray ££ or £££. Hamfisted person trying to force lid shut—distortion requiring panel beating and possible respray ££ to £££.)

## Interior

1. Examine seat and backrest. Check for damage. (Worn, thin or split covers. ££ each if correct pattern available.)
2. Tip seat forwards. Check for damage. (Scuffing and tears ££ per seat, if correct pattern available.)
3. Check dash. (Cracks, tears or scratches. Wrong instruments £ to ££.)
4. Check cleanliness and condition of hood. (From £ if dirty, ££ for some restitching or window

replacement up to £££ for B.L. replacement.)
5. Examine steering wheel and gear knob. (Correct parts fitted? Cracked or worn steering wheel £ if correct parts available.)
6. Test inertia reel seat belts, if fitted. (Should hold when tugged sharply £ each.)
7. *Post quarter-elliptic,* check door trim and door/window mechanism handles. (Wear and scuffing at base and rear of trim, buckling of hardboard backing, broken handles: £ to ££, if correct parts available.)
8. Ensure that the seats fold forwards and that the hinge mechanism has not collapsed. Check that the 'paddle' allows different backrest positions (where appropriate) and that seats slide and lock. (Stiff, unlubricated mechanisms £, or less. Replacement seat or frame repair £ to ££. Failure to slide easily could indicate weak and corroded floor £££.)
9. Wind both windows up and down—there should be no restriction. (Usually lack of lubrication, less than £. Worn mechanism £.)

## Mechanical

Ask owner to start engine. Let it idle—thorough warming-up takes quite a while on the road—this will help. (Does he/she let it idle on the choke? Harmful practice!)
1. Pull and push steering wheel and attempt to lift and lower at right angles to steering column. (Clonking indicates wear in column bush, loose column to body connections, loose steering wheel nut, loose column to rack clamp.)
2. *Post-Frogeye,* pull bonnet release. Is it stiff? (Seized mechanism or cable £.) *Frogeye,* check that bonnet emergency catch, twin automatic stays and supplementary rod stay are all in place. (Replacements may be hard to find.)
3. Open bonnet. Check for non-standard air cleaners, rocker cover. *Frogeye,* carbs and dynamo. (If originality is important £-££, if available.)

4. If oil cooler is fitted, does it leak? (Replacement £.)
5. Check engine/engine bay for general cleanliness and presence of oil. (Leaking gaskets/lack of detail care/blocked rocker box breather on later 1275 cars. Probably £.)
6. Listen to engine. (Tappets are generally most audible on 1275. Others should be quieter.) Bottom-end rumble, timing chain tinkle—non-adjustable—should not be audible. (Worn engine: timing chain and sprockets ££; worn crank £££.)
7. Is paint peeling around clutch/brake cylinders? (Carelessly spilt fluid strips paint £ + time.)

STOP ENGINE AND LEAVE FOR A FEW MINUTES.

8. Remove radiator cap SLOWLY with rag and beware of spurting, scalding water. Inspect coolant level and its general cleanliness. N.B. for models with expansion tanks the coolant in the tank is not a good indicator of the cooling system as a whole. Remove the cap in the radiator (*late 1275*), or the outlet elbow in the top of the thermostat housing (*1500*), bearing in mind the safety points already mentioned.
   Check for orange colour inside cooling system. Check for oil on top of water either in form of droplets or as brown 'gunge'. Remove dipstick and check for water droplets in oil. (Orange indicates rust and a long time since water has been changed or topped-up with antifreeze. Poor maintenance £ to £££ + . Oil in water or water on oil dipstick indicates head gasket problems—most common with 1500 and 1275. Probably £££ if head damaged or if overheating has caused associated problems.)
9. Remove engine oil filler cap. Look for yellow or brown slimy sludge or foaming inside cap. (Severe bore or valve guide wear ££ to £££.) Look for white foaming or 'goo' inside cap on later and U.S. models with emission control equipment. (Faulty ELC—Evaporative Loss Control-system £.)
10. Let car out of gear. Take handbrake off. Push car backwards and forwards a few yards. (Creaking wire wheels indicate need for rebuild or replacement ££ each.)
11. Inspect the fins of the radiator. (Newer Midgets appear to have greater problems with oxidation than older cars. Exchange radiator ££.)
12. Examine engine mountings for signs of previous removal. The engine mounts should have fine thread bolts and nuts, lockwashers on all nuts. Any wiring or other clips which were originally held by a bellhousing nut may have been left off when the engine was removed. Rubber mounted brackets should not be under obvious strain or show any sign of having been forced on back-to-front. (Previous engine removal is not necessarily a bad thing but it would be interesting to know why it was undertaken, what had gone wrong and who carried out the work?)
13. Jack both front wheels off the ground together. Turn steering wheel from lock-to-lock. (Roughness or tight spots indicates wear in steering rack. Replacement or overhaul ££.)

## Road Test

If you, the tester, are driving ensure that you have adequate insurance cover. Otherwise carry out as many as possible of the following tests with the owner driving.
1. Start up. Is starter noisy on engagement? (Worn starter dog £.)
2. Is it difficult to engage first gear? N.B. Pre-1500 cars' clutches should be light and even just a little 'sharp'. (Worn clutch and/or worn gear selector mechanism ££.)
3. Drive at 30mph. Brake steadily to a halt.
A. Does car "pull" to one side? (Failed oil seal behind rear drum brakes £. Oil contamination on front drum brakes £. Worn pads or shoes £. Seized callipers £ to ££.)
B. Do brakes rub, grind or squeal? (Worn pads or shoes £. But more if discs or drums ruined.)
4. Drive at 30mph in 3rd gear. Press, then release, accelerator four or five times. Listen for transmission 'clonk'. (Worn universal joint £. Worn differential ££. Worn Halfshaft/driveshaft ££. Worn wirewheel/hub splines ££.)
5. Drive at 40mph. Lift off accelerator. Listen for differential whine. (Worn differential ££, if severe or unbearably noisy.)
6. Accelerate hard in 1st gear to around 4000rpm, then lift off. Listen for engine knocking. (Worn engine bearings £££.) Also—
7. —does gearbox jump out of gear? (Worn internal selector mechanism £-££.)
8. Drive as in 6./7. above, but lift off in second gear, then repeat the exercise in third, road condition permitting. Does gearbox jump out of gear? Try the exercise, as far as is safe and practicable, in reverse gear, particularly (if possible) with earliest gearboxes. (Jumping out indicates worn selector mechanism £-£££.)
9. Drive at 45-50mph in 4th gear. Change into 3rd gear. Does gearbox 'crunch'? (Worn synchromesh £. Faulty/worn clutch ££.)
10. Drive at 25-30mph in 3rd gear. Change into 2nd gear. Does gearbox 'crunch'? (Worn synchromesh £. Faulty/worn clutch ££.) N.B. Gearboxes fitted to 1275cc cars had a straight-cut 1st and reverse gear which was always horribly noisy, so noise in this area need not suggest undue wear.
11. Do front wheels flutter or shake at speed? (Wheels out of balance £. Worn front suspension ££.)
12. Check that road conditions are suitable. With ratchet knob depressed, pull the handbrake on whilst travelling at 20mph or so. Don't risk a skid! (Car pulls to one side—faulty handbrake on that side. N.B. Seized rear wheel cylinders are a common problem on *quarter-elliptic cars* £.) N.B. In severe winter conditions, various parts of the handbrake mechanism can freeze simulating other mechanical problems.
13. When cornering, does the steering wheel attempt to return to the straight-ahead position when loosed? (If not, tight kingpins probably indicated £ + .)
14. In second gear at about 30mph accelerate hard, then decelerate

hard; don't brake. (If car veers to left or right, the rear axle is loose or the springs are faulty or [*Frogeyes*] the radius arm bushes have deteriorated or the radius arm itself has lost strength through corrosion. New U-bolts £. New rear springs ££. New radius arms ££.)

15.　At low speed, brake and listen for front end 'clonks'. (Loose wire wheels: retightening is free! But worn splines on wheels and hubs ££. Loose brake callipers: free retightening provided no wear. Brake pads moving within the callipers: no problem, provided that everything else is sound.)

16.　With the car stationary, operate the brake pedal. Apply light pedal pressure in repeated strokes. (If the pedal slowly works its way to the floor—even over a minute, the master cylinder is faulty. This problem more common to dual circuit systems £ to ££.)

17.　*Midget 1500*. Operate the red brake warning light or ensure that it illuminates when the key is turned to the ''Start'' position, then push on the brake pedal as hard as possible. (If the light illuminates, the rear brakes probably leak. Replacement wheel cylinder £. Sometimes only adjustment is required.)

18.　Accelerate from about 1000rpm in top gear, full throttle. (Pinking/spark knock probably indicates maladjusted timing. Can cause piston damage over a long period which = ££ or £££.)

19.　*Midget 1500*. Accelerate to 5000rpm then change up to second. ('Popping' though the exhaust indicates faulty emission controls— U.S. cars—or over-rich carburettor setting.)

20.　Accelerate up to 45mph in 3rd gear, then release throttle. Preferably use a downhill stretch. (Pronounced 'snapping' and 'banging' through the exhaust indicates burned out exhaust valves—pre-1275 engines particularly prone. (New valve and regrind £. Valve seat inserts plus valves ££.)

21.　At highway speeds (55mph maximum in U.S.A.) climb a slight hill with a very light throttle.

(Hesitation, coughing, 'snapping' or 'spitting'. (Indicates over-lean carburettor setting, can cause valve damage over a long period £ or ££.)

22.　Stop car. Apply parking brake firmly. Engage 2nd gear. Gently let out clutch—but depress again *as soon as car shows any signs of distress.* (If car pulls away, worn rear brakes £. Oil in brake drum £. If car remains stationary but engine continues to run, worn clutch ££.)

23.　Switch off engine. Does it run-on or 'diesel'? (Revs less than 800 on tickover, probably carbon build-up in cylinder head £ + time. Or over-advanced ignition. Early '70s models-on with anti run-on valve— the ELC system is faulty £.) N.B. 'Dieseling' may be a common problem in some parts where gasoline of a high enough octane is no longer available.

24.　*Midget 1500*. Have someone stop and start the engine several times while you, the tester, listen with the bonnet open for clonks around the base of the engine and further back, on a level with the gearbox. (Front end clonks mean front mounts have failed—weak mounts fitted pre-'76. Rear end clonks mean two of the four rear mounts have failed £.)

## Boot/Trunk Inspection

1.　Is the spare tyre inflated and with a good tread and does the wheel appear serviceable? (Replacement tyre—£, obviously! Replacement wheel £ to ££.)

2.　Is the jack available and does it work? (Replacement £.)

3.　*Post-Frogeye*. Is there a hammer for wire wheels—all wire wheeled cars—and a spanner for 1968-on wire wheeled cars? (Replacement £.)

4.　*Post-Frogeye*. Is there a key for the boot/trunk lock? (Replacement key if right number can be found, or even a replacement lock £.)

5.　Does the boot/trunk light illuminate, where fitted? (Switch bulb or wiring fault £.)

## Stage C—Dirty Hands

This is the level at which the car— by now being seriously considered—is given the sort of checks that make sure as far as possible that there are no hidden faults which could still make the purchaser change his or her mind. It might also throw up a few minor faults to use as bargaining points with the seller!

While Stage A took only a few minutes or so and Stage B took quite a while longer, Stage C involves a lot more time, inconvenience and effort, but if you want to be *sure*, it's the most vital stage of all.

**Safety: Ensure that the wheels are chocked when using jacks or ramps. NEVER go under a car supported only by a jack.**

If you want to make absolutely certain that every single potential corrosion area has been examined, refer to the list of body corrosion problems shown at the start of the bodywork chapter.

1.　Jack rear wheels off ground, one at a time, with parking brake fully on. Grasp wheel, twist sharply back and forth—listen for 'clonks'. If wire wheels fitted, do wheels move relative to brake drum? (Worn splines on hubs/wheels ££ per wheel.)

2.　Jack up front wheel at wishbone, partially compressing front suspension. Spin wheel and listen for roughness in wheel bearings. (Imminent wheel bearing failure £.)

3.　Grip front roadwheel top and bottom—ensure car weight cannot fall onto hand—and rock in the vertical plane. (Play indicates: wear in wire wheel splines/hubs ££ per wheel. Wear in wheel bearing £. Wear in kingpin £.)

4.　If wire wheels fitted, have an assistant sit in the car and apply the footbrake fully. With each front wheel in turn jacked off the ground, attempt to turn it sharply back and forth. Does wheel move relative to brake disc? (Worn wire wheel/hub splines ££.)

5. Jack each front wheel off the ground and support on axle stands. With a small jemmy bar or large screwdriver, attempt to lever both ends of the wishbone relative to its mountings. (Worn wishbone bushes, usually involving complete wishbone replacement ££.)

6. From beneath car, examine rear of brake drums and insides of wheels for oil contamination — compare clues given by visual inspection with earlier parking brake testing. (Failed oil seal/blocked differential breather £.)

7. Lift front carpets, check floor, inner sills and top hat sections for corrosion and/or repair. Probe suspect areas with a thin-bladed screwdriver and also tap it with a light hammer — corroded areas and also those repaired with fibreglass covered over with underseal will make a dull sound. Good metal will make a sharper sound. Check also for originality of floor — does footwell include shallow tray for heels to rest in? (Significant corrosion, possibly £££.)

8. Slide each seat forwards, lift rear carpets and check as detailed above. Check originality of floor — should have lateral (across car) strengthener ribs pressed into panel.

9. *Frogeye*, check very carefully around spring boxes both inside and underneath car. Compare repair pictures shown in bodywork chapter with appearance of car under inspection. (Significant corrosion £££.)

10. *Post-Frogeye*. Remove mud, if present, from around rear spring hangers. Probe for presence of corrosion with screwdriver. (Significant corrosion £ to ££.)

11. Examine and probe around inside or rear wheel arches and box section inside boot/trunk adjacent to inner wheel arch area and right to the car's backpanel. *Frogeye* — it will be necessary to empty the boot/trunk and crawl into the rear compartment with a torch.

12. Probe floor beneath sills with a screwdriver, including area beneath rear bulkhead and around spring boxes/front spring hanger. (Significant corrosion £££.)

13. From beneath car, probe boot floor with a screwdriver, particularly adjacent to rear apron and probe bottom of rear apron and bottom of rear wings. Probe and tap rear apron at its bottom curve, in line beneath number plate. (Significant corrosion ££.)

14. *Frogeye*. Check: front apron beneath grille on bonnet for corrosion; front and rear of wings — mounted on bonnet including supporting members inside bonnet. (Bonnet corrosion ££ to £££ if severe.) Check inner wings for corrosion or damage. (Replacement or repair £ to ££.)

15. *Post-Frogeye*. Check: inside front wings for corrosion to inner wings and to headlamp bowls. (Significant corrosion £ to ££.)

   Check: Bodywork around and behind grille. (Significant corrosion £ to ££.)

   Check: Leading edge of bonnet for corrosion and/or filler. (Repair or bonnet replacement ££.)

16. Sniff around fuel tank from beneath and look for evidence of fuel staining — dark patches — especially from front of tank and from the area where filler pipe joins tank. (Replacement ££.)

17. Inspect the engine for oil leaks. N.B. There will inevitably be some other than on a new or newly rebuilt engine.

   Check: Front seal on timing cover. (Not common but usually, on later cars, caused by blocked Evaporative Loss Control system £.)

   Check: Rear seal — leaked oil comes through gearbox bellhousing drain hole. (Rear oil seal replacement: £ + engine out. Gearbox first motion shaft oil seal replacement: £ + engine out and partial gearbox strip)

   Check: *Pre-1275 engines* — side covers — tappet inspection plates — on left side of engine. (Gasket replacement £.)

   Check: Around the oil filter (Spin-on canisters can come loose as can bolt-mounted type. Badly fitted rubber seal on bolt-mounted type £.)

18. Examine the front of the rear axle for oil leakage and oil thrown onto underbody. Slight leakage not uncommon. (Heavy leakage suggests faulty seal in nose of differential carrier, clogged vent or overfilled differential casing £.)

19. Grasp each shock absorber linkage in turn and shake it. (Worn bushes, linkages or shock absorbers £ each.)

20. Look for evidence of grease around grease point and seals. (Lack of servicing — £ to £££.)

21. Check condition of exhaust system and exhaust mountings. (Replacement exhaust ££.)

22. Check brake discs for deep scoring. (Replacement or reground discs £ to ££.)

23. Check as closely as possible visual condition of battery and terminals and also of battery tray on which battery is situated. (New battery £. Welding around battery tray £.)

24. From under the bonnet, grasp the throttle shaft — twin-carburettor models only — and attempt to shake it at each end. (Excessive movement results in an uncontrollable idle and vacuum leaks. Exchange or replacement carbs ££.)

25. Determine how much play exists in the clutch pedal. (If more than 1 inch or so, the clevis pin in the pedal/master cylinder pushrod is worn £.) N.B. Springs should be attached to both pedals

   Move the pedals from side to side. More than slight movement indicates worn pedal bushes or the bolt holding the pedals is loose £.)

26. Check the steering wheel for excessive free play by attempting to rotate it *lightly* with the car stationary and the front wheels on the ground. More than 1 inch at the circumference of the wheel is excessive. (Worn steering rack, replacement ££. *Late 1275 and 1500* — pinion endfloat in need of adjustment £: often caused by worn front shock absorbers £ each.)

27. Check front chassis legs as carefully as possible both from above and below for signs of bowing, wrinkling, welded repairs or any other signs of crash damage. Check too, inner wings and gusset plates adjacent to chassis legs for the same signs. If damage is found

check tyres for even wear indicating an out-of-line car. N.B. Some out-of-alignment does not show itself that easily. (Bodyshell out-of-line could need re-jigging, could even be scrap £££+.)

## Notes for Purchasers in America
*from John Twist of University Motors, Michigan.*

Ensure that there is a title plate on the Sprite or Midget (front right inner fender 1963-69) and on the top of the dash (can be seen from outside the car) and on the door sill from 1970-80. These numbers MUST correspond with the numbers given on the title—and all begin with H-AN (Sprite) or G-AN (Midget)—We've seen some MG1100 titles passed along with Midgets! Don't pay for and receive the Midget without getting the title. The title is your protection that the car is legally yours!

There is little protection for you if the car has been stolen—you can always call the local police and have a title check made to see if the car is 'hot'.

Most states require, prior to licensing, that a "Safety Check" be made by the local police if the car comes from out of state. The common items checked are: lights, brakes, Vehicle Identification Number, wipers, washers—and in some states the exhaust and other items have to be inspected. It's foolish to show up for the inspection knowing that a certain item is not working—call first to find out what is required.

The banks, savings and loans and credit unions will lend money on Sprites and Midgets but only to the amount shown in the *Blue Book* or National Automotive Dealers Association (N.A.D.A.) monthly report. These listings only go back ten years, or less, and the loan values are often well below what the purchaser may believe is proper for the car—but that is the way it is!

There are only a few exceptions—but you can attempt to "beat the system" by having several appraisals of the car done by dealers or reputable shops, affording the bank a better idea of what they are loaning the money for.

Whatever faults are found remember that all faults are repairable. If you want the car, use the cost of repair for leverage when conducting the final price with the owner. Any Sprite or Midget will require some repair and maintenance immediately after purchase—plan on at least £££ here for a complete lube and tune. [Author's note—probably only ££ in the U.K.].

Whatever the budget is, don't spend it all on the car leaving yourself shy of the money needed to do the repairs. Remember M.G.'s motto—Safety Fast!—and make sure you can afford to run your Sprite or Midget safely as well as fast.

## Buying—In Conclusion

Having examined a car in this sort of depth, it is likely that the prospective Austin-Healey Sprite or M.G. Midget owner will be confronted with an almost frightening array of faults. Although the price-check symbols will help in determining the most expensive problems, the following notes will help to provide some sort of perspective to those faults now all too clearly on view.

Body rot and underbody corrosion are far and away the two worst enemies of the Spridget range. Although the car is sturdily constructed any rot found should be viewed on the iceberg principle: for every spot or corrosion found on the outside, things will certainly be ten times worse on the inside and that includes the critical inner sills, inner door pillars, jacking points and other hidden or semi-hidden areas.

Upholstery can also be expensive to have repaired professionally, a problem which

afflicts owners of earlier, less well furnished cars less than those of newer Midgets. On the other hand, reconditioned seats and seat covers, and reconditioned dashboards from firms like Spridgebits help to soften the blow considerably. Good soft tops are relatively expensive while cheap replacements can be a poor fit, take so long to put in place and have such a short life that they are probably not worth considering.

Nearly all mechanical parts are readily available and will continue to be so for some time, partly because so many of the parts were originally built for so many cars that stocks are still fairly high (other than for unique items like the Frogeye dynamo) and partly because firms like Spridgebits are prepared to have them remanufactured. Therefore, in the main, the most tolerable faults in any Sprite or Midget, and especially one for restoration, are those within the car's mechanical components.

## The Extra-specials

Although it seems likely that the original Frogeye Sprites will go on to become worth quite a lot of money, only a handful of Sprites and Midgets are likely to become really valuable. In the main, these are the cars that by virtue of their history or background have got something special to offer. Most, but not all of the extra-special cars are known about and in good hands but a handful have vanished from view; any one of them would be a real find.

Included among the extra-specials must be the "works" cars, which vary amazingly in appearance and, indeed, performance. The first Targa Florio Sprite was, to all intents and purposes, bog-standard while the last of the racing cars were very exciting and potent pieces of machinery indeed (see "Heritage" chapter for details).

The "Super Sprite" was really something else again! The Healey company knew that a disc-braked Frogeye provided a platform which was safely capable of taking a far more powerful engine and, to prove the point, built the car code-named "XQHS". It was powered by a single-overhead-camshaft Coventry Climax engine which gave far more power than the basic unit. The Les Ireland-designed body included a front end which was even more frog-like than the original if that is possible, and featured the Healey trade mark of a swageline down the length of the car. The bonnet was full width and the fixed front wings led down to a conventionally shaped sill line. The performance of the car was so startling that the B.M.C. Management promptly banned it fearing competition with the existing M.G. and Austin-Healey range – so if you can find one of the remaining prototypes, grasp it quickly!

The Healey conversion of the Sprite into the Le Mans-style coupé (it was actually used on other circuits) has been copied by Lenham who supply a kit for converting the standard car. Both are attractive but the difference in their value is fairly enormous! Healeys put a tubular roof structure in theirs to add to rear-end stiffness while the Lenham look-alike depends upon utilising the basic strength of the car around which to build their GRP rear end.

Over the years, a number of GRP bonnets, rear-ends and hard-tops have been offered to the Sprite and Midget owner. In the main, they are likely to detract from the value of the car rather than enhance it, especially when the car has had to be cut about. The exception to this rule is, of course, the hardtop, which is simply a useful additional accessory. A works hardtop is likely to add more value than an aftermarket offering.

Lastly, a number of Sprites and Midgets have been converted into an entirely

different looking type of car. Premier among these in the UK is the Arkley, which looks a cross between a Morgan and a beach-buggy but whose well-proportioned GRP bodywork is mounted upon a cut-down Spridget floorpan. However, all such conversions are certainly a case of "Let the seller beware!" because they tend to be regarded very much as kit-cars on the open market, their value suffering accordingly.

However, it is the prospective owner who is determined to own a first class example of the marque who can find him or herself in the biggest dilemma. Is it best to buy a rough, but complete example and restore it to known standards or would an "original, low-mileage" example be preferable? In practice both alternatives have their disadvantages. A complete body restoration can cost a great deal of money if the work is carried out by a top-class firm making the commercial restoration of all but a few cars an uneconomic proposition – but then of course that is where this book comes in! The only way to be sure of getting rid of rust is to restore the bodywork and the only way to make economic sense out of the project is to do it – or to do much of it – yourself.

Popular myth has it that little used cars are the best buys but, unless it has languished in California's sunny climes, the older car with absolutely no rust inside its inner panels is so rare as to be almost non-existant. Even the lowest mileage examples are found to have some inner corrosion – invariably to the amazement of their owners if they are unfortunate enough to require crash damage repair.

Whichever option the enthusiast finally decides upon, there can be no doubt about which car should be avoided and can be detected using the procedures given earlier in this

chapter: it is the average-to-high priced Spridget, with glossy paint and chrome spinners shining seductively in the Spring sunshine, effectively blinding the would-be purchaser to the artificially smooth, plastic filled body and the endless expense and heartache to come.

Choose well to start off with – and enjoy years of motoring in one of the last of the simply enjoyable sports cars.

## UK tax exemption

Cars built before 1 January 1973 are exempt for vehicle excise duty ('car tax'). The important point here, especially for cars first registered in early '73 or later imports, is that the relevant date is the build date, not the date of first registration. If you provide the British Motor Industry Heritage Trust at Gaydon with the chassis number (VIN), they will give you the evidence you will need to claim tax exemption from your local Driver Vehicle Licensing Centre. Verbal confirmation is free of charge, but there is a charge for a letter of confirmation and a higher charge if you want a full Production Certificate, which provides a full 'Birth Certificate' for your vehicle.

## Classic Car Insurance

If you own a 'classic' Sprite or Midget, you can save money and ensure that you aren't caught in the 'old-car-not-worth much' insurance trap. Classic car insurance is usually cheaper than private motor insurance. This is because classic vehicles are generally used less than the main family vehicle and with extra care, making them a good risk as the likelihood of a claim is lower.

Naturally, enough, most insurance companies will set some restrictions to qualify for this. Models considered to be 'classics', are usually supported by an owners' club. In addition, insurers specify that the car must be above a certain age, in most cases 15 years old, though other companies have different age limits. In addition, the car must not be the main vehicle or be used for more than a specified annual mileage. To an extent you can choose the mileage that suits you, but the lower this is the lower the premium.

Above all, there is a cardinal rule that must be remembered when insuring your 'classic' Sprite or Midget. Make sure you can agree the value of your vehicle with your insurer. It's the only way to protect your investment, should the worst come to the worst.

One thing is for sure. If your vehicle is eligible, you really should consider an agreed value classic car insurance policy.

It cannot be over-emphasised that if the owner of an above-average Sprite or Midget wishes to protect the value of their car and not be in the position of having to accept the often derisory amounts offered by insurance companies on a take-it-or-leave-it basis in the vent of write-off, Agreed Value cover is essential.

B1. When buying an earlier car it's almost as important to have the correct, original parts with it as it is to have a car that is sound in the first place. One especially rare and increasingly expensive item on the second-hand market is the early type dynamo with special Lucas tach drive at the rear.

B2. To buy a car with all the correct detail fittings, and in as good condition as this, would cost rather a lot of money – say, around the price of the very cheapest new car currently available.

B3.  When buying any convertible sports car more than a few years old, it's essential to check that it hasn't sagged in the middle. This is a classical case of ''sag'' leading to an opened-up door gap at the front, bottom end . . .

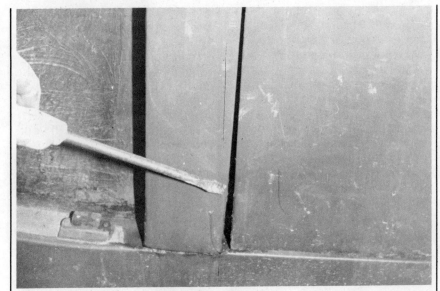

B4.  . . . On the other hand, if the gap is far too wide, it could mean that things weren't put together quite properly last time the car was repaired. The gaps at the rear door pillars can be telling too. Sagged quarter-elliptic cars tend to close their door gap at the bottom, while half-elliptic cars tend to open at the bottom, close at the top.

B5.  Mk. II Sprite/Mk. I Midget with 948cc engine is the rarest of all the cars, making it of increased importance that all the original equipment comes with the example being purchased.

B6. All Spridgets with a conventional bonnet are prone to suffering from corrosion at the bonnet front. It is especially important to check for filler here.

B7. Grahame Sykes of Spridgebits Ltd. tries the bounce test to the rear of the Midget. The rear suspension should be fairly stiff to start off with, so any undue bouncing indicates shot shocks. Condition of the front shockers is even more crucial to the car's handling.

B8. Corrosion around this inner wheel arch looks fairly innocuous but it means that the rear bulkhead is likely to be corroded too − and that's expensive to repair.

B9. This is a view of the floor with carpets removed on the left-hand side. It looks as though it needs ''a bit of welding''. It transpired that it needed a new floor, front-to-back, when we started poking.

B10.    Holes in the rear of the floor, viewed from underneath guarantee an M.O.T. failure in the UK, as they are close to load-bearing structures. Beware of cars that have been 'restored' (i.e. patched over) without attention to the underlying structure. Usually the quality of welding and the appearance of the repair gives the game away, but not always. Ask who 'restored' the car and ask to see detailed invoices, too. Cheap, top-class restorations don't exist.

B11.    ''It's just a little surface rust, sir.'' Except that behind that bubbling paint lies lots of ferrous oxide (rust!) − and this car needed new wings, sills, door pillars and door skins!

B12.    At the rear of the car, more typical rot-spots were to be seen. Filler won't cure rust damage − it only postpones the day when even more work will be required.

B13.    Door skins and the door bottoms, too, when viewed from underneath, are potentially very troublesome. Theoretically, Frogeyes, with their lack of wind-up windows, should be less rust-prone. But by now, they're of an age when door corrosion has often set in anyway.

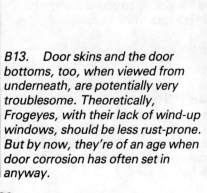

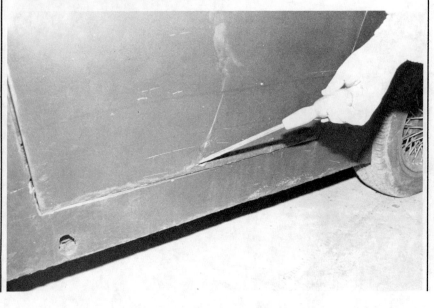

B14. After the bad news, the good! Spridgebits Ltd. and other specialists stock a huge range of repair panels which means that, given the time, the money and the know-how, virtually any Spridget is restorable. But allow for the cost in the purchase price.

B15. These Rostyle (Mag-effect) wheels were only available for a short while. If anything, they are probably more difficult to clean and to paint than the later, far more common wheels.

B16. All A-series engines are easy to repair, easy to get parts for and tough as old boots. Rebuilding one is still not cheap, however. This scruffy engine bay could only be restored with the engine out and after enormous endeavour. Check early 1098cc engine's bottom-end (those with ''10C.G.'' engine number) carefully.

B17. This engine bay has had the sort of time and effort spent on it which results in a beautiful appearance. But, oh dear! What a shame that the rocker cover, air cleaners and one or two other bits are non-original.

B18. The 1500cc Triumph engine found in later Midgets has a weaker bottom end than earlier cars. Check it with care.

B19. Many of those who enjoy using their cars through the Winter months find the alternator almost a necessity. They at least make the later cars more practical.

B20. Re-covering door trims where the original material was made from thermo-formed plastic can be a nightmare. Check carefully before buying.

B21. Disc brakes are far more efficient than the drum brakes fitted in the early days. The discs used are rather thin to start off with and deep scoring can necessitate the fitting of new ones.

B22.   Early cars' dashboards were often chopped about in order to fit all manner of bolt-on goodies and this can detract from the value of the car. Later cars are much more comprehensively equipped to start off with but check for scuffing, scratching or other damage.

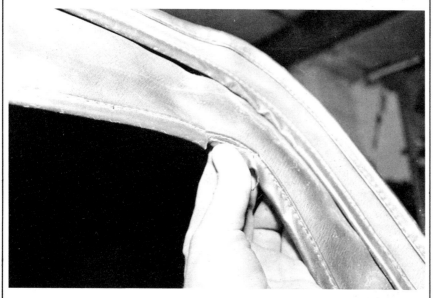

B23.   Hoods come in a range of prices and qualities, but the best hoods are expensive. Check for splits and cracks. Small ones can be repaired; large ones cannot.

B24.   Check also for pulled out studs or clips and for opaque windows. Light scratching or clouding can be polished out with metal polish and even clouding as bad as this can be repaired by having an upholsterer stitch in new clear plastic.

B25. In general, any sort of bodywork modifications − even the superb Lenham bodywork shown here − reduces the value of a car on offer.

B26. It is still possible to 'find' Frogeyes; this one coming from the proverbial barn. The author's bodyshop, The Classic Restoration Centre, restored this tattered shell . . .

B27. . . . to this. Which shows that anything is possible. They occasionally have restored bodyshells, like this one, for sale, making an easy restoration project. But that's cheating, isn't it?

# ③ Bodywork Restoration A

In many ways this section of the book is potentially the most useful one to the restorer. At the time of writing, Spridget body-work restoration has been covered in no other book and yet it is the most crucial area of the car. Poor bodywork reduces the life, safety and value of the Spridget while restored bodywork (in conjunction with a suspension rebuild) puts back the taut handling which the car possessed when new.

Those enthusiasts without welding equipment have several courses still open to them (quite apart from the obvious one of leaving it to the highly expensive – and completely uninvolved – professional). It is possible to hire electric arc welding equipment in most large towns, although this type of welding equipment is usually found to be too fierce for outer body panels even by the most experienced hands. For 'chassis' work and tack-welding inner wings or door skins, however, arc welding is fine. In the U.K. most Technical Colleges and Evening Institutes run evening classes where beginners can learn the rudiments of arc or gas welding.

Incidentally, brazing can also be carried out with an arc welder with the addition of the appropriate accessory.

Gas welding is far more versatile than arc welding, at least as far as thin-gauge metal is concerned, but gas bottles are more expensive to obtain and are far less safe to store and use. In the U.K. British Oxygen sell a pair of mini-bottles called a "Portapack" while there are a num-ber of independent concerns producing cheaper alternatives.

*"D'you think the setting might be a bit too high, Fred?"*

B1.   The Welding Centre produce a fully portable gas welding set which looks and feels more like a professional set than most others on offer. Used with a cylinder of Mapp gas, it gives a flame which is very nearly as hot as an acetylene flame. The only drawback is that the torch taps are a bit sensitive and also running costs are higher than for a full scale set, although the advantages of portability and lower purchase costs can more than balance this out.

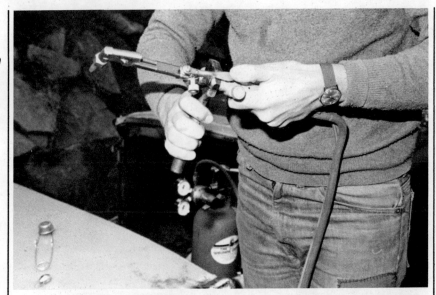

B2.   MIG welding is, as far as the DIY enthusiast is concerned, the Rolls-Royce of welding. The author's body shop uses the SIP Ideal 100 and its successor the Ideal 120 and both are as easy to use as drawing a line with a felt tipped pen — well, almost! It is certainly the most straightforward form of welding for the beginner to use and it also has huge advantages in that it creates far less distortion than any other form of welding.

B3.   MIG welding can be used on the thinnest metal and can also be used very successfully for spot welding with access only having to be gained from one side. Its disadvantages are its cost (it works out at around twice the price of The Welding Centre's better kits), the fact that it needs an Argon or $CO_2$ bottle to accompany it and its inability to heat or cut metal, but these are more than balanced out by its virtues if any quantity of restoration is to be carried out.

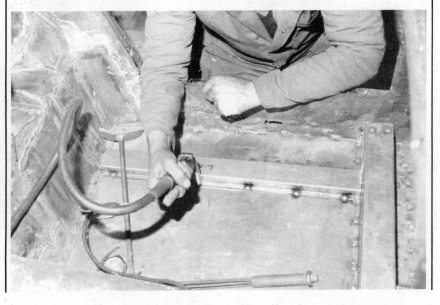

The fourth alternative open to the home restorer is to carry out everything except the actual welding. This is not as difficult as it seems and it saves the labour charges incurred for stripping, cutting out old metal, fitting new parts accurately and finishing off. It is also likely that an experienced welder will produce safer, stronger welds than the home restorer. In addition, the cost is not likely to be greater since no welding equipment needs to be bought or hired. On the other hand, there is the problem of transportation to and from the welder's premises — and doing it *all* youself is undoubtedly highly satisfying if the job is done well!

If this fourth alternative is chosen, the guidelines shown in this chapter are followed right up to the point where the repair sections are held in place with self-tapping screws or steel pop-rivets (aluminium ones are useless — they melt before the weld can be started) and then the welding alone is carried out by the professionals.

## Tool Box

At the start of every section, a "Tool Box" section appears, listing most of the tools and equipment needed to enable you to carry out the work. No list of "essential" workshop tools is presented here but simply the advice that it is safer and cheaper in the long-run to always buy (or hire) the best tools available.

## Safety

**At the start of every section is a "Safety" note. Naturally, safety is the responsibility of each individual restorer and no responsibility of the effectiveness or otherwise of advice given here nor for any omissions can be accepted by the author — "Safety" notes are intended to include useful tips and no more. Some more useful information on workshop practice and general safety measures is given as an appendix — you are strongly advised to read this appendix before starting any of the tasks detailed in this book.**

**Be sure to disconnect the alternator to avoid risk of damage to it when carrying out electric welding.**

---

# Stripdown and Examination

---

## Tool Box

Axle stands or ramps; a thin-bladed screwdriver; eye protection; paint stripper, rubber gloves and a scraper; notepad; bags and boxes for storing nuts, screws etc; a range of spanners (but mainly ½ inch and $^9/_{16}$ inch A.F.) and screwdrivers.

## Safety

**Paint stripper is damaging to skin and eyes — read instructions before use and wear gloves and goggles. Ensure that the car is firmly supported when lifted off the ground — a jack is NOT safe enough. Wear goggles when 'poking' beneath the car and beware of rusty, jagged edges.**

One of the project cars used for this book was a 1275cc Midget of 1968 vintage. The first task was to trailer it from Spridgebits Ltd., who obtained it for us, to the Author's own domestic garage where the

work was carried out to give the feel of an authentic home restoration.

*S&E1. The first task in carrying out a restoration of any size is to go round the car and methodically examine it, taking notes of all the problem areas. Of course your instincts tell you to make a start, to strip bits off the car straightaway. Once begun, this idea can be so infectious that you can lose yourself in a haze of releasing fluid fumes and rust dust, the excitement overcoming you until you reach the point of no return — and it's past closing time. Once graceful lines are now a tangled heap of metal on the floor and you haven't a hope in hell of remembering where all the bits came from. Perhaps the reader might see something of an exaggeration in this — but beware! It's not so far from the truth!*

*S&E2. Start examining the car from one logical point but don't be lulled into a false sense of security at this stage. That "slightly scruffy" appearance could well turn into a total rebuild. It usually does!*

S&E3.   The rear quarter of this wing had broken away — not only through rust but also because it had been bodged with filler at some time in the past, and filler is terribly brittle stuff. The presence of filler in these quantities meant that the whole wing was suspect.

S&E6.   Behind the trim board in the footwell was further evidence that corrosion had made significant inroads into the car's structure and we noted that a pair of footwell side panel repair sections would be needed.

S&E7.   The adjacent hinge pillar was found to be a sticky mess at the bottom but sound at the top. We made a note to buy a bottom hinge plate repair section and a full length cover section.

S&E4.   One of the few clues as to the condition of the car's internals comes from an examination of the jacking point. This one has collapsed allowing the jack to sink into the sill. Obviously the jacking point and the crossmember in which it is situated have corroded badly and will need replacement.

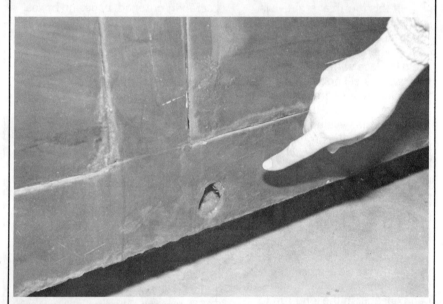

S&E5.   There wasn't even room to get the tip of the screwdriver blade into the door/door pillar gap so the sills and floor were obviously very weak. The point to note here is that it will be necessary to support the car off its rear wheels with the axle stands correctly placed to even-up the door gaps once again before welding up the sills and floor.

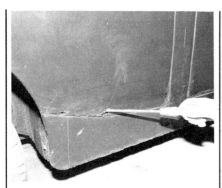

S&E8.    There was obviously some bad corrosion in the front wing base but we reserved judgement on that for the time being.

S&E11.    The front of the bonnet looked pretty ominous – it's a typical Spridget rot-spot. But we didn't examine it in depth until the bonnet was removed prior to engine removal (see relevant section).

S&E12.    Headlamp chrome rings were removed and then the three crosshead screws holding the headlamp units were taken out . . .

S&E9.    We had already established that the bottom of the door skin was bad enough to require replacement but from underneath the view was even worse. A door base repair section would save the day, however. We noted also that the door trims were wrong and that new ones of original type would be required.

S&E13.    . . . followed by the headlamp back. Headlamp wires were disconnected from the loom and tagged with numbered pieces of masking tape wrapped round them prior to disconnection so that they could be easily reconnected later.

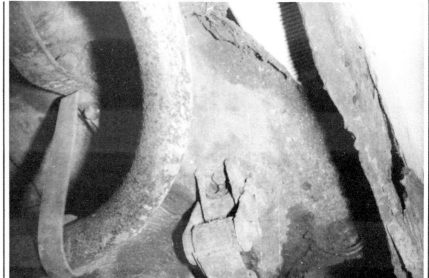

S&E10.    While ''down under'' we took a look under the boot floor, here viewed from beneath the right-hand rear wing. Repairs definitely needed!

S&E14.   The sidelamp units were similarly disconnected.

S&E17.   . . . before the side pieces were lifted away.

S&E19.   Rear lights are unbolted from inside the boot aperture. Again, the wires were tagged for ease of identification later.

S&E15.   Front bumpers were easily removed after undoing the two nuts holding the bumper irons to their mountings. The nuts and washers were put straight back onto the brackets to prevent their loss.

S&E18.   The grille surround base came off in exactly the same way.

S&E20.   Rear bumper bolts were undone in the same way as the front ones. If extra force is needed, try sitting on the floor and pushing the spanner with your foot.

S&E16.   The grille was already out of this car so we set about removing the grille surround. The crosshead screws had corroded and had to be drilled out . . .

S&E21.   We were not sure what size of rear wing repair would be required, or even whether a complete wing might not be necessary. We applied paint stripper to the whole panel . . .

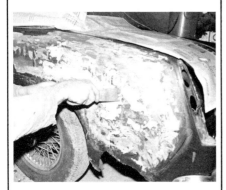

S&E22.   . . . before scraping the old paint off. Actually, this process can take several applications before bare metal is sighted. It is sensible to wear rubber gloves whenever handling paint stripper.

S&E23.   Finally, we sanded the panel using the angle grinder and found, surprise, surprise, that the wing was actually better than expected!

S&E24.   We carried out the same process with the front wing, then, when satisfied that enough had been seen, gave all the bare steel a protective coat of zinc based primer − cellulose compatible, of course.

The outcome of this early stage, this process of stripping for examination, should be that you are prepared for the worst if nothing else. You should aim to make yourself a list showing every job that you will need to do, and a list of all the repair sections needed along with their cost. This enables you to make a realistic estimate of the amount of time and money that you will need to dedicate to the project and so to pace yourself.

Incidentally, it is essential that, as every part, nut and bolt is removed, it is stored in a way that keeps it (a) safe from loss and (b) identifiable. One good way of doing so is to have a system of plastic bags, each one tagged with a masking tape label showing what it contains. All the bags can then be stored in appropriately sized boxes scrounged from local shops.

## Fuel Tank Removal

### Tool Box

Ratchet set for tank removal, open ended for petrol pipe removal; releasing fluid and a power drill for removing rusted-in bolts; large safe receptacle for catching and storing petrol drained from tank.

## Safety

Take note of information in the text and appendices on safety hazards. Petroleum vapour is far more dangerous than the liquid. Thus, a drained tank is less safe than a full one. Take great care to ensure safe storage and have the inside of the tank steam cleaned if it is to be stored for any length of time. For obvious reasons, attempting to weld a fuel tank can be lethal and is a task which should always be left to specialists.

The Sprite Mk II/Midget Mk I-on style of cars have a fuel tank which is virtually the same as that of the Mk I Frogeyes, the only difference being that the earlier cars' filler pipe consists of one steel tube welded to the tank top while, as the following pictures show, later cars' filler pipes are of different construction.

FTR2.  Start by draining all the petrol from the tank. Take the brass plug out of the bottom of the tank. Make certain that you have got an ample supply of suitable, safe and sealable containers in which to catch and keep the petrol. There's almost always more petrol in there than you think, so have some reserve containers on standby. Go to extreme lengths here to avoid the risk of igniting the fuel. One man was killed when, as he drained his tank, his central heating boiler, situated in his garage, started up and ignited the petrol vapour. Do the job outdoors if possible.

FTR4.  If the nut and bolt threads beneath the car have corroded to the point where you can't get them undone with a spanner, take an unorthodox route to getting the tank off. Obviously, with dangerous stuff like petrol about you must never apply a flame to the fixing bolts (especially since old fuel tanks are liable to seep petrol) and even the use of a cutting tool of some sort presents an unacceptable risk. So, WITH THE FUEL LINE STILL CONNECTED to the tank, with the FILLER NECK STILL TIGHTLY CONNECTED AND THE FILLER CAP IN PLACE, and with a jack or axle stand taking the weight of the tank, drill through the head of the captive bolt.

FTR1.  Tanks are fixed to the boot floor by a series of six captive bolts which are held in the boot floor with their threads protruding downwards. Note that once the tank is removed it is safest to store it with a wet rag stuffed into its opening. If it is to be stored for any length of time, have its interior cleaned for safety's sake. This gets rid of all the highly dangerous, highly flammable petrol fumes.

FTR3.  Next, slacken the nuts found holding the tank beneath the boot floor.

FTR5.  Next, from beneath the car, disconnect the petrol pipe which leads from the tank, and from inside the boot undo the clips which hold the rubber elbow connector to the tank top and to the filler pipe.

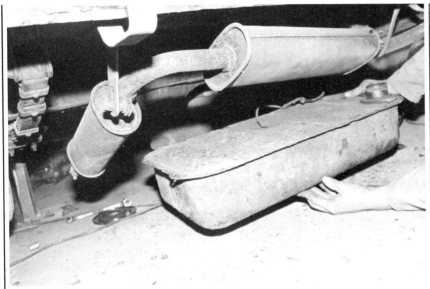

FTR6. Finally, take away the jack and lower the tank to the floor and disconnect the wires from the fuel level sender gauge.

FTR7. Frogeye fuel tanks are quite vulnerable around the area where the filler pipe joins the tank. Handle and store them with care otherwise the joint can easily crack. Take special note that when the tank is reconnected, the sender gauge wire must be connected first. It can be infuriating to forget it and have to remove the tank again.

## Bumper Bracket Mounting Repair (Midget)

BB1. The Midget was in many ways an extension of the old 'Frogeye' and that is shown to be quite literally true in the case of the bumper mountings which are an extension of the front of the chassis frame. To get the bumper up to the required height, raising brackets were used. These consisted of a flanged piece of sheet steel with another sheet steel channel spot welded onto it. The whole structure was bolted to the chassis frame.

BB2.    Start by making up a length of channel, slightly longer than will be required so that it can be cut to fit the flanged section later.

BB3.    After welding the two pieces together, resurrect the old bumper bolt (made of steel far too thick to rot out) and weld it to your new raising brackets. Remember when bolting the structure back on, that the towing eyes are held in place by the same bolts. Discourage further corrosion by painting the whole structure with a zinc-based, cellulose compatible paint before refitting it, thus ensuring that there is paint under the surfaces being bolted into place.

## Grille Surround and Undertray Repair

### Tool Box

A.F. spanners; ball pein hammer; tin snips; folding equipment; welding equipment.

### Safety

**Usual precautions when working with sharp sheet metal and when welding – see appendix.**

SG1.    First step in removing the grille surround is to unbolt it from both front wings. We had already removed the left-hand wing, so we took the right-hand wing off, too.

SG2.    The surround attaches to the wing via bolts into captive nuts held in the wing. One passes through the top . . .

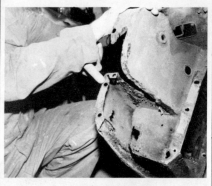

SG3.    . . . while others, at the bottom, screw into nuts behind the curved part of the wing at the front base.

1500 models only – two or three spot welds hold the undertray to each chassis rail. Clean-up the surface to expose the welds, drill through then chisel clear.

SG4.    Both splash guards were paper thin with rust. We repaired, or rather rebuilt, the most complex one with a hole for the air intake pipe, first.

SG5. There's no magic in fabricating a replacement panel like the one shown at the bottom. It's the result of meticulously careful measuring and marking, careful cutting out and accurate, crisp folding. The lip on the large hole and the flange on the right-hand edge have to be worked patiently and carefully and, admittedly, do require quite a measure of skill. Still, there's only one way to acquire it!

SG6. The bottom of this panel was badly corroded but the top half was perfectly sound.

SG7. A repair patch was made for the bottom half only. Note how the semi-circular hole was flanged by turning it gradually over a 90° edged 'anvil' held in the vice. Remember to allow enough metal for the flange when cutting out.

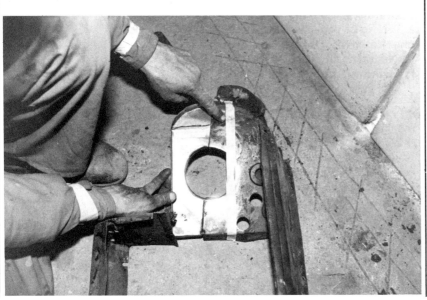

SG8. The repair patch was then offered up, and welded into place. Note how a piece of masking tape had been put across the sound metal before any work had begun. A single cross was placed on the tape and all measurements taken from the one, final datum point.

SG9. This is a view of the radiator/grille surround from below. The tray fitted beneath the radiator had rotted at its outer edges.

SG12. It was folded, leaving its mirror image twin on the other end to be made up and a new base section to be folded before the replacement tray was fabricated and fitted.

SG10. The front valence, which had originally looked quite sound, was taken off. It was found to be 75% beautifully shaped fibreglass with very little steel remaining. This is a really difficult panel to make up and it was with some relief that we learned that Spridgebits sell it as a ready-fabricated repair panel.

SG11. After making a card template, a repair for the edges of the tray was cut out, remembering to include correct flanges.

## Repairing a Kinked Chassis Rail

### Tool Box

As well as the usual range of workshop tools, the specialised equipment specified in the text and also, dependent upon the actual circumstances of the damage, a few one-off home-made tools could also be necessary.

### Safety

**Above all, be sure that the work has been done to a good professional standard. It would probably be wise to have anything but the simplest work checked over. Otherwise, follow the usual safety rules, especially if working under the car.**

It is an established fact that most sports cars end their life not through corrosion, but through the results of accident damage. Of course, most of those which are written-off by the insurers have corroded to the stage where any accident damage they sustain is no longer capable of being repaired at a realistic cost but the point is still there; that they end their lives crashed into oblivion. Sprites and Midgets are no less susceptible to

this unhappy event than any other sports car and, when front-end damage has taken place, the front chassis rails are prone to buckling.

Damage to the chassis rails could make a car difficult to handle, but it still might slip through an MOT test in the UK and you could even find yourself the owner of such a car. Even heavy damage is repairable with a professional body jig which holds the body firmly in place while pulling or pushing at the afflicted areas until they return to the required shape. The jig includes a set of guides against which to check the body for correct alignment in every direction.

Light damage can be repaired by the home enthusiast, especially if it is possible to hire a hydraulic body ram of the type illustrated here — they're the sort of thing that a half-decent tool hire shop ought to stock. We show how a lightly kinked chassis rail was pushed back into place, precisely.

CD1. The kink in the right-hand chassis rail can clearly be seen here, towards the top of the picture. We began by establishing just how far out the rail was. We took one of the shock absorber bolt holes as a datum point on one side and the bonnet locating hole on the other.

CD2.   We took a further check, this time back from the shocker mounting to the upright corner of the bulkhead . . .

CD4.   Lastly — and logically — the actual gap between the rails was measured comparing front, rear and damaged areas.

CD6.   . . . and across the line of the car.

CD3.   . . . and then, once again, the opposite diagonal was measured.

CD5.   Before carrying out any remedial work, it is essential to check that the car is on axle stands and on a level floor. Check the floor with a long spirit level along the line of the car . . .

CD7.   Then check that the axle stands — and thus the car (or bodyshell as in this case) — are dead level all round.

CD8.   The inner wheel arch strengthening gusset, which is being pointed to here, was found to be kinked, a result of the front axle line having been pushed back. We use the hydraulic ram, pushing forwards from the footwell end plate to push it back again. Chains and fixing pins should be part of any kit of body ram parts. Here, the right-hand end of the ram has a chain taken from it to the outer edge of the chassis rail mounting. As the ram is pumped up, the chain pulls the mounting point back into place.

CD9. Of course, the footwell end plate is nowhere near strong enough in itself to take these sort of loads, so it was reinforced with two baulks of strong timber: one between the toe board and the floor crossmember and another back from the crossmember to the heel board.

CD10. Meanwhile, back in the engine bay, things were moving fast! We used a bottle jack, supported with a timber on one side and with a steel plate to spread the load a little on its ''top'' surface, to help push the rail back into place.

CD11. Alternatively — even preferably, since far higher loads can be exerted — a professional tool can be used.

CD12. One of the front struts had been ripped off this car in its accident. Replacing the strut alone would have been more problematical than cutting off the whole front section of the chassis leg and welding on a replacement from a scrap car — at least this is one of the few parts that virtually never rots, so should be available in good condition from a parts car.

Of course, after every stage in the procedure shown, alignment checks were taken and notes made of any movement found. In practice, it will almost certainly be necessary to carry out all the necessary pushing and pulling a number of times. It is far better to attempt to move each area a little at a time rather than trying to push it all the way in one go. The different parts are dependent upon one another and so are likely to move in sympathy with each other.

If any doubts remain as to the thoroughness or accuracy of the work, or if home DIY methods do not completely achieve the desired effect (and don't forget to check height of chassis rails too — all too often, one will lift relative to the other in an accident), take the car or bodyshell to the professionals. A misaligned bodyshell can be a lethal danger on the roads — don't take chances!

## Front Wing Removal/Front Wing (Inner and Outer) Repair

### Tool Box

A range of A.F. spanners; releasing fluid; heat source (such as a welding torch or butane lamp).

### Safety

**Ensure that nothing flammable is accidentally ignited whilst stubborn nuts are being heated.**

Many manufacturers extol the virtue of bolt-on wings as though they had only just been invented! Spridgets have used them ever since the Frogeye made its last leap into motoring history, and removing them is a piece of cake!

Here the author with the aid of one of The Classic Restoration Centre's panel beaters shows just how simple it is. Note that the grille and the grille surround have first been removed from the car, along

54

with the lights and other trim. The colour of this wing is grey because we wanted to find out how much rot and corrosion there was beneath the paint; so we stripped all the old cellulose off with paint stripper before removing it from the car — it's easier to handle that way — and then we painted the bare metal in zinc-based primer. We didn't want further corrosion to set in even before we had done something about repairing the last lot!

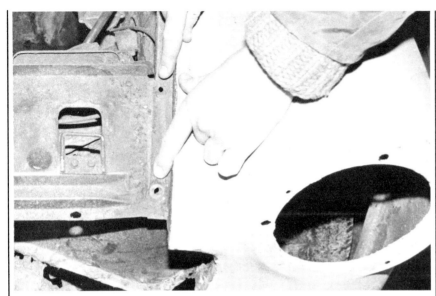

FWR1.    First the two bolts holding the front wing to the bonnet lock platform are removed.

FWR2.    Beneath the grille the front wing is bolted to the apron with three nuts and bolts at the rear of the join shown here. They tend to go fairly rusty so be prepared to soak them well with releasing fluid before commencing work and also be ready to use heat to help free them. Even a butane cartridge-type blowtorch should give enough heat to do the trick.

FWR3.    Three more bolts are arranged in a vertical line behind the footwell trim panel. They screw into captive nuts held in the wing structure itself.

FWR4.    On the principle of leaving the easiest until last (but also because it holds the wing stable until the last minute, allowing you to remove all the other bolts easily), take out the bolt which passes through the end of the rain channel and into another captive nut held in the top corner of the wing panel.

FWR5. And then it only remains to lift the complete wing away. Refitting must be carried out in the exact reverse order but there is one important point to make: Don't tighten the bolts up until all the bolts are in place, and check all alignments carefully before final tightening, leaving those bolts found inside the footwell until last.

FWR6. Spridget front wings usually seem to deteriorate first in the bottom corner, as shown here. Although the rest of this wing was sound, the bottom corner had broken away.

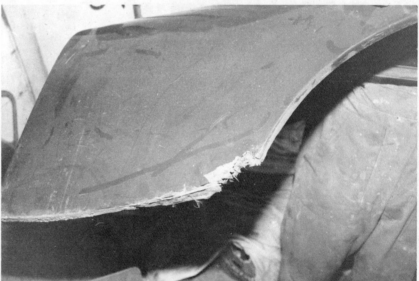

FWR7. Quite a large fibreglass patch was pulled out from behind the corroded area and a cut was made back to sound metal. The rest of the wing base was sanded back to bare metal just to make absolutely sure that no more rot lurked behind the paint.

FWR8. The repair patch was flanged to the right shape then stepped so that it fitted the wing flush after it was welded into place. For more extensive corrosion in this area, a repair panel is available which covers the entire lower reaches of the wing and which includes the correct mounting brackets.

Mk I Frogeyes and the later Sprites and Midgets all have virtually the same inner wings. That may seem surprising in view of the difference in the appearance of the cars' outer panels, but the only difference is in the flange fitted to Spridgets' inner wings to correspond to the fitting of the bolt-on outer wings.

*FWR9.    One of the first places to deteriorate on the later cars is this lower quarter, near the place where it joins the bulkhead. Making a repair section is a relatively simple matter. It may be easiest to fold the repair out of flat steel and shape it in situ after tack welding it into place. Of course, if the repair section has to be made any larger, it will be necessary to form it and shape it before it is fitted.*

*FWR10.    These are the remnants of a 'Frogeye' inner wing (note the lack of a flange compared with the earlier shot). As usual, the inner panel has remained quite intact, while the top panel has corroded at the join with the outer panel which is barely hanging on at all.*

*FWR11.    On the other side of the car after cutting away part of the top panel, we decided that more drastic surgery was needed. First, we took a piece of card and pressed it against the outer panel, making a fold and a dirty mark (workshop fingers are usually enough!) feeling through to all the edges of the steel. Just for good measure, each straight line was marked over with a pencil and ruler and measured to check its size. The top flanges were also measured and marked onto the card.*

FWR12. Back to the other side (they are, of course, symmetrical, so the same card template can be used for each side, suitably reversed) and the top panel was removed after drilling out all spot welds . . .

FWR13. . . . and then chiselling the joints apart.

FWR14. Replacements were made by cutting out the templates then placing them on steel sheet, drawing round them and cutting out to suit.

FWR15. With a pair of sections of angle iron cramped in the vice (and held closed at the other end in a woodworker's cramp), the cut-out steel for the top panel was folded over using a piece of wood between hammer and steel to prevent any hammer marks damaging what was to be a finished piece of steel.

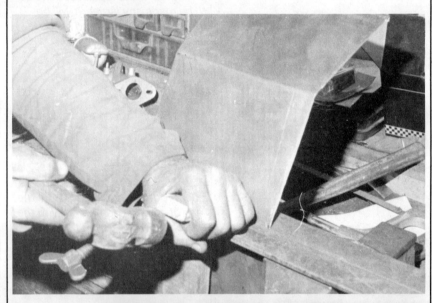

FWR16. After welding both repair sections in place, the only damage that remained was to the inner panel. It had been accident damaged at some time in its life and it looked as though the slight rippling which covered the entire surface was going to be difficult to get rid of, so a thin scrape of filler was used to disguise the damage. Careful panel beating would have done the job in time (although unskilled hands would probably stretch the metal and make it worse); it's all a question of how far you want to go.

These inner panels are also often damaged because they are leaned upon, or even sat upon while the bonnet is up and servicing is being carried out. When the section becomes old and rust weakened, such maltreatment can just about finish it off and give the restorer extra work to do, So check out the possibility that it might have happened to your car before you start.

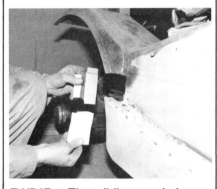

FWR17. The mildly corroded Midget inner wing shown in the first shot in this sequence was repaired after first cutting out a card template to the shape of the repair patch required and then making up a steel section to match.

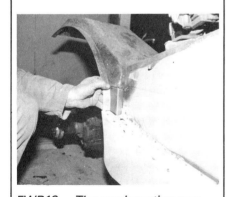

FWR18. The repair section was made with let-in flanges, designed to sit behind the existing panel and so disguise the repair – all the more important with the 'Frogeye' repairs where they will be visible with the bonnet open.

FWR19. It is possible to buy complete front inner wings as repair sections and if one of those is used, follow the above sequence with the obvious difference that you will not have to make up the panel yourself. Panels are available like this one, which covers the usual corrosion areas, both smaller and larger panels are also available. The smaller one covers just the arched part of the inner wing and the larger one includes the whole inner panel not shown here. Also, slightly different panels are available for Frogeyes and for later cars; Mk I's inner wings have a turned under flange, while Spridget-shaped cars have the external flange shown here.

In the past, inner wing sections bought from less reputable firms have had a poor reputation regarding their quality of fit. Make as certain as you can that the ones that you buy are of the correct shape – even a small deviation can cause great problems. If you are going to collect such a panel for yourself, it could be worth making up a template of the wheel arch shape, as shown earlier and taking this along to check the fit.

## Bulkhead Repair

Only the most badly corroded cars rot out at the top of the bulkhead, but it happens. The following sequence shows a Mk. I Sprite bulkhead being repaired, but all models are basically similar in construction.

BR1. Under the shreds of old filler, we found strong evidence of corrosion. The front of the bulkhead was also damaged where holes had been crudely punched to allow the passage of wiring.

BR2. Ray, one of The Classic Restoration Centre's body men, investigated the extent of the damage by grinding down to bare metal with the sanding disc on the angle grinder. It's sensible to wear a face mask when doing this in case fibreglass has been used – powdered fibreglass dust can be lethal!

BR3. Drill out the spot welds from the area to be renewed . . .

BR4. . . . then chisel the welds apart.

BR7. Next, Ray patched the damaged areas on the front of the bulkhead. Again the MIG welder was ideal because there was virtually no resulting distortion to contend with.

BR10. Rubber gloves were used to protect hands against the corrosive effects of paint stripper. Paint stripper must be kept out of the eyes – it's best to wear goggles.

BR5. Make up a repair section for the one to be renewed. Cut out the corroded metal . . .

BR8. The top quarter of the bulkhead was pushed in a little, perhaps as the result of past accident damage. Ray made a screw-in end for the slide-hammer and screwed it into the windscreen mounting. The slide-hammer was then used to pull the bulkhead back into place.

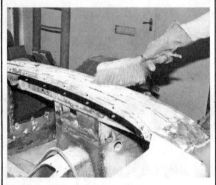

BR11. The stripped paint was swept off and – surprise, surprise – more paint! This always happens, so . . .

BR6. . . . and weld in the new section.

BR9. Before any filler was used, we stripped all remaining paint from the bulkhead top. Note how the paint wrinkles after the application of stripper.

BR12. . . . you usually have to be prepared to go through the process several times until you reach bare metal.

BR13. After filling a curve like this, use an easily bent solder stick to check that the curvature of one side matches that of the other.

DP2. The plate to which the hinge is bolted is seen here. It's made of really thick plate so it won't corrode, but its surround will.

DP4. . . . and open at the bottom.

## Hinge Pillar Replacement

The hinge pillars are dreadful trouble spots on all Sprites and Midgets. They are one of the first places to show evidence of serious corrosion when the rot sets in and as a result they have frequently been repaired − often badly. The owner often cannot see much wrong with the car even though the doors can be moved up and down and the pillar is a bit bubbly at the bottom. So the hinges are crudely reinforced and the pillars filled. Consequently, the door pillar proper goes on corroding away inside until the time comes when it can be ignored no longer − and by then the job is quite a big one.

DP3. Frogeyes and Spridgets close their frontmost door gaps at the top as the 'chassis' corrodes . . .

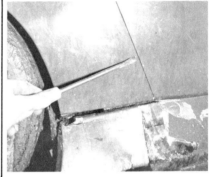

DP5. Spridgets follow the same pattern at the rear − they close at the top and open at the bottom but note − Frogeyes, because of the different type of loads fed into the bodyframe, close up at the bottom.

DP1. The bottom door pillar is the first one to go. Obviously, when it reaches this stage, there's no point in attempting to remove the hinge from the plate let into the pillar. Simply cut the whole thing out in one piece.

DP6.    First stage in removing the old door hinge pillar, after removing the door and hinges of course (they simply screw and bolt into place — use an impact screwdriver to remove the hinges from the doors), is to cut off the hinge pillar outer skin. This is best removed by grinding the edge of the skin until the corner is ground away, or at least until the metal is thin enough to be cut easily with a bolster chisel.

DP7.    It really isn't very sensible to handle razor sharp steel without gloves. Ray, The Classic Restoration Centre's body man who carried out this piece of work hates working in them. Ah well, they're his fingers! Normally, the door pillar skin would need chiselling away from the bottom hinge plate but this one was so corroded that the hinge plate came away with the outer skin.

DP8.    This pillar proved to be a double skin — someone had bodged a repair in the past. Spridgebits can supply a great selection of door pillar repair sections. Between them, they satisfy the owner who has found just a relatively small amount of corrosion and wants to do the job properly by cutting out and replacing, say, just the bottom hinge section, through to the replacement of the whole pillar such as that covered here.

DP9.    The rear of the hinge pillar comprises the side of the passenger (or driver's) compartment tunnel. Ray cut away the remains of the hinge pillar but left as much of the rear plate in place as possible.

DP10.    Because of the rust, the cutter was not working all that cleanly and in any case we did not want to get so close to the back panel that we burned right through it so there was some cleaning up to do with a cold chisel.

DP11.    Three things to note here: The first is that part of the lower backplate had corroded badly and so all of the corroded area was cut away. Second, the screwdriver is pointing at the two captive nuts to which the door check strap is fixed. These must be left in place if at all possible or the captive nuts must be replaced if the backplate has to be replaced in that area. Third, the Spridgebits complete hinge pillar is shown being held up. This contains the plates to which the hinges bolt, held within cages which allow them to move a little so that the hinges can be adjusted; a good authentic fitting.

DP12.    The sill had been replaced on this car in the not too distant past but the cowboy who had fitted it had cut a slot in the top to allow it to be pushed over, rather than fitted under the hinge pillar. The sill top had to be plated before the backplate could be repaired using flat steel sheet. Note the grips which allow the welding rod ends to be used completely − quite a saving over a period of time.

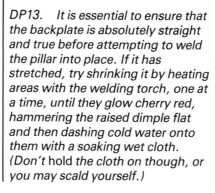

DP13.    It is essential to ensure that the backplate is absolutely straight and true before attempting to weld the pillar into place. If it has stretched, try shrinking it by heating areas with the welding torch, one at a time, until they glow cherry red, hammering the raised dimple flat and then dashing cold water onto them with a soaking wet cloth. (Don't hold the cloth on though, or you may scald yourself.)

DP14.    Before attempting to fit the pillar to the car, fit it to the door itself. A magnetised screwdriver can be very useful here as first the hinge arm had to be slid into the door, then a washer has to be slipped in place over its hole beneath the inner door skin (on the top here with the door facing outside-down) before the screw is inserted through the holes which can be seen in the inner door skin. To make matters worse, the screws are short and can't be held in place with the fingers − hence the need for the magnetised screwdriver! Fit the hinges to the moveable plates in the door pillar in a centralised position.

DP15.    Our pillar did not quite go into the corner formed by the sill top and the backplate and, although Spridgebits' panels are notably well made, you can expect a little fiddling about to get the pillar to sit flat and flush.

DP16.    With everything shipshape, offer the door up into the aperture, engaging the locating peg on the rear door pillar into the door.

DP17.    Ensure that door gaps are accurate all round by cutting small packing pieces from thin wood and resting the door upon them.

DP18.    Measure the door pillars from side-to-side and if they have sprung in at some time, 'encourage them to go back out again by wedging in a piece of wood from the transmission tunnel.

DP19.    Somehow, the bulkhead top had closed down a little, so we improvised a body jack out of a small trolley jack and a length of timber, jacking the bulkhead up again until it was where we wanted it.

DP20.    While on the subject of checking door gaps, don't forget to check that the distance between door and sill top flange is correct. If it is too wide, the door seal will not keep out the howling draught and if it is too small the door will not shut on the rubber. The fit of this area is less important than the level of the door on the outside. It is always possible to dress the flange a little, one way or the other.

DP21.    In cases of severe corrosion such as we found here, it may be necessary to carry out some patching upwards of the hinge pillar, under the bulkhead.

DP22. When all the gaps are as accurate as possible, braze the hinge pillar in place. Don't weld it fully yet — the most successful body repairers are pessimists! Braze can be softened with the torch and the pillar position adjusted. Weld can't be moved in this way.

DP23. We found that we couldn't do anything about the fit of the curved part of the door at the front where it matches the curve in the bulkhead. Somebody had bodged a repair in the past and the bulkhead was simply too big in this area.

DP24. Although the repair didn't fit properly, it was sound and so we tailored it by simply 'welding' down the edge of the panel. This reduced it in size slightly and left it as sound as ever.

DP25. A problem which afflicts Frogeyes and the early Spridgets with quarter-elliptic springing, is that as the strength goes out of the car's frame because of corrosion, the door gaps close up at the bottom. The door gaps close up on the later half-elliptic cars too as they corrode, but they close-in at the top and that problem is best put right when the floor and sills are repaired, by restoring the body to its original shape, but the Frogeye cannot readily be restored to correct shape in the same way, particularly if repairs have subsequently been carried out to the sills, locking the body into its new shape. Here a line is drawn a centimetre or so back from the edge of the door shut pillar . . .

DP26. . . . then the cutting torch, a Monodex cutter or some other non-distorting method is used to cut down the drawn line. (Note how the cutting torch is held at the correct angle for cutting through thin steel sheet.)

DP27.   The cut is widened to the amount which the door pillar has to go back, using tin snips. If the pillar has to be moved back by more than a couple of millimetres, it may be necessary to remove the sills and use a body jack to get the whole structure back into shape.

DP28.   Next the pillar is tapped evenly back and the joint welded back up. Make absolutely sure that the pillar is straight and true before welding. ⇨

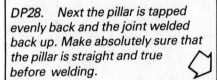

DP29.   Last of all, when the door has been found to fit properly and the hinge pillar is welded into place, weld the hinge pillar cover plate into place, making certain that it lies level with the door, the bonnet when it is shut in the case of the Frogeye, with the front wing in the case of all later cars, and also with the sill and door lines.

DP30.   When fitting the pillar cover plate to a Frogeye, close the bonnet to check fit. Spridget front wings have to be hung in place to carry out the same check.

DP31.   When The Classic Restoration Centre restored the Practical Classics magazine's Midget, we removed the hinge pillar after the outer sill had been removed. The reason for fitting the new hinge pillar before the sill was that the sill can then be fitted to the pillar.

DP32.   The door pillar on this car had rotted to just below the level of the top hinge. A full-size Spridgebits repair section was cut down to fit and located in the same way as the Frogeye pillar already shown.

DP33.   The hinge pillar cover plate can be fitted with the front wing still attached at its front end, by lifting the rear of the wing out of the way. But frankly, you might as well go to the extra trouble and take the wing right off.

DP34.   When fitting the cover plate (and shorter versions of the same cover plate are available), ensure that the door and wing gaps are right and that the three holes, through which the wing bolts pass, are properly aligned.

DP35. We spot welded the plate into place using the SIP Spotmatic with extension arms to reach round the obstruction. Of course, the pillar could be tack-welded using gas or MIG, but spot welding is by far the easiest way.

## Door Skin Renewal

Fitting a new door skin is an ideal introduction to serious bodywork repair for the novice because, although it involves some fairly drastic cutting and some fitting, there should be no problems with achieving a good fit provided that the correct approach is followed, and the range of repair sections available means that no origination needs to be carried out — all parts are bought ready formed.

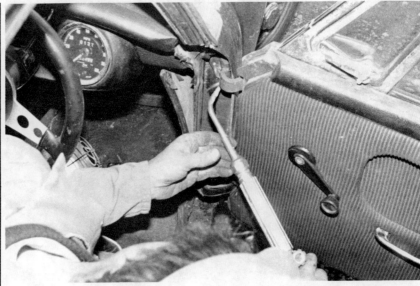

SR2. First, remove the door, but leave the hinges on the door — refitting them can be fiddly. It may, of course, be necessary to apply some heat to stubborn screws. An impact screwdriver is also useful.

SR3. On the other hand, if the bottom hinge pillar is in as bad a state as this, it's best not to get too involved in trying to get screws out at all. It's then quicker in the long run to take the door off the hinge.

SR4. And don't forget the other alternative (only practicable if the hinge pillars are to be replaced) of drilling the bolts out.

SR1. When this number of rust bubbles have formed along the bottom of a door, it's time to fit a new door skin. Carefully inspect the door bottom, too. It may well be that the door base has rotted out, in which case a repair section for that area will also have to be fitted.

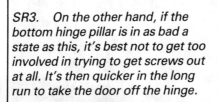

SR5.   If you have any doubt about whether a couple of tiny rust bubbles really do mean that there's a ton of filler in there covering a rotten door, it's a simple matter to grind out the surface to check whether there is, in fact, filler behind it all. (Wear a mask to protect against harmful dust). This door was found to be O.K. and we got away with a small patch.

SR6.   Its cousin on the other side was in a worse state, so Ray began by drilling the spot welds out of the top face of the door.

SR7.   Then the top piece of metal – the top fold of the door skin – was parted from the section below  with a bolster chisel.

SR8.   Next, Ray ground the corner of the fold all the way round the door; the front and rear vertical edges; the bottom edge; the outer edges of the top.

SR9.   Once again, the final cut through the thin steel was made with the trusty bolster chisel. Ray hates wearing gloves – but beware! This steel is very thin, very sharp and very dangerous. You really should wear thick leather industrial gloves.

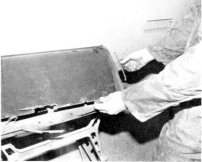

SR10.   The two top corners may need to be finally cut through with a hacksaw, then the redundant skin can be lifted away. Look how the fold which originally wrapped around the outer edge of the frame, has separated from the loose skin.

SR11.   The old door base was rotten, so Ray cut it away after carefully marking around the repair section first to ensure cutting it to the right size. He chose to use oxy-acetylene but a hacksaw with the blade turned at 90° to the frame would have done the job at least as well.

SR12.   The door base repair section was offered up to check its fit, trimming the existing frame to suit.

SR14.   Because MIG welds are rather higher than gas welds (although the lack of distortion more than makes up for this slight disadvantage), the welds were ground down.

SR16.   The new door skin, held at the top here, was also painted on the inside. It was then placed face down and the door frame placed inside its flanges.

SR13.   After making absolutely certain that the frame was true and square, the base was cramped into place (note that a small overlap is allowed for). The SIP MIG welder was used to run a series of seam welds along the edges of the joins.

SR15.   Before going any further, Ray sanded all rust from the edges of the door frame, then the edges were painted, together with the repair section and any other bare metal with cellulose-compatible zinc-based primer.

SR17.   The frame fits snugly into the folds of the door skin, which are already turned at right angles, the holes in the frame top must be aligned with the holes in the door skin top fold.

SR18. With the door held flat, the fold was partially turned over all the way around, before going back to the starting point and hammering the fold a stage further. Finally, hammer the fold down and hammer it flat, interposing between hammer and steel the end grain of a piece of wood to avoid damaging the metal. Don't try to hammer the fold all the way over in one place and then try to move on to the next. If you did so, you could find that you stretch the metal, making it extremely difficult to get it flat and smooth again.

The final stage is to make a few tack welds to hold the skin firmly in place, especially at the top face. You really ought to refit the door to the car before carrying out the welding just to ensure that the door has been reassembled true and square before taking the irrevocable step of welding up the door skin.

## Sill Jacking Point Repair

Every now and again someone will fit new outer sills to a Midget or Sprite without giving any consideration to the structure beneath. Then it becomes almost inevitable that the jacking point will collapse when the jack is used and the new sill becomes damaged. It wouldn't be terribly expensive to replace the complete sill, but when an owner came to us and specified that he wanted the sill left in place and a repair panel made up, we devised the following method at

The Classic Restoration Centre. It's an ideal project for someone who fancies trying out a bit of more advanced panel beating.

JP1. First, the damaged area was cut out with a really sharp bolster chisel.

JP2. Then, we found a tube of the right internal diameter. It had to be the size of the jacking point aperture, less the width of the turned-in flange.

JP3. It was also necessary to position it correctly on the repair panel, of course! Note how the ends of the panel have been 'let-in' to form a shoulder which will sit behind the level of the sill.

JP4. The hole was centre-punched and drilled all the way round, using a piece of scrap wood to prevent damage to the workbench. It is always wisest to clamp a piece of steel down very firmly before drilling in this way. It could spin on the drill and cause almost as much damage as Bodicea's chariot wheels!

JP5. A larger tube and the ball of a ball pein hammer were used to turn over the edge of the flange.

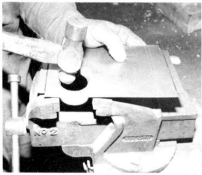

JP6. And then, to turn it over more sharply, the open jaws of the vice were used as an anvil.

JP7.    The shoulders on the repair
were sprung into place, the repair
panel fitted pefectly – and the
customer's original sills were saved!

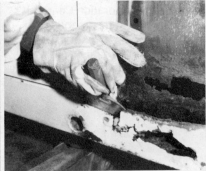

SR3.    Chisel round the front of the
sill (this one had disintegrated
beneath the front wing) and around
the door hinge pillar.

SR4.    Continue to cut along the
top of the sill . . .

## Sill Removal and Refitting

All Sprites and Midgets, from first
to last, used exactly the same sill
structure, the only alteration being
to the 1500 models which had two
jacking points instead of the one
situated just to the rear of the front
door pillar fitted to all other cars.

SR1.    This car's front wings had
been removed prior to removal of
the sill (see appropriate section for
details). Note the mis-match in the
chrome strip line at the rear of the
door. This shows that the car has
sagged in the middle, and this
MUST be remedied before new sills
are fitted.

SR2.    Open the car's door and
place a stout baulk of timber
beneath the floor just inboard of the
sill line. Jack the car up so that
some of the weight is taken on the
jack but not so far that the wheels
are off the ground. Carefully check
the door level and door gaps all the
way round, lowering or raising the
jack as necessary to attain the
correct door fit.

SR5.    . . . and join up the cuts above the jacking point.

SR8.    The old sill then has to be folded down (it's safer by foot!) . . .

SR11.    The story is taken up on another M.G. Midget. Here the old sill is shown being removed.

SR6.    Chisel across the sill, adjacent to the door shut pillar.

SR9.    . . . before removing the sill completely by cutting all the way along the bottom seam.

SR12.    As well as checking the door gaps visually, the author is here measuring to make comparisons with the other side and to ensure correctness.

SR7.    Then, on this car, since the wing at this point also needed replacement, the wing itself was cut through. Where the wing is sound, the cut must be made beneath the wing/sill seam.

SR10.    The inner sill was tested for soundness by tapping it strongly with a cross-pein hammer. After establishing whether the sill should be renewed or not, the remnants of the seams have to be removed by drilling out the spot welds − visible after cleaning rust and paint from the surface and looking for their shallow indentations.

SR13.    The car was lightly jacked up from beneath and, to make absolutely certain that there was no folding in the middle, a length of stout timber was knocked tightly in place between bulkhead top and heelboard.

SR14.    This replacement inner sill is of a stout thickness of steel and contains all original cut-outs. Check that any cheap alternatives on offer are as good.

SR17.    One of the points to watch when fitting the inner sill is that it overlaps the door bottom by enough to provide a lip to clip on the rubber draught-proofing strip.

SR19.    A hole is provided in the sill through which the jacking tube passes. It should be welded on firmly.

SR15.    Before fitting the inner sill, any nasties such as these sill remnants must be removed as well as cutting out the old inner sill.

SR18.    An important location point is in the area of the box section which cuts across the floor in line with the jacking points. The old flanges should be retained if possible when the old inner sill is cut off. Note that the bare metal has been primed but that a strip, top and bottom, has been left bare to enable the spot welder to work.

SR20.    With the new inner sill in place, it is possible to start closing off the inner wing area because there's now something to weld to!

SR21.    The footwell side plate is likely to be as rotten as the inner sill. The Spridgebits repair section is stoutly made but, strangely, is too short — or at least ours was.

SR16.    The new inner sill is lightly tacked into place at the rear. Access has been greatly enhanced, of course, by the fact that in this case the lower half of the rear wing has also been removed. The untidy bits at the bottom are remnants of the old floor which is still in place at this stage.

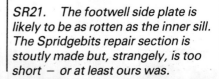

SR22.   We made our own and stepped it so that it appeared flush from the inside of the car. The outside is covered by the wing, of course. It may be best to make up the complete section from top to bottom where it is to be used on a Frogeye because this area shows up clearly when the bonnet is opened.

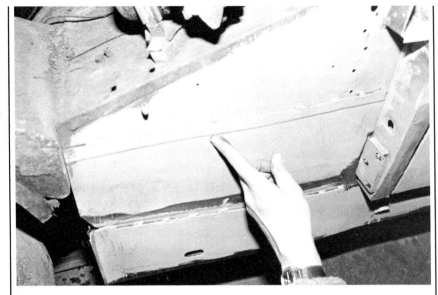

SR23.   Next, it's time to fit the outer sill. Genuine B.L. (or Austin-Rover) sills are the best ones to use; others may not fit as well. And again, in the case of Frogeyes it's important to note that the top of cheaper sills at the front often have joints in them and these, too, show when the bonnet is opened up.

SR24.   We spot welded the sills together, top and bottom, after first going to a lot of trouble to ensure that the door fit was right . . .

SR25.   . . . and later the hinge pillar and its cover were gas welded to the top of the sill.

## Floor and Rear Axle Mounting Renewal

Frogeyes and Spridgets share a virtually identically-shaped floorpan, the only difference being in the shape at the rear where the springs are mounted. It is possible to replace the floor with flat sheet steel but it will then lack the correct strengthening flutings at the rear and in the shallow footwell at the front. If the rear of the floor is rotten, it almost certainly means that suspension mountings are also rotten. Replacing them is a moderately difficult job on the half-elliptically sprung cars but on the quarter-elliptic cars (Mk I and II Sprite, Mk I Midgets) the job requires a black belt in bodywork! First-timers have been known to repair quarter-elliptic spring mountings but there are several potential trouble spots to watch out for.

The following sequence contains 'edited highlights' from several jobs carried out at The Classic Restoration Centre and between them they give an approach to follow which we have found to be effective. You should always, in our view, fit a new floor after the sills have been fitted in place, but before repairing the spring boxes or hangers.

*FRA3. It is, of course, necessary to remove the old floor first. Measure and record the positions of 'Frogeye' passenger seat supports first.*

*FRA4. These supports don't come with replacement floors, so cut off their undoubtedly rusty retaining bolts, and keep the supports for future use.*

*FRA1. Lying flat on the ground is a Spridgebits replacement floorpan complete with all the correct pressings (and also four holes at the rear which are used for half-elliptics but not for quarter-elliptic cars). On top of the floor is a top-hat replacement section, to the rear of it is a spring box capping while behind that is the all-important spring box itself. In his hand, Dave, one of The Classic Restoration Centre's panel beaters, holds a chassis frame reinforcement/shock absorber mounting plate.*

*FRA2. The rear of the car has to be supported on quite high axle stands. The front corner of the boot floor is the best place to put them. Make sure that the door fits remain good — place a trolley jack and strong piece of timber to spread the load under the transmission tunnel to lift the centre structure if it should prove necessary to adjust the door fit in this way and, in any case, to take the downward load you may place upon the car while working on it.*

FRA5. If no cutting torch is available, a sharp chisel will do the job almost as well.

FRA8. Hold the floor accurately in place from beneath using a combination of axle stands, clamps, scissor jack or whatever you have available to hold such a large piece in place. Weld the floor into place all round except — if you are to carry out further repairs there — at the rear.

FRA11. The 1 inch internal diameter tube has been welded to the support and the inner sill into which it fits and the whole jacking point has been welded to the floor and painted.

FRA6. Leave the crossmember (or as much of it as is sound) in place. Measure the crossmember-to-heelboard gaps on both sides and make absolutely certain that no closing up has taken place.

FRA9. Cut out a new crossmember, if it has to be renewed, and mark out on the floor where it is to go and also where the jacking point is to be fitted.

FRA12. Paint the inside of the crossmember . . .

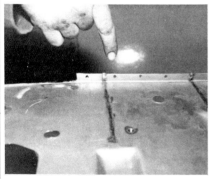

FRA7. Before offering the new floor up, drill ⅛ inch holes along the length of its flange. If you are using a resistance-type spot welder, this won't be necessary, but if you intend to MIG spot-weld, it certainly will. If gas welding, drill slightly larger holes.

FRA10. Make up a new jacking point. Make a support to fit neatly inside the crossmember. Here it is being drilled to take the jacking tube.

FRA13. . . . and weld it into place. Be careful not to buckle the floor by seam welding the whole thing with gas in one go. Once again, the MIG is supreme in these circumstances.

FRA14. Unfortunately, the replacement floor is not always as wide as the original. If the old floor is perfectly sound around the transmission tunnel, cut it to match the new floor with a suitable overlap. Otherwise, patch in a new section of steel.

When you first look at the heelboard of an early Sprite or Midget, it is really difficult to imagine how it all goes together. Basically, its structure is like a tall, thin triangular section. At each of the extremities, a box protrudes into the bottom of the box, into which the rear springs slide. Beneath each box is a tapering reinforcement plate with flanged edges. Confused? The following sequence should help.

FRA15. The outer edges, from where the springs have been removed (See: Frogeye Rear Axle Removal) are obviously badly corroded. The outer heelboard must be tapped thoroughly to reveal any further corrosion. This one was rough!

FRA16. If the shock absorbers are still in place, remove them now. The bolts (one of which is shown in place here, pass right through the radius arm mounting) can be rather stubborn, so be prepared to have to apply heat.

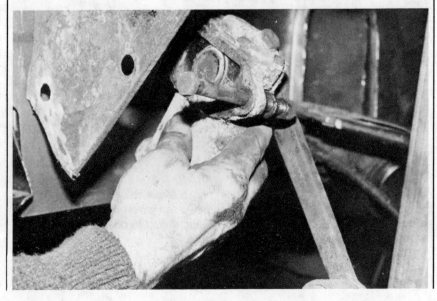

FRA17. Then unbolt the radius arm mounting from the spring box (already removed, in this shot). The bolts extend forward; the holes in the side are for the shock absorber.

FRA18. From behind the radius arm mounting — and note that this shot was taken from the other side of the car — the spring box can be removed.

FRA19. Back to the left-hand side of the car, this is how the spring box mounting area appears.

FRA20. Now, remove the remnants of the heel board outer panel. Note carefully how it all goes together: The bottom flange is the rear of the floor; the left-hand flange is the new inner sill; behind it is the outer sill. To the left of centre is the shock absorber mounting plate while to the right of centre is a heelboard reinforcer which is left in place. It is MOST IMPORTANT that the shock absorber mounting, no matter how corroded, is left in place at this stage.

FRA21. The spring box can be removed equally well from the front or from the back. Drill out the spot welds holding the spring box cover plate in place, then remove the spring box.

FRA22. The new heelboard outer is offered up next and secured precisely in position.

FRA24. This is how the spring box fits on the other side. The left-hand side of it (as you look at the picture) has had the rotten steel removed. The bolt threads protruding forwards are from the radius arm mounting which must be bolted up in place both through the heelboard to the spring box and also, to ensure that the mounting and the spring box are both in the correct place, to the shock absorber mounting plate.

FRA26. Then, take off the radius arm mounting again . . .

FRA23. From the front again, the new spring box is eased into place. It is best to leave the final tidying up until you are sure of location for new panels, but beware of sharp, rusty edges.

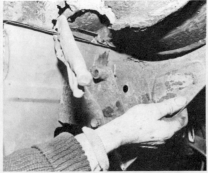

FRA25. After ensuring correct location of adjacent parts, the shock absorber mounting plate can be cut out. Drill out the spot welds.

FRA27. . . . and weld the heelboard outer panel fully in place.

FRA28. When we first repaired this area the Spridgebits repair panels were not available, so we had to fabricate our own. The following will be useful for those who are unable to get hold of fully made-up repair panels. The spring box base was left in place.

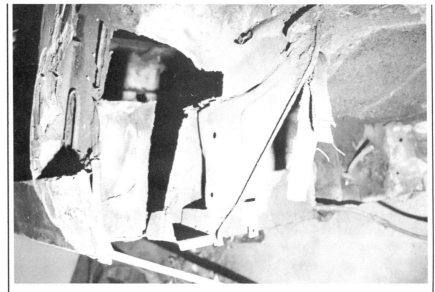

FRA29. A replica was made of the section to which the radius arm mounting was bolted using a carefully constructed card template The threaded fixing 'nuts' were cut out and welded accurately to the replica (right).

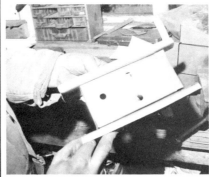

FRA31. They were held together, in situ, as shown here.

FRA33. Viewed from inside the cockpit, the D.I.Y. spring boxes.

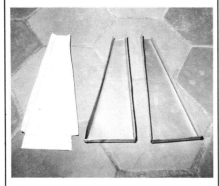

FRA30. Two triangular side supports were constructed, again using a card template based on the originals.

FRA32. The same technique of bolting them to the shock absorber support and radius arm mounting assured accuracy.

FRA34. With the radius arm mountings bolted back on for reference, the replacement shock absorber mounting plate can be fitted.

FRA35. Ours didn't quite fit. The angle between the top and front edges of the 'triangle' wasn't sufficiently closed in, so a slot was cut to enable some adjustment to take place.

FRA38. The bottom support plate, in this case, fouled on the bottom of the shock absorber mounting plate, so it was necessary to saw it off.

FRA41. Two bolts pass upwards into the threaded end of a plate like this . . .

FRA36. After being correctly positioned, the plate was welded up with the MIG. No captive nuts were provided for the exhaust pipe mounting bracket although holes were stamped in the panel.

FRA39. While the axle is off the car, take the opportunity to clean and paint it. Don't forget to use heat resistant paint on the drums and backplates.

FRA42. . . . and a U-bolt passes round the spring and down through the support plate shown here.

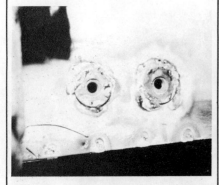

FRA37. When this is encountered, it is essential that captive nuts are welded or brazed into place – there's no way of getting into the back of the panel once it's closed off.

FRA40. Lift the axle on a trolley jack and slot the spring ends into the open mouths of the spring boxes.

FRA43. Bolt the spring box cover plate in place using the front two bolts only, and ensure that the holes in the vertical face align with those in the spring box.

FRA44. If any (or all) of the heelboard inner is to be replaced, make up a repair panel and slide it into place.

FRA45. Then drill the mounting holes right through.

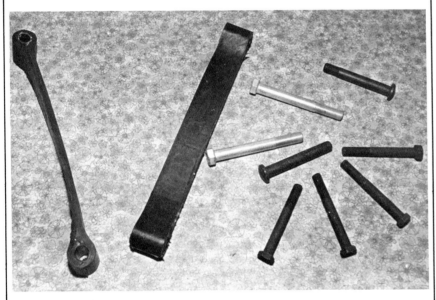

FRA46. New bolts were used for the check straps (left), the spring mountings and the radius arms.

FRA47. Check straps stop the suspension dropping down too far if the rear of the car takes off — remember it is a 'Frog'!

FRA48. New radius arms should normally be fitted as old ones are usually severely rust-weakened. Protect the insides of the new ones by injecting Waxoyl into them.

The finished repair to the spring mounting area has put the bulk of the designed strength back into the car. It's not a simple job but, with careful checking for fit and dimensional accuracy at each stage, the job is D.I.Y.-able, even if at a relatively advanced level.

FRA49. Most half-elliptic repair panels are somewhat different and much simpler. The floor and outer heelboard are virtually the same but, from top to bottom here are: spring mounting plate; rear floor repair section; inner heelboard (or rear bulkhead) repair section.

FRA50. Fitting is fairly self explanatory. The spring mounting plate bolts up through the rear floor, but it cannot be repaired without opening up the heelboard in the equivalent area to the Frogeye's spring box. Remember again, to check that door gaps are even and, if necessary, correct by holding the car up level and true on axle stands.

## Rear Door Pillar Base Repair

DP1. After removing the rear wing of this Midget it was obvious that the base of the door shut pillar had also rotted. The corroded steel was cut out as shown.

DP2. Then a cardboard template of the repair section to be built was made up.

DP3. A sheet of steel was marked using the template, cut out, and folded in the vice. Here, the steps to allow it to sit flush are being let into the panel.

DP4. The finished article is fitted and welded into place. Note that the remnants of the outer wing have been removed from the door shut pillar. The spot welds have been drilled through and the remains chased away with a chisel.

## Rear Outer Wing Renewal (Frogeye)

The following picture sequence shows how to replace a complete Frogeye rear wing. The general principles can be applied to the later Sprites and Midget rear wings and also to the Frogeye front wings, although, if anything, they should be easier to fit because there is no inner wing to which they are attached. The crucial thing with Frogeye front wings is their fit to relative door pillar and sill line.

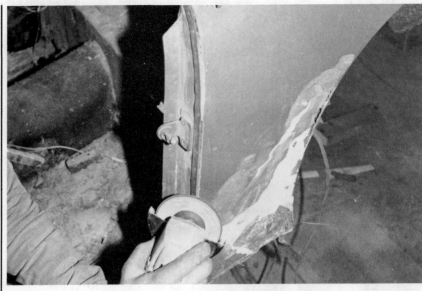

ROW1.    This Frogeye rear wing had appeared fairly sound . . .

ROW3.    The angle grinder was used to take off most of the corner, where the wing flange joined the door shut pillar.

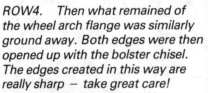

ROW4.    Then what remained of the wheel arch flange was similarly ground away. Both edges were then opened up with the bolster chisel. The edges created in this way are really sharp — take great care!

ROW5.    Next, the wing has to be cut near its join with the centre panel. There are a number of ways of doing it. One is to drill a hole in the panel . . .

ROW2.    . . . until we sanded — and sanded — and sanded! And found that it was, in fact, full of filler. It had to come off!

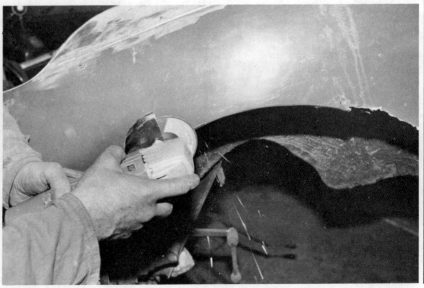

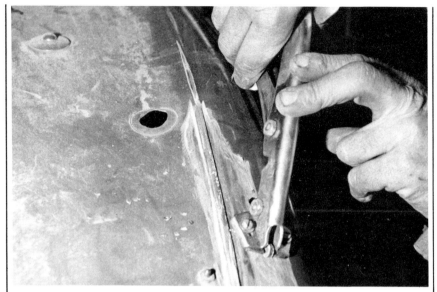

ROW6. . . . and use a panel cutter such as this Monodex. This curls a thin swarf of steel upwards between the two anvils which lie flat on the steel. It doesn't distort the steel at all, but it's very slow.

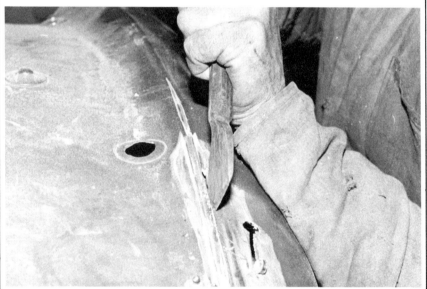

ROW7. Distortion wasn't a problem here, so we showed how a bolster chisel can do the job. It's quite a lot faster but harder to control. A power jig saw would be another alternative.

ROW8. We ended up using the 'old faithful'; the oxyacetylene cutting torch. Used at an angle, so that the flame is cutting through the maximum amount of steel at a time, it's quick and, with practice, it becomes a remarkably clean method of cutting sheet steel. The drawback is that it's an expensive way of doing it.

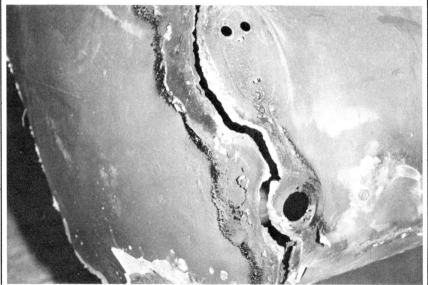

ROW9. These cut lines show clearly that a narrow strip was left around both rear light mountings.

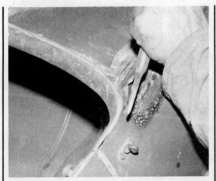

ROW10. Rather than risk melting the aluminium trim rail, the last part of the cut was made with a bolster chisel.

ROW13. With the wing out of the way, the end retaining bolt for the aluminium trim strip could be seen. It is incredibly difficult to get at with the wing in place.

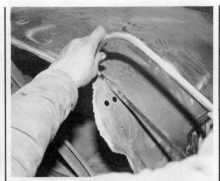

ROW16. A hacksaw was used to cut through the wing remnant at the top of the rear light mounting.

ROW11. Remember to take off the hood fixing turnbuckle before the wing is scrapped.

ROW14. The trim strip was removed to avoid any risk of damaging it later on.

ROW17. The spot welds around the rear light mounting . . .

ROW12. There's something very satisfying about lifting away a wing that has just been cut off.

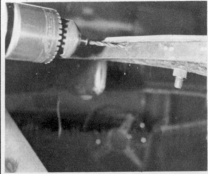

ROW15. The remains of the wing and the wing beading were held by spot welds. The centre of each spot weld was drilled out.

ROW18. . . . and around the rear flasher mounting were drilled out.

ROW19. Similarly, the spot welds at the door shut pillar were weakened. It is usually necessary to use a ⅛ inch drill and then to make the final break with a bolster chisel.

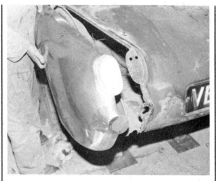

ROW20. The Spridgebits-supplied new rear wing was, for a hand-made wing of its shape and curvature, a surprisingly good fit.

ROW21. There didn't seem any point in using the blank lamp mounting plates fitted to the wing so, once again, we drilled out the spot welds.

ROW22. The actual wing fitting is quite a fiddle but not especially difficult. It is necessary to use lots of clamps and/or self tapping screws to ensure that the wing is a perfect fit before welding it in place.

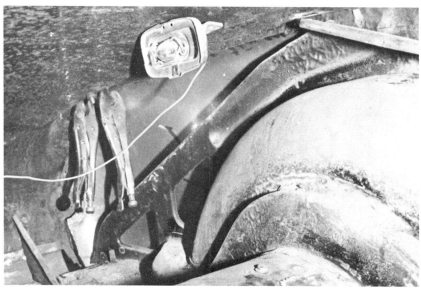

ROW23. Unfortunately, there is no escaping the fact that the top flange/beading has to be welded from inside the boot, the welder having to work in a very confined space. When carrying out work in a space of this size, great care must be taken to avoid toxic fumes. MIG welding, in particular, is known to produce fumes which can be dangerous under these enclosed conditions.

ROW24.    Tack-weld the wing top, taking care not to damage the beading at all, or spot weld/tack it from inside the car.

WR2.    Here, the wheel arch repair panel is seen fitted and tack-welded in position.

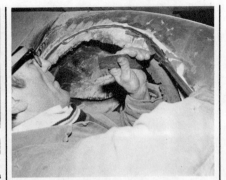

WR4.    After placing the repair section against the wing and drawing round it. the old steel has to be cut away leaving a suitable overlap.

ROW25.    Then fit the base accurately. We had to cut a slot in this wing and bend the bottom flange upwards by almost half an inch to make it fit properly.

WR3.    On the other side of the car, you can see that the bottom of the repair panel supplied has to be cut off when a rear lower section (see WR1) has been fitted first. This is most certainly a point in the favour of this repair section – it's better to have too much, so that you can cut some off, than too little.

WR5.    Occasionally, the repair panel has to be tailored to fit. Here the panel is being snipped prior to opening it up a shade. If the adjustment is very small, the imperfection in the curvature will not be noticeable.

## Rear Wheel Arch Repair (Frogeye)

WR1.    If the rear lower section has to be renewed, fit the repair panel for this area first, but make absolutely sure that its front edge is in line with the normal position of the wheel arch flange which may have rusted away.

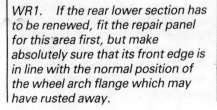

WR6.    This repair panel was slipped behind the cut edge of the old wing, forming a small overlap. The bespoke way of carrying out the work is to produce a stepped edge so that the two panels sit flush with the overlap behind the wing. ⅛ inch holes were drilled at regular intervals . . .

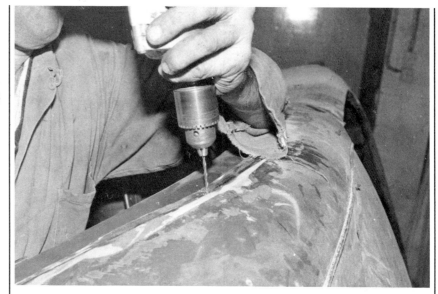

WR7.    . . . and self-tapping screws used to ensure a good, tight fit.

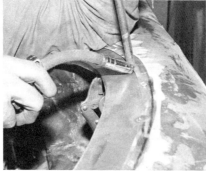

WR8.    Where small gaps existed, they were held closed while the SIP MIG welder seamed them into place.

WR9.    The old wing had ''bellied'' at this point, possibly where stresses had been set up by earlier welding. It was shrunk back by heating a spot to cherry red with the gas welder, hammering the raised heated dimple flat, then slapping a soaking rag on top of it. Be careful to cool the rag each time, to avoid the risk of being scalded.

WR10.    On the other side of the car it was necessary to make a flat patch to fit between the repair section and the door shut pillar. This was simply marked up in situ, cut out, and welded in place.

## Rear Inner Wing Repair (Frogeye)

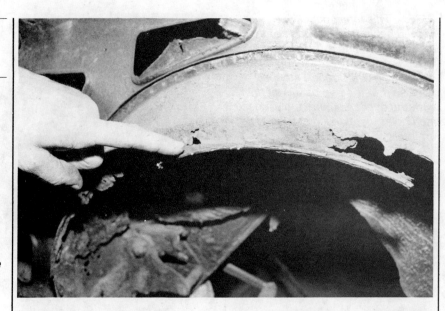

FRI1.   With the whole rear wing out of the way, it was easy to see just how rotten a typically rotten wheel arch can be. Virtually all of the corrosion had taken place in the flange and the vertical section leading from it.

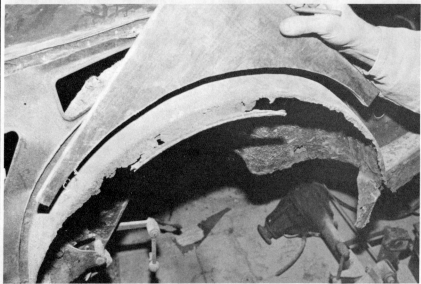

FRI2.   No repair sections are currently available for this area, so we set about developing a D.I.Y. method of making one. First, we cut a piece of 10mm thick plywood into the exact curve of the wing. Note that we only attempted to make it half the circumference of the wing arch. Handling a piece any larger than this would be difficult and wasteful of steel.

FRI3.   The wooden former was used to mark out a piece of steel to the correct shape and size . . .

FRI4.   . . . and the steel for the repair section was cut out.

FRI5.   Using a combination of the bench vice and grips, the steel was clamped to the wooden former and the flange folded over. The other pencil line which can be seen here is for a fold to cope with the curve in the inner wing.

FRl6. The same former was used to create these inner repair sections where only the wheel arch outer was being repaired.

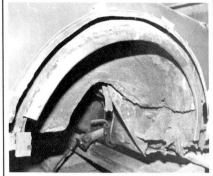

FRl7. These repair sections MUST be fitted with constant reference to the shape of the new outer panels by offering the outer panel up at regular intervals. An alternative preferred by some people is to fit the outer panel first and then fit the inner panel from beneath. For the less experienced this has the distinct advantage that the inner panels are more likely to fit properly and from that point of view the method can be recommended. But it does mean that the panels are far less 'get-at-able'.

FRl8. A note regarding the rearmost inner wing section, where the double curve almost turns back on itself: try snipping the innermost fold to help the steel to curve, then trim and weld up the steel neatly.

FRl9. The final step is to weld the inner and outer wing flanges together. They can be spot welded — and indeed that is by far the quickest way of doing the job — but spot welds don't prevent further damp penetration. A better solution is to neatly seam the two flanges together with a small nozzle and flat, unobtrusive welds.

## Wing Beading Renewal

Bubbles of rust along the tops of the wings, seemingly oozing and bursting out from under the edges of the wing beading are the outward signs of something really horrible happening beneath the surface.

The wing beading is the strip that runs along the top of the joint between wing and body at the rear of all the cars and along the top and front of the bonnet on Mk I Sprites. It is actually a T-section with the upright pushed down into the joint between the flanges on the wing and the inner panel. All three sections (both flanges, and the beading) were sandwiched together and spot-welded when new so that theoretically there is only one way of renewing the beading should it corrode badly, and that is to take off the entire wing, painfully drilling out all the spot welds, and then reassemble with new beading.

However, this is a very time-consuming business so, because time is money (*customer's* money!) we devised a cheaper alternative at The Classic Restoration Centre. It's not a purist's solution to the problem — but then, not everyone can afford the money or the time to be a purist.

WB2.    The old wing beading is easily chiselled off and the remnants can be ground off with a small angle grinder.

WB3.    The cavity between wing and centre panel will be full of rust and half-corroded metal. Try chasing some of it out by using a ⅛ inch drill as a router. The chances of breaking the drill bit are high, but that rust has got to come out.

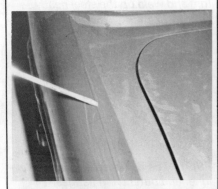

WB1.    Wing beadings were fitted to the tops of all rear wings. By virtue of their age, Frogeye wing beadings are far more likely to rot out than those on later cars.

WB4.    Fill the cavity with braze as a way of strengthening and sealing the joint and forming a base for later stages.

WB5.    The braze will undoubtedly spread each side of the joint. Linish it back to bare metal with a sanding disc.

WB6.    Apply plumber's solder paint over the joint and over a narrow band each side of the joint.

WB7.    Gently heat the area covered in solder paint until it 'flushes' and tins the joint area (i.e. covers it with a thin coat of 'tin', or solder).

WB8. While the solder is still molten, wipe it smooth with a thick cloth.

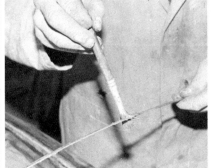

WB11. Spread flux onto the bottom of the strip and onto the wing joint.

WB13. Cut the beading off to length with a junior hacksaw, holding the saw at the angle shown. Leave the beading sticking out by ⅛ inch, or so.

WB9. Now it's time to fit the wing beading. The beading at the bottom is as it comes from suppliers such as Spridgebits. You need only the top strip for this job.

WB12. Heating the job slowly, not intensively as in welding or brazing, but by passing the torch rapidly over it, melt solder into the area where the beading strip is held down to the wing joint. Use a piece of wood to hold the work down. The heat in the body panels will keep the solder molten for a surprising length of time!

WB14. Then hammer the excess beading flat and over the edge of the wing, sealing the end of it off neatly.

WB15. Rub down the beading edge to remove surplus solder using a folded piece of 80 grit paper.

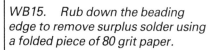

WB10. Grip the tongue of the strip in the vice, turn your hacksaw blade through 90° and cut the top off.

WB16. If there are a few hairline gaps between beading and joint, don't risk sweating in more solder — it could cause the beading to lift again. Wipe in a little filler using the end of your finger to ensure a thin, even, smooth coating. Try not to get filler into the ribbing in the beading strip — it then loses its 'originality'.

## Rear Quarter Inner Panel Renewal

RQI1. Here a rear quarter inner panel has been fitted prior to welding on the outer panel. Great care has always to be taken to ensure that it aligns perfectly with the outer panel. Forming a dish-shape can be quite difficult, but the solution for the amateur who hasn't become quite that skilful is to make up a more roughly shaped panel or to cut the steel, fold it to the required shape and re-weld it once it is in position. This method is not likely to gladden the heart of the perfectionist but it is sound — and it is far cheaper than having to pay bodyshop rates.

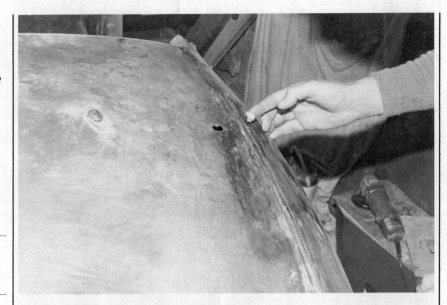

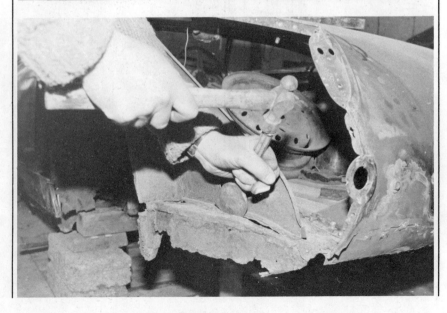

RQI2. The old inner quarter panel was cut off using a bolster chisel across the top face.

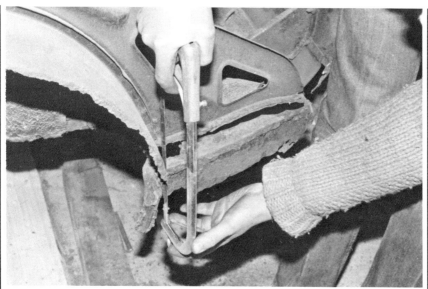

RQI3. The vertical face was cut with a hacksaw to avoid disturbing the inner wing which was, by now, not attached in too many places!

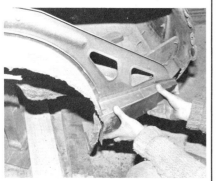

RQI4. A replacement panel was made up, folded and flanged, then welded at the top. It was deliberately left too short so that, after the wing was fitted, the base of the inner panel could be made up to suit it.

It must be emphasised that this method of repair does not exactly replicate the original shape of the part. Instead it provides the home repairer who does not have the finest skills with a way of repairing a complex but unseen shape with a soundly constructed replacement.

## Rear Lower Wing Repair (Spridget)

We fitted a lower wing repair section to the *Practical Classics* Midget at The Classic Restoration Centre. At Paul Skilleter's suggestion (he's *Practical Classics'* Managing Editor), we paint stripped the whole rear wing and found, as is usually the case, that the upper part of the wing was very sound indeed. The lower parts of the wing, front and rear and especially the whole of the wheel arch area was a disaster zone.

RLW1. This Spridgebits wing repair section was very comprehensive, including all the flanges required and was a very good fit indeed. All repair sections seem to need some tailoring but the amount needed by this one was minimal.

RLW2. The repair section is held in place and the top edge marked out with a pencil. Note that the bare steel has been painted with primer to prevent any rusting.

RLW3. A new line was marked a little way down from the one previously marked, to allow for the overlapping shoulder on the repair panel. The old wing was cut off, leaving a narrow flange at the front . . .

RLW4. . . . and the same at the rear.

RLW5.   At this point, the remnants of the old wing fell away; there was nothing holding it around the bottom at all. For details of how to remove a wing where it is attached in these places and of how to remove the spot welds around the 'hull' below the rear lights, see the section on Frogeye rear wing renewal.

RLW6.   The inner wing had also disintegrated in the same area.

RLW7.   And this was all that remained of the boxes at the tail. It is important to keep all the bits that remain when things get as bad as this. They can't, obviously, be used again but they can be used to give reference points when making replacements.

RLW8.   The outer repair section has to be put on and taken off a number of times when carrying out the next stage in the operation. We fixed it with clamps, then decided upon a suitable datum point from which to take all our measurements.

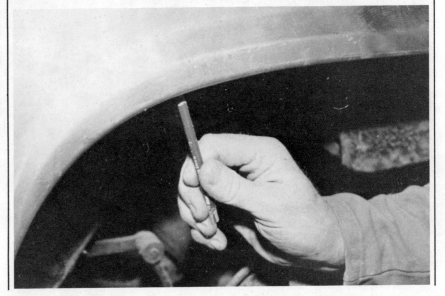

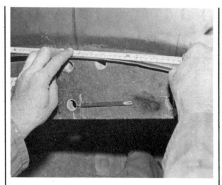

RLW9.    That point was transferred to the inside of the wing . . .

RLW10.    . . . and a small piece of steel, large enough for a part of the inner wing to be drawn around, using the outer wing as a template.

RLW11.    The part-repair section for the inner wing was then cut to shape.

RLW12.    This is a cut out part-repair for another part of the inner wing shown here held against the outer wing. Note that it is oversize to allow for the shape of the flange.

RLW13.    The curved flange was folded, a section at a time, by clamping the workpiece to a piece of angle iron which, in turn, was gripped in the vice.

RLW14.    To dress the flange, the dolly was held against it while it was hammered from the other side.

RLW15.   At times it would have been very tedious to keep taking the wing off and putting it back on again. Then a profile gauge (available from home D.I.Y. stores) like the one shown here is really useful.

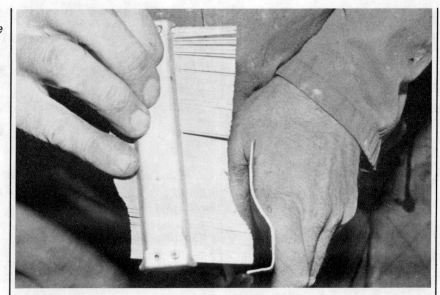

RLW16.   In the end though, it is necessary to make the repair fit the wing itself. For a cheap 'n' cheerful rebuild, it would not be necessary to make the shape of the inner wing replicate exactly the shape of the outer, although obviously, the shape and size of the flanges would have to match. In fact, it could be argued that if the two pieces of steel were a little way away from each other, the whole area would not be so rust-prone.

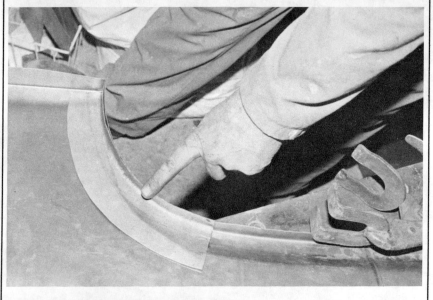

RLW17.   Once all the pieces are made up, they can be clamped and welded into place. At this stage it is ESSENTIAL to fit the outer wing in place and check the fit.

RLW18.    When it comes to fabricating this area, you can see why it is important to keep as much of the original metal as possible to provide references. The top of this section is in two pieces. It looks as though the inner section is the same shape as that of the Frogeye; while the outer section looks as though it was 'tacked-on' to allow for the extra width of the later cars.

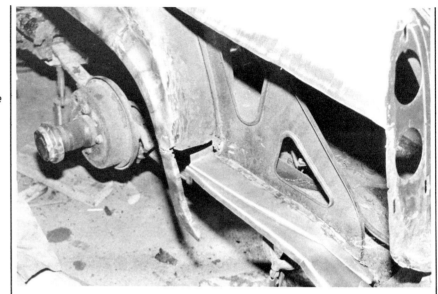

RLW19.    With the outer section spot welded into place, the inner wing was complete. We used the SIP Spotmatic spot-welder here; it's quick, efficient and probably the cheapest of all welders to run.

RLW20.    Complete Spridget rear wings are still available from Austin-Rover. See Frogeye rear wing replacement section for fitting tips.

## Rear 'Chassis Rail' and Boot Floor Repair

Although the Sprite and Midget range was of monocoque construction, there was an integral 'chassis' built into the structure of the car designed to give strength in the same way as an old-fashioned separate chassis but constructed as part of the bodywork. The rear 'chassis rails' are at first difficult to detect because of the very fact that they are part of the bodywork but, as the following photo sequences show, they quickly make themselves obvious when rust takes a severe hold.

From inside the boot of the Frogeye these rails can be seen snaking their way over the rear axle tunnel at the outer edges of the boot floor (they are of course a lot easier to see behind the seats and inside the lift-up boots of later cars) while from outside, they appear to be no more than part of the rear inner wheel arches. On the bodyshell that Ray can be seen repairing at The Classic Restoration Centre, the entire outer length and some of the inner portions of the box section had rotted through. Most cars, even the bad ones are not usually as bad as this one.

RC1. Part of the rear box section outer section has been cut out and repair sections cut out of 18g steel have been tacked and clamped in place over the front part of the box section. Ray is using The Welding Centre cutting torch to cut out yet more rot found further back. A good motto to stick to is: "If in doubt, cut it out!", but try to leave in flanges if they are good enough because it gives you reference points to work to.

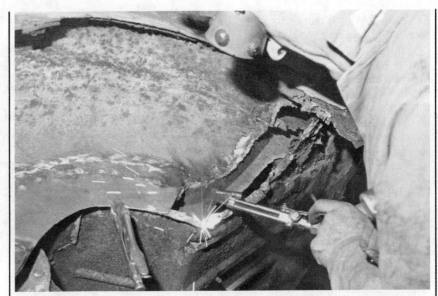

RC2. The flanges themselves and anything else which is going to be welded must be cleaned up thoroughly beforehand. An angle grinder is absolutely perfect for the purpose. A grinding disc can be used (but be sure to use one which has a central recess and is thus designed to take side loads. Flat discs are meant for edge loads only and could shatter with disasterous consequences if incorrectly used). For light gauge metal, lightly rusted steel or steel with tricky curves in it, a 36 grit sanding disc mounted on a flexible rubber pad might be preferable.

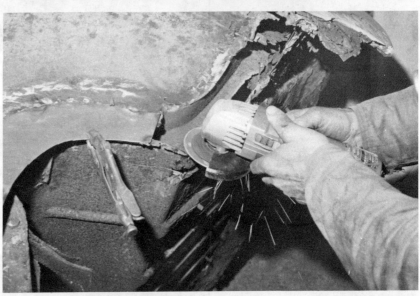

RC3. At this stage and to gain better access it was decided to remove the lower part of the rear wing which was due to be replaced by a repair panel anyway. It is important to cut back as far as sound metal and it is equally easy, even at this stage in the proceedings to be taken in by the presence of body filler. Fortunately, it is very brittle, even in the huge chunks with which this bodyshell was plagued, and it breaks away easily with the assistance of a pair of mole-type grips.

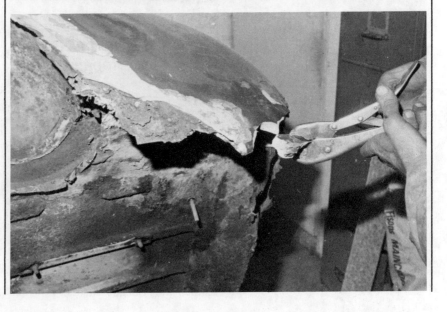

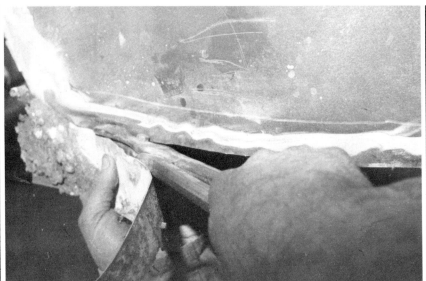

RC4. After placing the new repair section in position and scribing along its top edge, the old lower portion is cut away leaving a generous flange against which to attach the repair section. See relevant section for more detailed information.

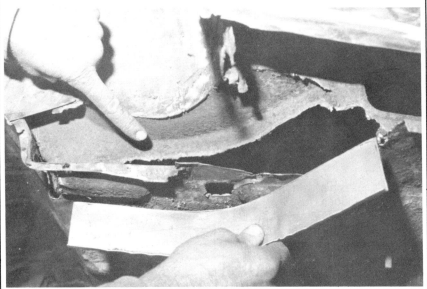

RC5. Bear in mind here that the bodyshell is on its side and that this shot is roughly equivalent to lying on the floor and looking up through where the rear wing should be. With the old rear wing lower section out of the way, it became obvious that the inner surface of the box section had rotted out too, and so it was cut out and a repair patch made up for it.

RC6. After final shaping, the patch is welded into place, again using equipment supplied by The Welding Centre which we found to be light and particularly well suited to this type of repair. Note that the final shaping involved forming a fold to meet the inner panel which runs parallel to the rear wing and − most importantly − a flange was formed onto the bottom of the repair patch to give something substantial to weld the bottom of the member to.

RC7.  With the box section repairs at an appropriate stage, it was time to turn our attention to the boot floor itself. The rear of the floor appeared to be quite bad, but that is best dealt with at the same time as the rear apron which runs across the rear of the car beneath the rear number plate. Viewed from directly underneath the car, the only obvious rust in this area was at the bottom corner of the rear of the axle tunnel. That was where we made a mistake!

RC8.  We followed our usual approach of marking out a piece of card against the job . . .

RC9.  . . . before cutting it exactly to shape. Expect to take a little time to trim the card precisely but console yourself with the thought that card is far, far easier to cut to shape than steel sheet!

RC10.  When the card is cut to size, place it on a sheet of 20g steel sheet and draw accurately around it.

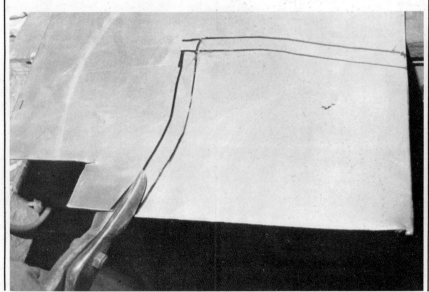

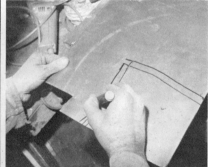

RC11.  Then remove the card and add on enough material to allow for a flange to be folded.

RC12.  And simply cut around the outer marks.

RC13. Many people are unnecessarily wary about making folds in curved material but using the home set-up shown here, it is surprising what can be accomplished. Two pieces of straight angle iron are held in a bench vice and the protruding end of the angle iron is supported with a baulk of light timber held to the angle iron with an ordinary woodworker's G-cramp. The potential for using this set-up for folding long lengths of steel is obvious – you simply slacken both the vice and the G-cramp, insert the sheet to the point where it is to be folded and retighten the vice and clamp before folding the steel over in the normal way.

RC14. On this occasion, the angle iron was being used as a firm surface against which to fold over a curved flange. Start at one end and hold the fold against the edge of the angle iron. Tap the fold a little way over then move on a couple of centimetres and tap the next part of the fold over a little way, being careful the whole time to have the marked out fold against the edge of the angle iron. When the entire flange is folded over by, say 10 degrees or so, go back to the beginning and tap the flange over, bit by bit, about as far again. The whole process should take a good four or five passes before the whole flange is folded over. Try to do it in less and the steel will stretch and distort the repair panel.

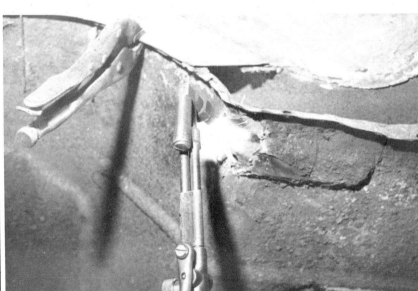

RC15. The rotten steel is then cut out . . .

RC16. . . . and the repair panel tacked into place. It was at this stage that the rear part of the boot floor was tackled (all the conflagration is caused by filler and fibreglass flaring up — always have a fire extinguisher handy!)

RC17. It was then that we realised that much more of the boot floor was corroded beyond redemption than we had at first realised. You can see here how this particular section taken from the boot floor has begun to go 'filigree' — rust has got at it from the inside leaving the outside looking fairly sound but in fact as thin as tissue paper in places.

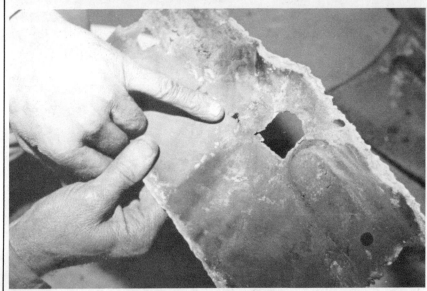

RC18. You are looking at the rear quarter of the car with the bodyshell tipped on its side and with the lower portion of the rear wing removed. The bottom part of the structural member found behind the rear wing had rotted at its bottom flange and so a new flange section was made up . . .

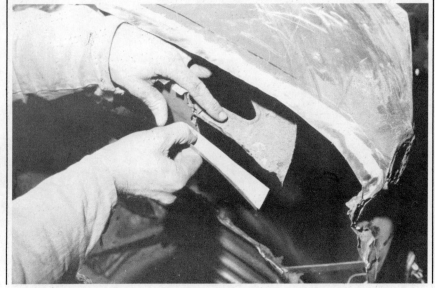

RC19.  . . . and welded into place, giving something substantial to fix to. Note how the correct curve of the section has been retained.

RC20.  Once again, using the card template method, a repair section was made up ready to fit . . .

RC21.  . . . and tacked into place. Note that this repair section has been left short of the rear apron so that a one-piece repair piece for that area can be made up.

RC22.  The front flange on the repair section had to be made to fit around the rear axle tunnel bottom edge. Rather than fold it first and then find that it did not quite fit, the steel was left unfolded, then once the repair panel was tacked into place it was heated to a mid-red colour using the welding torch all along the line of the fold.

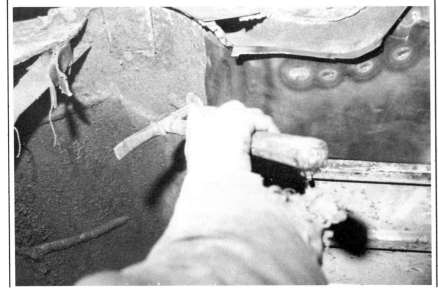

RC23.  The fold could then be made using the metal underneath as a former, secure in the knowledge that it was sure to be a good fit.

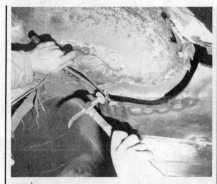

RC24. To flatten the fold out properly, Ray held the spoon (a flattened and slightly curved piece of steel) over the fold while hammering it down. This produced a sharp fold. Finally the fold was tacked into place.

RC25. The boot floor section having formed the bottom part of the box section, a piece of 18g was cut and shaped and the outer surface of the box section (really a continuation of the inner wing) was closed off.

## Rear Apron Repair

Although on the face of it the rear apron appears to be a fairly well protected area — at least in comparison with the MGB's which is open to the elements — it can still rot out, especially in conjunction with the rear of the boot floor. Frogeye's rear aprons are only different from the later cars in the complexity of their shape. So if you can repair a Frogeye's nether regions — and you *can* if you follow this sequence — you can repair any Spridget.

RA1. It is best to repair the backs of the rear wings before embarking upon this area, so that there is a definite line to work to. Note, however, that the outer reaches of the apron, on each side, curve back a little, matching the line of the whole rear panel. Before commencing work, sand the entire area to establish exactly where rust and body filler ends and steel begins.

RA2. Mark out the area to be cut away using a straight edge.

RC26. At the front of the same box section, the rest of the outer face of the box was cut out and renewed.

RA3. Working with a straight edge is far, far easier than attempting to repair against a random wavy line. Cut out all corrosion from the boot floor, too, in the same way.

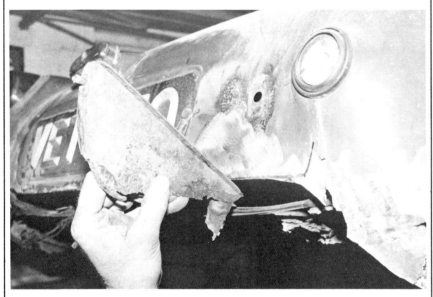

RA4. A roughly triangular bracket (or what is left of it) is fitted behind each bumper mounting and bolted to the floor and rear panel. Remove each of them.

RA5. In order to make a replacement, place the bracket on a piece of card and mark round it.

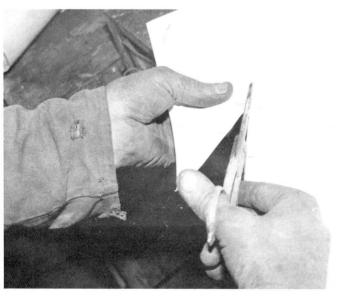

RA6. Then make a card template from which replacement brackets can be fabricated in steel.

RA7.  Unless your arms are ten feet long, this is the only time that you will be able to get a dolly to the back of the panel on a Frogeye (Spridgets are of course much easier — you just open the boot lid). Don't forget that 'Frogs' are particularly prone to having bumps — and thus dents — in that area. So check that a smooth surface in this area isn't just filler. It might be too late to do anything about it later.

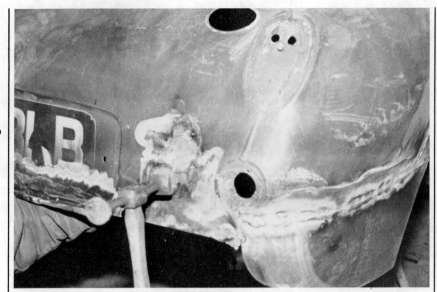

RA8.  Before going any further, grind the cut edges of the repair flat and free of burrs.

RA9.  Where the indent for the number plate has to be repaired, take a 3-D note of the shape to be attained with a profile gauge.

RA10.  Start by repairing the number plate area. We used home D.I.Y. methods here: two lengths of angle iron gripped in the vice; a wide bolster chisel used to make the initial 30° or so bend.

RA11. A dolly with a curved face was then held against the steel while the bent-over steel was dressed up again, giving the curved let-in shape found around the edge of the number plate recess.

RA12. Where a little adjustment is needed, don't be afraid to use unorthodox methods.

RA13. With the repair cut to shape, drill the edge of the rear panel.

RA14. We used the SIP MIG-welder with the spot-welding nozzle fitted as shown.

RA15. Very great care was taken with aligning the repair panel accurately before it was clamped in place and spot-welded through the holes already drilled. Of course, virtually any welding system could have been used but this was quick and gave little or no distortion.

RA16. Where the corrosion damage is less, the repair panel can be much simpler, as shown. Indeed, when the number plate area has been repaired and a sound straight edge formed, this is the next step to take in any case.

RA17.   Because of the size of this section, we drilled holes and held it in place with self-tapping screws.

RA18.   Next, the rear boot floor repair section is held in place. Simply hold a flat piece of steel up against the underside of the boot floor and draw around the curve of the rear apron repair section.

RA19.   The rear of this boot floor repair section has to be flanged. Mark it out a couple of centimetres away from the line you have just marked and cut out the steel to that shape. Then fold the metal in the vice — by hand if the repair is long enough to give decent leverage — until it is roughly to the correct angle.

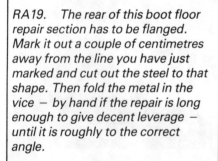

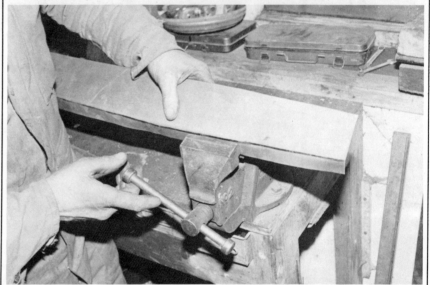

RA20.   Then go all the way along it again and hammer the angle square. Using the vice without the angle iron allows the required curve to remain in the steel.

RA21. If the fold comes out with a number of 'flats' still evident from the vice jaws, dress them out on the bench using a dolly.

RA23. Place the boot floor repair section in place on the car and mark out the flange to the correct depth. Hold it in place with self-tappers if necessary.

RA25. Ray positions the repair panel with great care. It's easy to change its position now but awfully difficult after it's been welded in place.

RA22. If necessary, restore the sharpness to the bottom of the fold with the bolster chisel. Obviously, it doesn't need to be too sharp.

RA24. A useful tip: hold the section in the improvised jaws of the two pieces of angle iron held in the vice. Beware of thin pieces of swarf! They can be razor sharp — dispose of them carefully.

RA26. Ray chose to tack the panel into place using gaswelds. It's a little easier to use on surface-rusted steel than the MIG welder.

RA27. Back to new steel and the SIP MIG comes into its own once again. The bottom of the flange could well be seam welded to prevent the ingress of any moisture although spot-welding could be quickest. Note how the ends of the rear apron repair have been left a little short. They are to be made up with a flanged section which will be fitted with the correct piece of beading (available from Spridgebits).

RA28.   As mentioned earlier, the rear panel can take an awful bashing. Even after dents have been planished out with a hammer and dolly, a trace is bound to remain. Highlight the high-spots such as these shown here by filing across the top of them; the high spots will, of course, look shinier than the surrounding area.

RA29.   After applying a smear of filler and rubbing it down, find an old can of aerosol paint (MAKE SURE THAT IT'S COMPATIBLE WITH WHATEVER PAINT YOU ARE USING) and spray a very light dusting coat onto the repair. Hold the can quite high so that the paint is almost dry before it hits. Final rubbing down with a block will expose any high-spots that may remain.

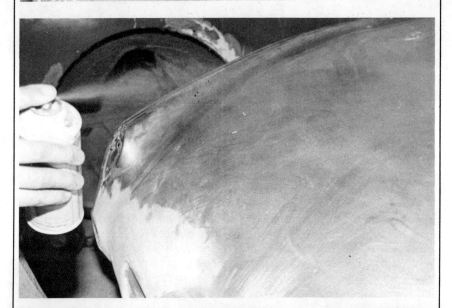

## Breaking A Body Shell

BS1.   This body shell looked OK in some places but nevertheless it was just about beyond economic redemption. This made it a suitable source for a replacement rear end centre panel which was desperately needed for another restoration. The author shows how to cut off the panel required.

BS2.    It is in these circumstances that The Welding Centre's welding pack really comes into its own. It is light enough to be taken to where the work is and yet man enough for the job when it gets there. First of all I tried cutting with the welding torch. This is perfectly adequate for most small cutting jobs if the oxygen is turned up high; and it's quicker than having to change over to a cutting gun if you are in the middle of a welding operation.

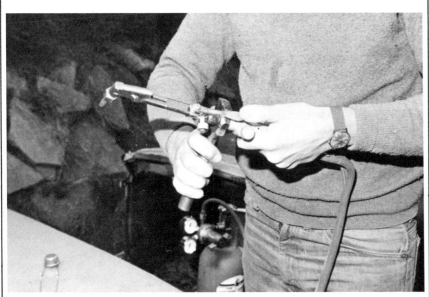

BS3.    This was a larger scale cutting job and so the welding torch was unscrewed from the gun and The Welding Centre cutting torch screwed into place. Setting the gun up for the first time takes a little while but once it is set up (i.e. when the screw which controls the amount of extra oxygen fed into the flame when the cutting lever is pressed is just right) very little future adjustment should be needed. Too much oxygen and the flame is blown out; too little and the flame remains relatively red and cuts are blobby and untidy.

BS4.    The correct way of cutting car bodywork is to hold the gun in its normal flame setting with the unburned, blue part of the flame just a shade away from the work. As soon as the steel melts (which only takes a couple of seconds), the torch should be turned so that the flame is angled sharply in the direction which you are going to cut. At the same time, the cutting lever is depressed and almost instantly a neat cut will appear in the metal. A little practice is required to learn how quickly to move the gun: too quickly and you overshoot the hot metal and the oxygen coming through the gun no longer cuts the steel; too slowly and the cut will not be clean and neat.

*BS5. Voila! The back taken off the car like taking the lid off a giant tin of corned beef. Note that I cut an inch or two outside all spot welded seams. All that remains is to sand off all the seams with a power sander to help find all the spot welds before drilling them out with a one-eighth inch drill. The redundant ribbon of steel will then come away easily with the help of a bolster chisel.*

## Respraying

It's galling but it's true that the only part of a rebuild that most people notice is the respray . . . you can spend hundreds of hours making a car sound, original and dimensionally perfect but unless it ends up with the sort of shine that almost hurts you to look at it, the car will be generally classed as an also-ran. Respraying a car to a high standard is not at all easy but the Spridget owner has two things going for him. First, the car is small, easy to get round in a confined space — and best of all — it doesn't have a roof, which is one of the trickiest parts to spray successfully. In addition the owner-enthusiast has time on his side and if things go wrong, there is usually enough time to put them right.

Whilst on the subject of time, it cannot be over stressed that the most time consuming part of respraying a car is in its preparation. Preparation means: removing all rusted metal and replacing it with new (as detailed in many other places in this book); fitting panels that align correctly with one another; making all surface areas both flat and smooth (and don't be mistaken — they are not at all the same thing); and providing an environment which is warm, dry and free of draughts and dust, in which to carry out the actual spraying process.

The choice of spraying equipment is also rather important.

Some recommend that a 'pro'-type compressor and spray gun are hired rather than a cheap spray set purchased. However, the typical hire shop set up can have three distinct disadvantages: the cost is usually high if the unit is to be used over a reasonable length of time; the user does not have the opportunity to get to know the whims and foibles of the particular set before it has to go back again; and worst of all, the equipment usually leads a hard life and is frequently half worn out or sub-standard in some other way. The author's first respray was carried out on the front drive, using a cheap airless sprayer, which is little more than a powered garden sprayer. It was desperately slow and there was a lot of arm-aching cutting back to do afterwards but the results were among the best the author has achieved! The point of this little homily is that the care and time taken in preparation and spraying are worth far more than the most expensive equipment.

A low cost spray system with a great deal to commend it is that manufactured by Apollo Sprayers of Birmingham, England. It does not use a compressor in the normal sense but instead a fan blower similar to that used in a vacuum cleaner. The pipe to the spray gun is large bore because the air supply is high volume, low pressure which has the advantage that there is less compressed air rushing around, whipping the dust off the walls and ceiling of the typical small domestic garage. On the minus side are the facts that the blower cannot be used to power other tools and also the short duty-cycle of the blower unit which means that it cannot be used continuously for long periods. Even so, the quality of spray achieved can be remarkably high with this unit.

*R-A. A big-hearted little system is that used by SIP in the Airmate Jet 30. This uses a very small compressor built along conventional quality lines and comes with a matching spray gun. This is the sort of unit that would make an ideal alternative to hiring a large compressor for a week or two, especially since the compressor unit can itself be used for other lightweight duties around the workshop.*

R-B. Airmate compressors rise in size up to the type of unit that will do a worthwhile job of work for the most serious of enthusiasts. Because they are fitted with an air receiver, a quantity of air can be stored which allows some leeway for the fluctuations in demand caused when heavier duty tools are used. These machines are perfect for those who want to equip themselves with a full 'pro'-style one man workshop at DIY cost.

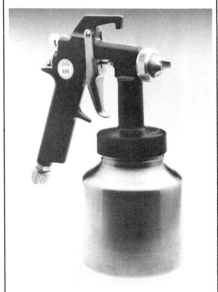

R-C. SIP also manufactures a quality spray gun suitable for the conscientious enthusiast. Known as the 'Jade', it can operate in a variety of modes and gives a high quality finish without having to go right up to the high cost and high air consumption of the full blown (if you'll excuse the pun) professional spray guns.

R1. Many older cars have been sprayed with 'synthetic' or 'coach paint' both of which are terms for oil-based paint. Produced primarily for commercial vehicle refinishing it is often used by those who inhabit the cheaper end of the car sales market. Oil-based paints are a lot less expensive than cellulose but can take a long time to dry and in the usual domestic environment can act like flypaper and a dust trap combined! Its major disadvantages are even greater in that it cannot be flatted with wet-and-dry for a long time after is has been used (so what do you do if you get a run?) and if cellulose paint is sprayed over the top, it sets up a reaction which gives the appearance not dissimilar to that of paint stripper. This door had been painted in oil-based paint so we stripped it right off.

R2. The rest of the body was stripped off too. Even when cellulose has been used throughout, you can still get to the stage where one coat too many will cause the crinkling and crazing patterns that mean 'reaction'! It is essential that all the old paint is stripped off if top class results are the aim.

R3. Some nooks and crannies are almost impossibly difficult to get at unless you are prepared to spend an age with scraper and sandpaper. We used a small sandblaster powered by the SIP compressor to get the insides of the door pillars back to bare metal.

R4. The inside of the bonnet was covered with surface rust, so it too was sandblasted. Sandblasting is extremely thorough but it does have a major disadvantage: before any spraying can be carried out you have to go around the car, first with a powerful vacuum cleaner, then with an air-line, to make sure that no particles of sand remain trapped in any of the body's channels and crevices. Otherwise they can easily fly out during the spraying operation and ruin an otherwise perfect job. After sandblasting, this area was painted then covered in spray-on underseal.

**R5.** When you are satisfied that all the old paint and surface rust has been removed, go around the body and true up any faults with a hammer and dolly but do not be ashamed to use body filler as a form of glorified stopper to make profiles absolutely right. Use the spreader as a shaper and attempt to get the shape about right with the surface of the filler, but leave it slightly proud. As well as saving the stuff, you are more likely to end up with a satisfactory, ripple-free finish if you don't have to sand too much off.

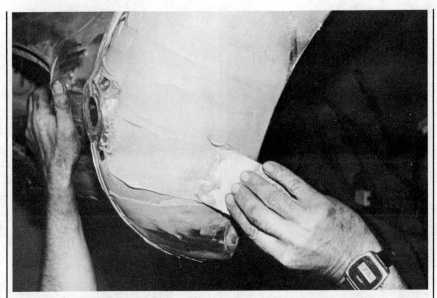

**R6.** In general, the longer the surface of the sanding block, the truer the finish. Use the sander in several directions and thus reduce the risk of creating ripples. Be prepared to spend quite a long time making surfaces absolutely true. If you are not sure how things are going (and filler can be deceptive; it flatters to deceive), run your hand flat across the surface to feel for ripples or even spray a light coat of gloss cellulose aerosol paint over the surface. The shine will show up any imperfections.

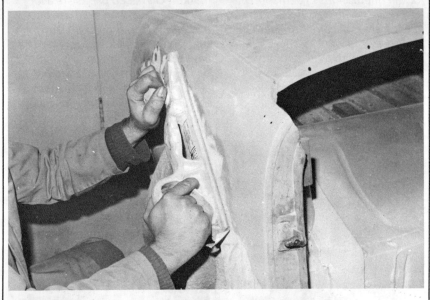

**R7.** It's always best to spray the interior of an open car first. The interior surfaces are far less critical than the outer panels and the paint will bind on any particles of dust that may have escaped your attention, rather than leaving it free to land on wet paint whilst spraying the exterior of the car.

R8. Use of a power sander can cut down time spent on sanding quite considerably. Rather than buy expensive purpose-made sanding strips, save money by cutting your own from the rectangular sheets of 'frecut' paper sold by the paint factors.

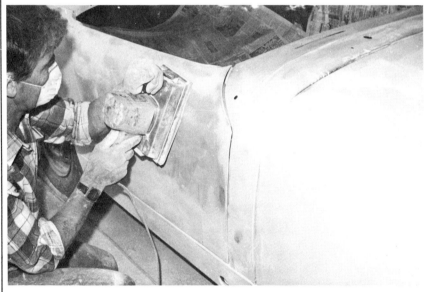

R9. The power sander can be used on convex surfaces but should be deployed with care to avoid cutting right through to bare metal. Obviously, it cannot be used on concave surfaces, where it is best to wrap the 'frecut' paper around the curved side of a sanding block, or use it freehand.

R10. After masking off the interior, we sprayed the outer panels with primer. You can also use a high build 'spray putty' which, if used in moderation, gives a good depth for flatting without too much shrinkage. It has to be sprayed on pretty thick and so cannot be used with the very low powered spray equipment.

R11.    After priming the body, flat it down very thoroughly using wet-and-dry paper (which, in spite of its name is always used with water) or use fine 'frecut' paper which has the advantage that it can be used dry. Whichever system is used, start with a medium grade of paper, then go over the whole job a second time with a fine grade.

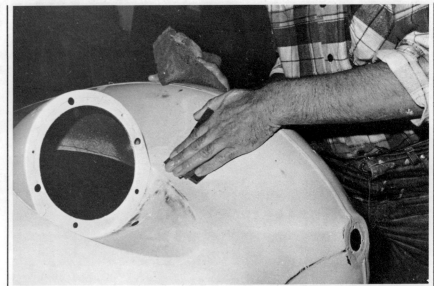

R12.    Flatting will show up any blemishes which you may have missed earlier. This small 'ding' is typical of the sort of damage that most Frogeye bonnets seem to sustain. As well as being visible, it could also be felt as the hand was run over it.

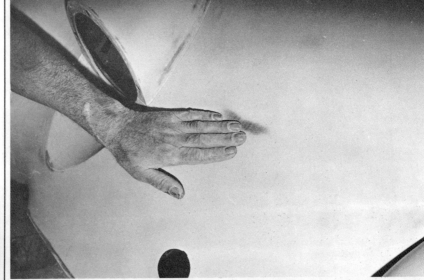

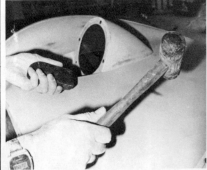

R13.    A rubber mallet and a dolly with a slight surface curve were selected to rectify the problem.

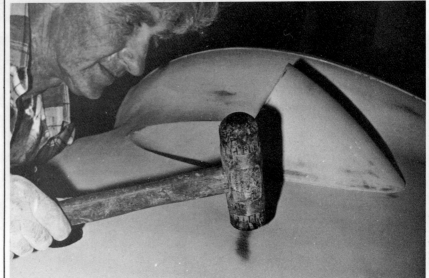

R14.    With the dolly held beneath the raised dent, it was firmly but carefully hammered flat.

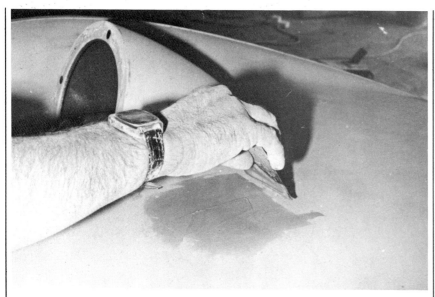

R15. A smear of stopper paste was wiped over the repaired dent. A thin skim of filler could have been used as an alternative.

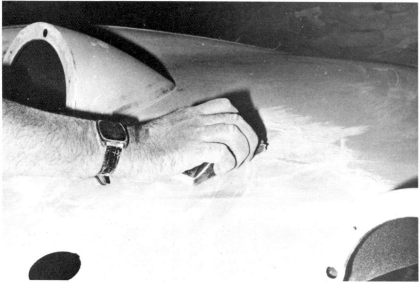

R16. The repair was re-flatted, going through the grades of paper, before being spot primed and flatted once again.

R17. With the flatting completed, it was time to start spraying. In this case, the masking of a denuded body shell was simple but it is always important to mask off wheels, interior and engine bay because overspray can reach into the most surprising places.

R18. The 'fiddly bits' were given a coat first of all. Here, rear light and beading areas were given a going over.

R19.    It is most important that door shuts are sprayed at this stage, not forgetting the edges of the doors themselves. If the insides of the doors are to be painted, they are best sprayed beforehand whilst off the car in the same way that the inside of the bonnet was sprayed while the bonnet was removed.

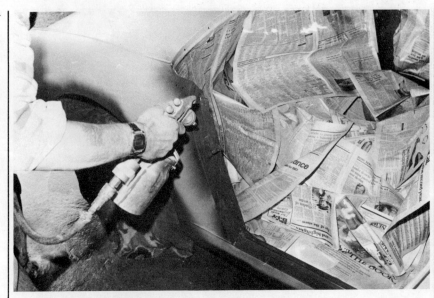

R20.    Panel joints and panel lips were also given a quick 'blow over'. It's surprising how these bits and pieces can be missed when spraying the rest of the body and to go over them later will add unnecessary overspray.

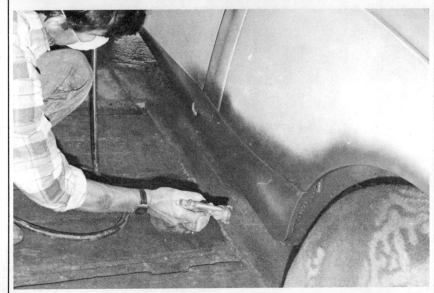

R21.    Wheel arch lips are not to be missed out . . .

R22.    . . . nor the headlamp pod edges. If you try to spray these small areas while spraying the major panels, it is all too easy to put on too much paint and cause a run.

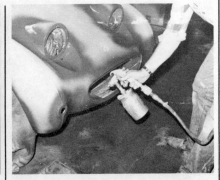

R23.    Make sure that all potential dust traps such as the radiator opening have been blown out with the air-line before spraying commences.

R24.   Although those areas that are going to be covered by trim will never be seen, it is vital that they are painted too, so that there is no edge to the excellent paint finish.

R25.   Finally, the whole car can be sprayed, a panel at a time, working from one 'corner' steadily around the car. Make certain that no draughts can blow over the car for several hours after painting, otherwise paint will 'bloom', i.e. take on a milky appearance. After allowing the paint to harden off for several days, any over-spray or relatively dull areas can be polished to a high gloss with paint cutting paste and plenty of elbow grease.

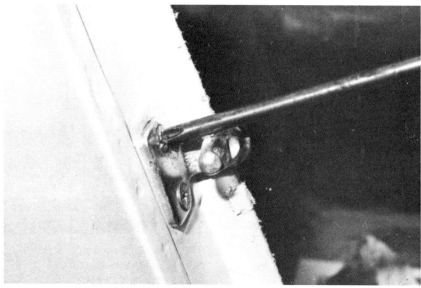

R26.   Later, the car can be fitted with all the small ancillaries such as this striker plate. Take care to adjust correctly with the door draught excluder rubber in place. A well fitting door is visually most important.

R27.   This is the stage when your 'filing system' for small parts will be put to the test. With an excellent paint finish many of the fittings and small parts which once looked acceptable will now seem to need renewal or re-chroming. Allow for this in budgeting. These are the rear hood clips.

R28.   If you are rewiring the car, put the electrical components in place and locate all the wire endings  before connecting them neatly into place.

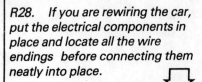

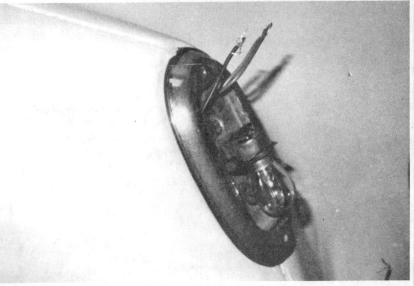

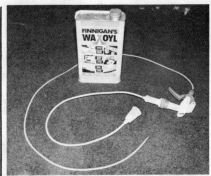

RP1.   Finnigans 'Waxoyl' is probably the most well known DIY rust inhibitor. It is shown here with the low-cost injector gun designed to reach well into box sections. Apply it liberally. In winter, heat the tin in hot water to thin the liquid or thin it down with white spirit.

## Rustproofing

After having put so much time and money into rebuilding the body, it would be the height of folly not to do something about preventing, or at least delaying, further corrosion. The only way of doing so is to inject a rust retardant into all of the enclosed box sections, for that is where serious corrosion takes place The cost of doing so is relatively small and the rust inhibitor fairly pleasant to handle. But having once injected the stuff, make a point of repeating the operation every year or two at the most, in conjunction with a thorough steam cleaning and close examination of the underbody and repainting where necessary. Many people have mixed feelings about the use of underseal and prefer paint only, on the principle that any deterioration in painted steel can clearly be seen and rectified at an early stage. Underseal can only be a problem if it becomes slightly loose and allows moisture to be trapped. Steam cleaning, however, will remove loose underseal before it has a chance to cause problems. The choice is an open one, and must be left to individual preference.

RP2.   Holts make a similar product called "Inner Shield" and also market a similar injector kit.

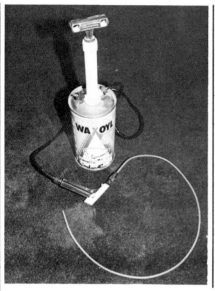

RP3.    Finnigans also sell a super-de-luxe injector which takes the form of a pressure can and spray which operates on the pump-up garden sprayer principle. Once the initial can of fluid has been purchased it can be topped up from a standard can.

RP4.    A far more thorough and professional internal covering is obtained by using the DeVilbiss SGB-602 anti-corrosion spray outfit. Cheaper systems leave something to be desired in that the spread of inhibitor can be very patchy whereas this unit gives a spread equivalent to original manufacturers' latest specifications. Here, the air intake of the bonnet is being coated. The bottom half is quite a complex structure so make sure that all internal surfaces are reached.

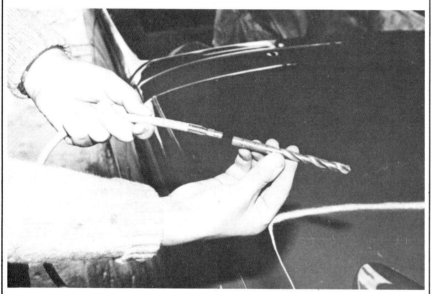

RP5.    The SGB uses a larger bore tube than the Waxoyl or Holts models, so it was necessary to select a much larger size of drill bit. Make sure that you lay in a stock of rubber plugs before commencing.

RP6.    Injecting the crossmember is easy on all cars: simply insert the probe through the jacking point. Make sure that plenty of fluid runs around the jacking point itself.

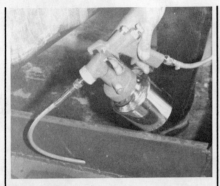

RP7. Similarly, the inner sill should have an opening tailor-made for insertion of the probe. If not, simply drill on in an unobtrusive spot and plug it afterwards.

RP8. The quarter-elliptic cars' longitudinal member will have to be drilled before it can be injected.

RP9. Before injecting the spring box/rear bulkhead area, study the section from this book on its repair, so that you can ensure that you drill holes in the right places and cover every nook and cranny. From the point of view of the strength of your car, this is a most crucial area, so future corrosion is to be avoided at all costs.

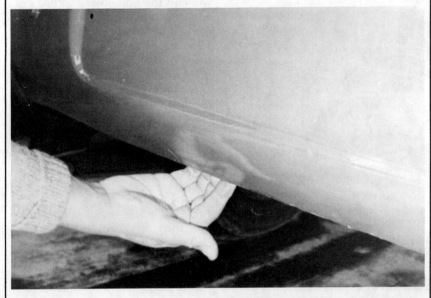

RP10. Some areas, such as this one at the base of the rear valence/boot floor joint, can be injected without drilling holes. Crawl inside the rear panel (Frogeye), but beware of the fumes; open the boot lid and spray from above on later cars.

RP11. There is little point in showing every area to be sprayed because many of them, such as the front and rear "chassis" box sections, the door hinge pillars and door shut posts, are a matter of common sense. However, don't forget the joint between inner and outer wings which is sprayed from inside. The Frogeye bonnet corner fillets pictured here and the underside of the bulkhead should also be sprayed, but use the short probe supplied with the cheaper kits or buy yourself a hand-held garden sprayer. The spray probe would probably coat more in rust inhibitor than you bargained for!

# ③ Bodywork Restoration B: The Heritage Shell

Some people want to own a Midget or Sprite that is totally original; others just want to enjoy one of the greatest little sports cars in as good a condition as possible. If you belong to the latter group, then restoring your car around a Heritage bodyshell could be the way to go. But do take note that these brand-new Rover-Heritage bodyshells are, at the time of writing, ONLY available for those Midgets and Sprites with conventional semi-elliptical springing. They're not at present available for any of the early cars: 'Frogeye' and Mk II Sprite or Mk I Midget. But do check with your dealer to find out if Heritage have somehow been able to schedule the construc-tion of 'Frogeye'-type assemblies. (It is certain, by the way, that new 'original' Mk I Sprite bonnets will never be built, because the original tooling has been lost.)

The *advantages* of rebuilding around a new shell are quite extensive: You can rebuild your own car even though you may not be able to weld; you will probably spend less than having a badly rusted shell properly rebuilt

(though shoddy jobs are cheaper!) and, best of all, you will have a totally sound, strong, properly aligned and safe structure in which to drive around when the job is finished. And, as a marvellous bonus, all shells are now zinc coated by Heritage for the ultimate in rust protection.

The *disadvantages* are also there, of course. New shells are 'fit-alls', with mountings and holes for all models of this type, chrome or rubber-bumper. There-fore, your car will never be totally original again. (Mind you, if lots of old steel has to be cut away and replaced, it won't be truly original anyway …) However, if the work is done properly, value should not be affected. And you must be aware that there will be a *lot* of fitting up to do. Open the bonnet of your car and take a look at the number of clips, pipes, wires, stops, nuts and bolts under there. All will have to be removed, cleaned or replaced and refitted – time-consuming stuff! If you're doing it yourself, that can be part of the pleasure, but if you're paying someone else, do be aware that the high labour

element can make a Heritage rebuild at least as expensive as a conventional rebuild.

In the end, if their Spridget is completely rusted out, there can be no better or safer way for most DIY enthusiasts to rebuild their cars than around a Heritage shell.

This Chapter shows how to go about re-shelling your Midget or Sprite in an entertaining way, but one that was, nevertheless, a speeded-up version of a normal real-life situation.

In 1991, Heritage launched their MG Midget and Austin-Healey Sprite bodyshells in the most dramatic way imaginable. Within the space of two working days, mechanics from a number of leading MG specialists completely stripped an original but sad donor car and rebuilt the parts into one of the brand new shells at the 'MG World' car show at the National Exhibition Centre near Birmingham.

Stirling Moss drove a ratty but lowish mileage 20-year-old Midget into Hall One at 10 am on the Saturday and parked it next to a brand new, ready painted Heritage bodyshell. A swarm of blue-overalled locusts descended upon the heap, and less than 30 hours later – no more than 45 minutes behind schedule – the reconstructed car, stripped and rebuilt down to the last throttle stop, was driven out again. And the hundreds of spectators, drifting past the on-stage show, saw for themselves that it IS possible to rebuild a Midget in a limited number of hours. At least as important, they saw that it could be done at low cost, making re-shelled Midget motoring among the best value on four wheels.

## The Background

The whole thing began in the mists of time when Heritage's powerhouse and Assistant MD, David Bishop, sat down with two of the largest Heritage approved suppliers, Moss Europe and Brown & Gammons, to discuss this celebration of the launch of the new Midget bodyshell. B & G had already quoted one Steven Guest, the owner of a rusty but otherwise excellent Midget, for the replacement of a shell, and he agreed to allow his car to be the subject car in the show. Most of us would have jumped up and down with excitement at the prospect – first show rebuild of a Midget; S. Moss in driving seat; ultra-rapid completion – but Steve is a real cool dude! He calmly gave his approval.

It was decided that each of the two specialists would supply two of their best mechanics, while one of the restoration specialists who works at Studley on the Heritage historic fleet would make up the team of five. Ron Gammons and Graham Paddy, the man behind Moss Europe, would do the running commentary, with valuable contributions from David Bishop and Stirling Moss himself. The Friday evening prior to the show saw the teams getting to know each other – they had never before met, let alone worked

together! – and plans were made. Piece of cake. Can't go wrong. Saturday, everybody strips down, cleans, paints; Sunday, we screw it all back together. Doddle. Easy. What's yours? Or was it going to be so easy?

The first problem, at least from this writer's point of view, was that the rebuild team decided to ask Mr Moss to drive the car in to the show an hour earlier than was originally planned, so as to have an extra hour on the car. Result: no useful photographs of the event – just the snap shot shown here. The next problem was that not one of the five photographers in attendance was the master of his camera's fate. For one thing, the Gang of Five mechanics were there to work and, quite rightly, *nothing* was going to stop them! None of the shots shown here was posed; all were snatched as the mechanics, streaming with sweat almost from the off, worked non-stop at the job in hand.

The remainder of the problems, in truth, were what made the whole project worthwhile. Most of us, if we had been carrying out this work, would have cheated. We'd have slackened off nuts and bolts, ensured that nothing was rusted solid and even surreptitiously replaced the odd component, but the Brown & Gammons/Moss Europe team were having none of it. The car was virtually

untouched, save for the overnight application of releasing fluid; and the stripdown and rebuild difficulties were exactly those that would be experienced by the home restorer. Consequently, the step-by-step sequence of events described here will be of enormous value to the home restorer intent on building a totally sound, budget price sports car. As Graham Paddy said: "We wanted to show how you could create a superb Midget without throwing money at it."

*Please bear in mind when following this picture sequence that many of the photographs will appear to be not in the correct order. This is because a large number of people were working on the project vehicle all at the same time; so much so that there was almost a blur of hands and MG Midget parts! The pictures have been reorganized into an order that makes them simpler to follow, but it does mean that some of the surrounding parts can mysteriously appear and disappear as the sequence progresses! The reader's understanding is requested in the hope that he or she will find the sequences easier to follow than would otherwise have been the case.*

*BS1. PPO 1K waits in the dull and dingy wings at the NEC ready to make its entrance on to the stage.*

BS2. Heritage's David Bishop discusses with Stirling Moss the incredible achievement of the Heritage organization in managing to put the MG Midget and Austin-Healey Sprite bodyshell back into production.

BS3. Brand new bodyshells can be ordered from all the leading specialists, and can be purchased either with or without front wings, bonnet and front grille surround assembly, but all come with doors and boot lid. It is probably false economy not to purchase the complete assembly that we see being built up in the subsequent shots.

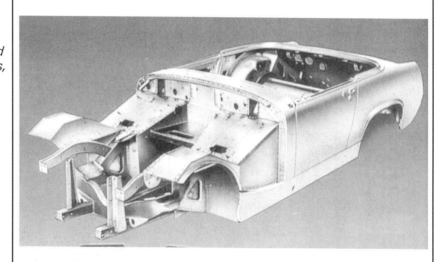

BS4. David Bishop (left) now turns to Ron Gammons, who discusses, for the benefit of the surrounding audience, the work that is being carried out on the new bodyshell which was painted before having been brought to the show. In the background, work has already started on stripping away PPO's former identity.

BS5. And here is the reason why a new bodyshell was such an economical option for this car. It was relatively low mileage and with almost all of its original parts intact, but was suffering from an almost terminal degree of rust. Bearing in mind the fact that most Midgets and Sprites are not worth a fortune, the only really economical way of carrying out this work is to try to reuse as many of your old parts as possible, and if you should be looking for a car to purchase with a view to reshelling it, the condition and originality of ancillary components should figure very highly in your calculations.

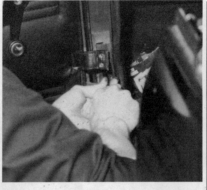

BS7. One of the first jobs was to remove the doors so that access to the old shell would be improved. Here the door check strap is being unscrewed . . .

BS9. Bonnet and boot stays are generally perfectly serviceable, but make absolutely certain that you retain all of the clips and fittings. The best way of doing so is to screw them back into place on the ends of the stays themselves the instant you have removed them.

BS6. The exhaust system had been replaced only a few months earlier, so it was carefully removed ready for reuse.

BS8. . . . and then the screws holding the hinges to the A-pillars are removed. These will rarely come out without a fight, and an impact screwdriver will be an admirable investment. Alternatively, try tapping the head of your screwdriver while a partner attempts to turn the screwdriver with a molegrip firmly clamped to the blade. Ensure first that screwheads are thoroughly cleaned out to provide the maximum purchase for the screwdriver.

BS10. Removing the bonnet is best carried out with the assistance of a second pair of hands. If the bonnet on your car is sound or only requires a small amount of remedial attention, you may be able to sell it and recoup at least some of the cost of your new bodyshell.

BS11. Before attempting to remove the windscreen, the centre stay must be unbolted from the dashtop . . .

BS12 . . . and once the retaining screws are removed the screen easily lifts away. The aluminium screen surround will probably clean up beautifully; small scratches in the screen itself can be dealt with by using a polishing kit from one of the suppliers, such as Frost Auto Restoration Techniques or The Eastwood Company. The sealing rubbers for the doors, however, will almost certainly need replacement.

BS13. Sidelamp lens removal is a must, if only to keep lenses and bulbs as spares . . .

BS14 . . . while headlamp bezels will almost always clean up satisfactorily and can be reused on the new shell.

BS15. Sidelamp units, on the other hand, are rarely serviceable since they have usually been attacked from the rear by the dreaded rust.

BS16. Normally speaking, the same can be said of headlamp bowls and their rubbers, although you will quite often come across those that have been replaced just a short time earlier and which can, of course, be refitted. By taking the trouble to paint and Waxoyl the backs of them before reassembly you will extend their life considerably.

BS17. Rear lamp units are far more likely to be usable since they are not exposed to the elements. You will greatly improve the appearance of the units if, after removing them, you scrub the lenses, inside and out, in hot soapy water. This removes all the ingrained dirt and allows the lenses to shine almost like new lamps. You will be surprised at the extent to which this 'lifts' their appearance; otherwise you may be surprised at how dull they look against your car's new bodywork.

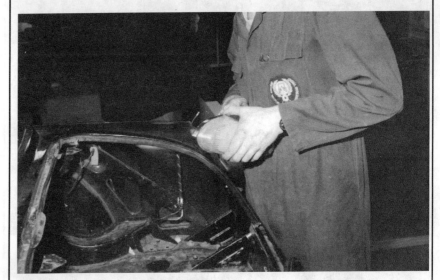

BS18. Strip out every ancillary from the boot, including (on the outside) the number plate and the number plate lamp wiring.

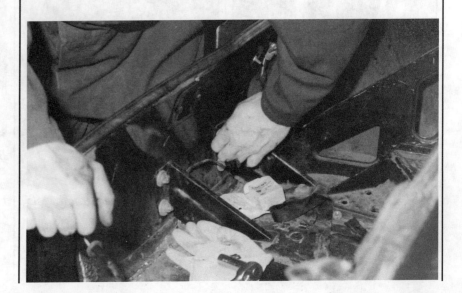

BS19. At the opposite end of the car, items such as the horns will be eminently reusable and will even look the part if you take the time to wire brush them clean and give them a coat of paint.

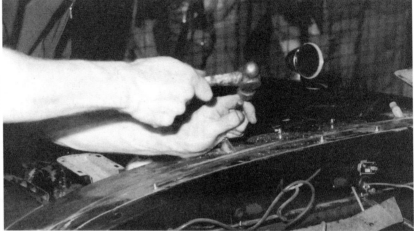

BS20. There is a great temptation to almost tear parts off the car, but you should be mindful the whole time that you want to be able to reuse as many of them as possible. Even though the cost of individual small parts may not be very great, when added together the cost of several dozen of them can be quite considerable! Here, the nut holding the windscreen wiper mechanism to the bulkhead has been found to have been rounded off previously. It is being drifted free with a small cold chisel, which may well ruin the nut but it should be a simple matter to find a scrapyard replacement. Whenever you accidentally or deliberately damage parts, make a careful note so that you can purchase new ones all in one go. Otherwise, you are sure to need the very part that you have forgotten to buy in order to get on with the job!

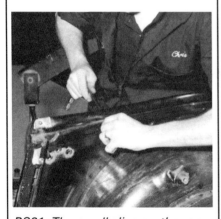

BS21. The small clips on the rear of the body, onto which the soft-top is clipped down, must be removed with very great care. They are made of soft metal and are easily sheared or damaged.

BS22. Chrome-plated self-tapping screws pass through the centre of special studs for holding the carpet in place. These should also be removed, and it is at moments such as this that your storage facilities will be put to the test. If you have a roll of sandwich bags handy you can pop all the screws and clips from one area of the car into a bag, stick a piece of masking tape on to the bag and write an instant label describing what the parts are and where they came from. As you take parts off the car, you might think that you can't possibly forget where they have come from; but when it comes to it, you will find you won't remember *where* quite a lot of them come from unless your filing system is well organized.

BS23. Here's another of that huge number of items that can be reused on your new bodyshell. The bonnet release mechanism will bolt straight on to your new bodyshell, but do remember to allow sufficient time for things like cleaning up the mechanism, painting and greasing it, stripping out the release wire and greasing it, or replacing the release wire if it appears frayed. If you can imagine how long that will take, and multiply it by all the hundreds of items that are fitted to the car, you begin to realize what a miracle it was that the Brown & Gammons and Moss Europe specialists did the job so quickly. But there were rather a lot of them and they do all know the cars inside out; while, if you are a perfectionist, you might want to go even further than they did in preparing and preserving the parts before they are refitted to the car.

BS24. You will also have to allow many hours for cleaning and polishing chromium plated parts before they are refitted. Just looking at how much space these few items take up shows the large amount of floor area that you will need to carry out the work properly.

BS25. And here's a reminder of an item that is not to be forgotten! The chassis number is held to the bodyshell with a pair of pop rivets. Drill them out carefully, taking care not to damage the chassis plate, and rivet it on to the new shell. You can buy a new chassis plate and have it stamped with the correct number, but for authenticity there is nothing quite like the original plate complete with its original number stampings.

No matter how difficult it is, contrive to hang on to the old bodyshell until the new one is completely fitted up. You will inevitably forget to remove something or other: in fact you won't even realize that some parts are not part of the new shell and have to be carried over from the old one. If you throw the old shell away before you have completed the work, you are sure to find that there was something left on it that you will need later on. The other reason for keeping the old bodyshell is because you will need a reference point to see where many of the components were fitted. The new Heritage bodyshell will have holes and cutaways where your old one had none. This is so that the new one can be used with a variety of model changes, whereas your original shell, of course, will have been tailor made for your particular model of car. Consequently, there may be occasions where there are so many possible fitting positions

that you won't know the correct one for your car without referring back to the old shell.

*MS1. The car was raised off the ground and supported on axle stands before the wheels were removed. You must make sure that if you are working on a car supported by four axle stands that they are stable, so that there is no risk of the car slipping off when working underneath. When you encounter stubborn nuts and bolts, such as on spring shackles, there is a great temptation to use enough force to pull the car right off the axle stands if you are not careful. The best approach is to leave two wheels on the ground for as long as possible, chocking them to prevent the car rolling in either direction. When you have*

*to work with all of the car off the ground, adopt a belts and braces approach: leave your trolley jack lightly supporting the car, or even rig up some ropes to take the weight up to the beams on your garage roof, should the car topple off its axle stands.*

*MS2. Take very great care when disconnecting the oil pipes from the oil cooler. In fact, if you can leave the pipes connected to the cooler, so much the better, since it is extremely difficult not to cause leaks and perhaps even destroy the top of the oil cooler as the pipes are removed. The best approach, if you have to remove the pipes, is to unbolt the oil cooler from the front pan of the car, as shown here, and then to* unscrew the pipes from the top of the oil cooler. Do not, however, use just one spanner as this mechanic is doing: have another spanner locked on to the hexagon, which is a part of the fitting flange on the oil cooler, so that as you unscrew the oil pipe, there is no risk of screwing the entire flange off the top of the oil cooler and destroying it. These are relatively expensive items, and if you can save them for reuse later, so much the better.*

*MS3. You will have to unbolt the oil pipes from the engine block, of course, but you may be able to leave the splash plate, through which the oil pipes pass, still attached to the pipes while you remove the whole assembly from the car. You can then pull the pipes from the splash plate ready to clean it up and paint it later.*

## Mechanical Stripdown

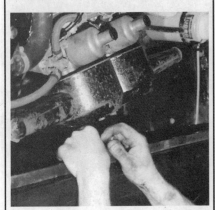

MS4. Now, preparations are being made to remove the engine from the car. You will at least have to take the air filters off the carburettors, and you may be well advised to remove the carburettors as well since there will then be no danger of damaging them. Note that the chassis plate referred to earlier is directly underneath the air filters – just visible in this shot – and if you decide to remove it at this stage, do take care to label it and keep it safe. Alternatively, leave it on the car until you want to transfer it to your new bodyshell.

MS5. All the other engine ancillaries will also have to be disconnected, such as heater pipes, throttle and choke cables . . .

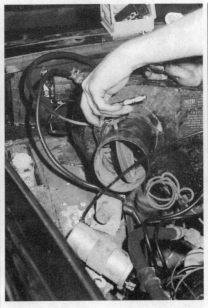

MS6. . . . and while the heater control flap cable does not have to be disconnected at this stage, the heater tap cable will have to be removed from the engine if the Midget is of a later vintage than this one.

MS7. The earlier type of heater tap and the coiled wire for the oil pressure gauge can be seen in this shot. When disconnecting the oil pressure gauge from the block, take very great care not to accidentally destroy the pipe. Replacements are very expensive since you will have to replace the whole of the water temperature gauge/oil pressure gauge unit. Watch the copper pipe carefully as you undo the union screwed into the block. If you see the pipe turning as you undo the nut, stop, try to straighten the pipe where it enters the union (without kinking it) and apply releasing fluid. Work the union backwards and forwards, gripping the pipe as carefully as you can with pliers, and it may also be beneficial to apply some heat, though not to the pipe itself since you might melt the copper. In a few cases, despite your very best efforts, there may be nothing for it but to sacrifice the pipe and face buying a completely new temperature and pressure unit. If that happens, console yourself with the thought that you can buy exchange ones, trading in your old unit for a newly refurbished one.

MS8. Where the Midget is concerned, it helps to take off the steering rack before lifting the engine out. Four bolts hold the rack down to rack mounting brackets on the front crossmember. You have to knock down the locating tab washers first.

MS9. Before you can lift the steering rack out, you will, of course, have to split the ball-joint connections from the ends of the rack, and also disconnect the steering column end by undoing the pinch bolt where the end of the steering column joins the rack and carefully drifting out the pinch bolt. It isn't enough just to slacken the nut off, since the bolt passes through a recess which prevents the end of the steering column from pulling off the rack even if the nut and bolt come loose.

MS10. Meanwhile, beneath the car more hands were at work. The Midget's engine and gearbox have to be fetched out together, and on many models it is not possible to get at the connection between the front end of the prop shaft and the back of the gearbox. Here, the prop shaft is being unbolted from the differential so that it can be lowered and then pulled back off its splines on the back of the gearbox. On these earlier models you have to replace the prop shaft on to the back of the gearbox as it is being lowered into place, but that comes later.

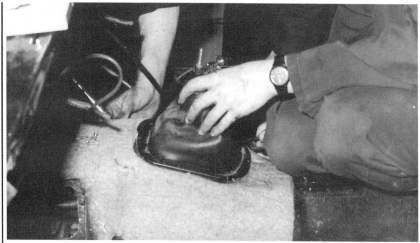

MS11. And here are more items that can be reused, and must therefore be kept carefully. After removing the gearknob, the gearstick gaiter and mounting bezel can be removed and you should hang on to the self-tapping screws holding the bezel in place, resorting to another of those trusty plastic bags, and perhaps taping the bag to the bezel for safe keeping so there is no confusion about where they belong.

MS12. With the gearstick in the neutral position, the three bolts holding the gearstick down can be removed – replace them into their threaded holes in the top of the gear box extension as shown here – and be absolutely certain to disconnect the reversing light switch.

MS13. When you undo the engine mounts, disconnect one of the engine mounts from the engine front plate and the engine mounting tower, but on the other side unbolt the tower itself from the car's bodywork, removing all four nuts and bolts. That way the engine will lift out a lot more easily.

MS14. Once out of the car, the gearbox can easily be unbolted from the engine and then pulled free. Take care not to damage the clutch as the first motion shaft is withdrawn from the back of the engine. That means not resting the weight of the gearbox on the clutch as it comes free. If you've never done it before, look into the gap between engine and gearbox as you pull one from the other and support the weight of the front of the gearbox until it is completely clear of the engine.

MS16. One of the Brown & Gammons mechanics has the engine suspended over a drip tray while he applies engine degreaser to every nook and cranny. You may wish to consider steam cleaning the whole of the engine bay and the underside of your donor car before stripping any of it down. This had been done in the case of this car before it was brought into the show, and it certainly reaps benefits in terms of pleasant working and being able to get at all the relevant nuts and bolts. If, however, you are not able to strip the car down immediately after having it steam cleaned, you would be well advised to invest in a few cans of WD40, or its equivalent, and squirt a coating over all of the mechanical components. This will help prevent rust from setting in immediately, and will also have the added benefit of assisting in the removal of seized threads.

MS15. It is false economy to even consider reusing the clutch unless you know it to be of very recent vintage. The release bearing on this unit had come apart. The copper thrust washer is *not* supposed to be separate from its housing (shown towards the top of this picture)!

MS17. Here the gearbox is being degreased. If you can rig up your own degreasing tank, so much the better. It doesn't have to be a pumped system such as the one shown here: a simple tank with degreasing fluid in it, and a brush to scrub the components to be cleaned, will suffice. All you have to do is replace the fluid at fairly regular intervals. (It is an oil derivative and should be disposed of carefully. Put it in an old oil can and take it to your local authority oil disposal depot. Never *tip the fluid down the drain* or into the soil.)

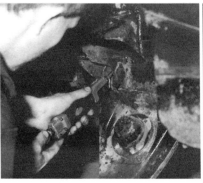

*MS18. It is worth taking some time in cleaning the carburettors. Buy a proprietary brand of carburettor cleaner from your local motor accessory store and spray that on liberally. (You'll need a drip tray, or similar surface, to work on.) This will help you to remove old gaskets which must be scraped carefully from flanges, taking care not to scratch the flanges in any way. You should then check the flanges for cracking or distortion. In an extreme case you may*

*have to consider purchasing new, reconditioned or good second-hand carburettors. Before dismantling the twin-carb assembly, you would be strongly recommended to photograph it in detail because, for the inexperienced mechanic, it's almost impossible to remember how it all goes back together again. Remember also that immaculate carburettors add to the engine bay appearance enormously: another reason for spending some time on this area.*

*MS21. Midgets and Sprites are notorious for the fulcrum pins seizing up and being impossible to remove. In an extremely sensible move, the Moss/Brown & Gammons mechanics decided to use a power hacksaw to cut right through the fulcrum pin . . .*

*MS19. Shock absorbers are service items and you may as well reuse them if they have life left in them. You could even consider just unbolting them from the bodywork and leaving them attached to the axle; certainly until the whole assembly is off the car and on*

*MS20. Where the front suspension is concerned, you will have to disconnect the anti-roll bar and the steering rack (if not already done).*

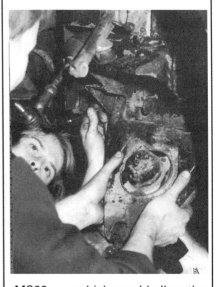

*MS22. . . . which would allow the otherwise impossible-to-remove wishbone pan to be taken away easily. Having said that, this fulcrum pin decided that it would allow itself to be unbolted and removed in the normal way.*

MS23. The anti-roll bar, having been disconnected from the front suspension assembly – note the way in which the mounting plates have been left in place on the end of the anti-roll bar (a far simpler way of removing it) – can then be unbolted from the car's bodywork. You are strongly recommended to replace the anti-roll bar rubbers, since they have a lot to do with the effectiveness of the anti-roll bar and, in time, the old ones become soft and fairly useless. You won't need to disconnect the stops that sit up against the ends of the rubbers, but you will undoubtedly need to do some sanding, cleaning up and repainting.

MS26. . . . and bolted to the rear floor either side of the rear bulkhead front plate.

MS24. The exhaust system is another service item, and this one was to be reused, as described earlier. Alongside it you can see the rear spring which is best disconnected once the exhaust system is out of the way.

## Bodywork Build-up

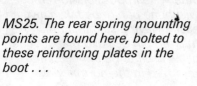

MS25. The rear spring mounting points are found here, bolted to these reinforcing plates in the boot . . .

BB1. Although not strictly a part of the bodywork, the process is exactly the same – the wiper motor is wire brushed prior to painting.

BB2. When painting aluminium parts, it is essential that you spray on a self-etch primer, otherwise the paint will simply flake off again. Smoothrite is said to adhere well to aluminium parts without the need for such primer, although it will inevitably be less brittle and longer lasting with a primer beneath it. Smoothrite is just a touch too 'plasticy' looking, but if you can live with that, it's about the right depth of semi-gloss finish that you would expect to see under the bonnet.

BB3. It all depends how far you want to go, whether you want to strip down the grille and remove the chrome or mask it off . . .

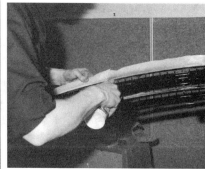

BB4. . . . and spray paint the black parts of the grille black. Do remember not to use a full gloss paint for this, since the original was satin finish and a full gloss will look very garish.

BB5. More grille aperture parts receive the spray paint treatment. As you can see, there's not too much overspray with aerosol and it's really the most convenient way of painting so many small fiddly parts that you may not want to paint all in one go.

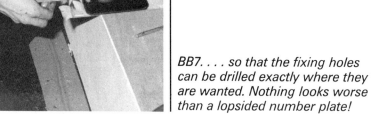

BB6. The old number plate backs, of course, will be reused, but new number plates are a must. They are cheap and lift the appearance of the car considerably. Note the care being taken here to ensure that the mounting holes are measured precisely . . .

BB7. . . . so that the fixing holes can be drilled exactly where they are wanted. Nothing looks worse than a lopsided number plate!

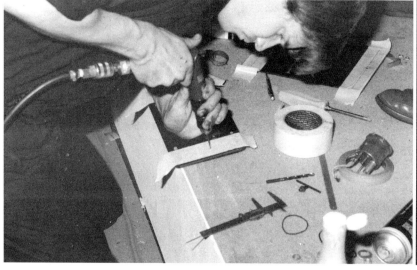

BB8. The bumper irons have all been sandblasted and painted with zinc-based paint and Smoothrite (Hammerite would be just as good) and the insides of the bumpers will also benefit from a coat of paint or a coat of Waxoyl. Mounting bolts should all be dipped in grease or, better still, in copper-impregnated grease such as Copperease which comes in tubes and tins. This is better than anything at stopping threads from rusting and bolts from seizing up.

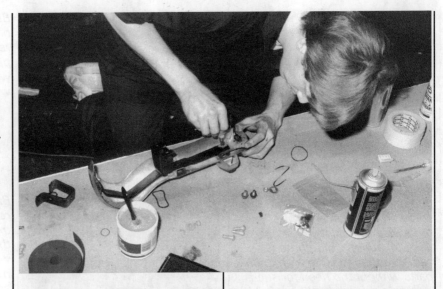

BB9. Go to a lot of trouble to clean the chrome work. A little bit of black tarnishing in the nooks and crannies won't have been noticeable on the old car, but on the new one they will stand out like greasy finger nails on a ballerina. Even if there's some rusting and pitting on your bumpers, you'll be surprised at how you can improve them. In the worst possible cases, use a scouring pad, but don't do so on chrome that's in good condition because you risk taking off some of the plating. However, if you can get rid of the worst of rust pitting, your bumpers will last you at least until you can afford to buy new ones. Wax them every time you wash the car and you'll be surprised how long they last before the rust shows through again.

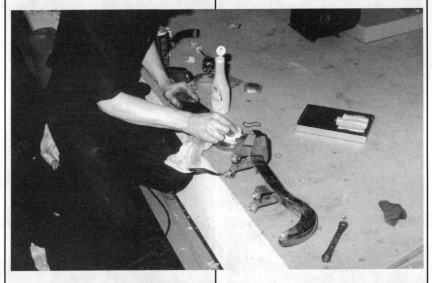

BB10. When refitting the bumpers, take the greatest care that the ends of the bumpers don't gouge your lovely bright new paintwork. You could wrap a rag around them or mask off the paintwork itself with some plastic sheet.

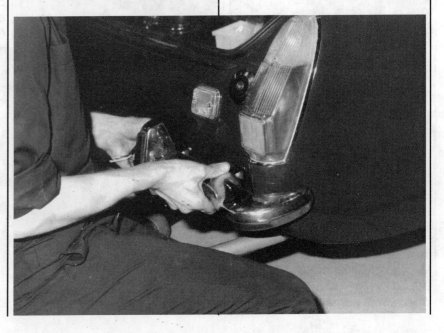

BB11. The front bumper mountings on this car had rusted out very badly and were replaced with new ones. Note also the nice shiny new nuts and bolts that are starting to appear beneath the car. Each of them is bright zinc-plated and will last a lot longer than the originals, especially if a good coating of Waxoyl is applied over the top.

BB12. Most parts of the old headlamps were rescued. Having been cleaned up, they were found to be in good condition, and even the rubbers were reusable. The rubbers themselves will respond well to some boot polish or black trim cleaner before being fitted back on to the car.

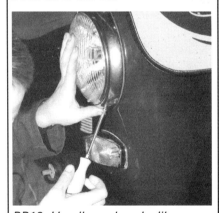

BB13. Headlamp bezels, like bumpers, will often clean up and are capable of being reused – adding considerably to the cost savings that you can make, so that a Midget reshell need not be an excessively expensive operation.

BB14. Graham Paddy, of Moss, refits the matt black grille aperture trims. They had to be masked off as well before they were painted, of course, so that the chrome rims – cleaned up before painting – remain visible and shiny.

BB15. The serviced wiper mechanism is refitted, and the fixing nut (the one that had to be chiselled to make it turn) is replaced. New rubbers are fitted beneath the angle distance pieces: if you don't do so you will be asking for a wet leg next time it rains!

BB16. This is a bit of a knee trembler! Trim fixing holes have to be very carefully measured before they can be drilled. You are strongly recommended to use a wide piece of masking tape and make the marks on that in felt pen or pencil. You can't use a centre punch for starting the drill because, of course, that will dent the panel, but you could hold the drill in place and turn the chuck by hand half a dozen times or so until the tip of the drill just begins to bite into the steel. This will provide you with a 'start' from which, with the additional benefit of the masking tape, the drill should not slip.

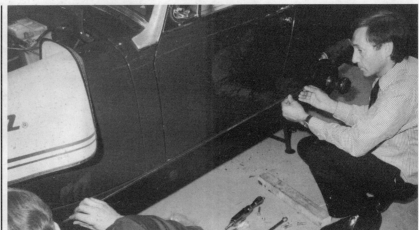

BB18. . . . and run more Waxoyl down the back of the chrome strip to be fitted here, and on to the mounting clips themselves. Anything you can do to keep rust at bay is worth thinking about.

BB19. Viewed from low down, the old rear lamps and reversing lights are reused . . .

BB20. . . . and the number plate bolted back into position. If you have to open up any of the holes in the bodyshell, be sure to paint some zinc-based primer followed, when it is dry, by Waxoyl around the edges of the hole to prevent rust from taking a hold.

BB17. Put a dab of Waxoyl into each hole before pop riveting the mounting clips . . .

BB21. As some electrical items are fitted you will inevitably need to run the wiring into place, and don't forget to add grommets where necessary. You will curse and swear if you forget and have to disconnect significant parts of the wiring in order to get grommets in place afterwards.

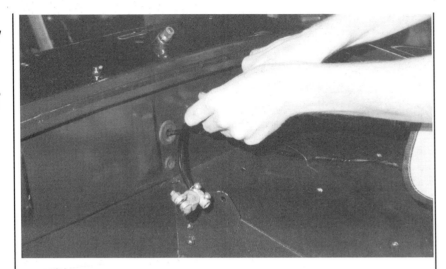

BB22. The fuel pump is not part of the bodywork at all, of course, but you could say that its mounting bracket is, and here it is seen having been bolted into place beneath the rear of the car.

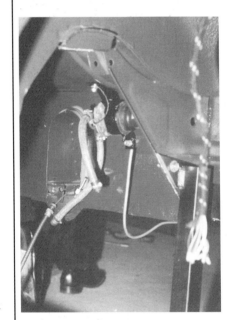

BB23. The bonnet, of course, had been taken off to facilitate fitting up, and you may wish to leave it off for as long as possible.

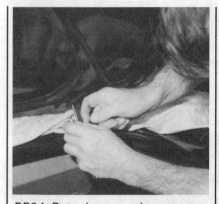

BB24. But when you do come to fit the boot and the bonnet, more than one pair of hands will be needed. You will also need some thick cloths to lay across the bodywork so that the boot (in this case) can rest on the bodywork without causing any damage. Use a pin to line up the hole in the boot lid hinge with the threaded hole in the boot panel, and then hand-tighten the mounting screws into the other two holes. As with all the threads on the bodyshell, they should have been chased out first with a tap to ensure that there is no swarf in place and also to ensure that the captive nut is not fouled by the metal of the panel to which it is fitted – a not uncommon occurrence.

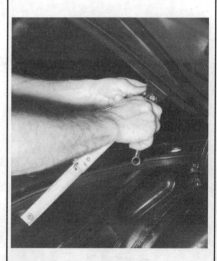

BB25. You will now be pleased that you put the special mounting bolts and nuts back on to the boot and bonnet stays so that you know exactly where to find them when refitting the stays.

BB26. If you want the boot lock to operate the correct way round, start with the locating dowels at top and bottom while the T of the handle goes from side-to-side . . .

BB27. . . . then, when the boot lock is open, the T-handle will be running up and down, moving to side-to-side when the handle is in the closed position.

BB28. Purchase new paper gaskets for the door closing plates which are screwed to the B-posts. We have known some filing to be required here before the screws will go in properly, but you can expect a little variety between bodyshells of this sort. If it happens, don't get too annoyed: just thank your lucky stars that you are one of the lucky few who can buy a new bodyshell for his or her classic car!

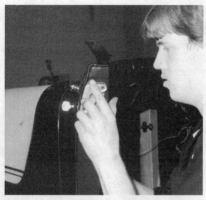

BB29. Similarly, you will be able to get hold of new gaskets for the door latch mechanism where it fits to the door . . .

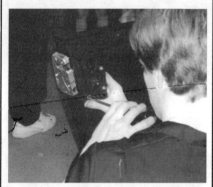

BB30. . . . and the door handle and lock mechanism can also be screwed into place.

BB31. Check carefully that the lock works and operates the locking mechanism.

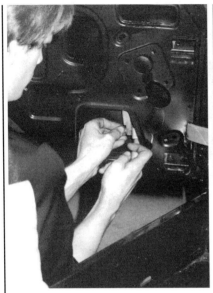

BB32. The door quarterlight bracketry is fitted to the door, and the quarterlight bolted to it.

Waxoyled the insides of the doors before fitting any of the mechanism, but that would have made an extremely messy job of inserting all of the machinery, such as the winder mechanism being offered up here.

BB35. After fitting the glass, the rear runner can be offered up into place and bolted in.

BB36. Don't despair if there are a number of holes for which you can't find a use. Heritage doors are made to suit a number of different models and there maybe holes that your model doesn't need.

BB33. This strip of metal, folded into an elongated S shape, makes it much easier to pull the new door seals on to the door. Once again, to attempt to reuse this item would be a false economy. The old ones are usually brittle and cracked and, in any case, you don't want to run the risk of too much water running down inside your shiny new doors.
BB34. I suppose you could have

BB37. Modern cars always have a waterproof covering between the door casing and the door panel to stop any of the moisture that gets down inside the door from damaging the door panel backing. Graham Paddy fits self-adhesive sheets over the door apertures here. You could use a plastic sheet with a good quality waterproof tape or impact adhesive to hold the plastic all the way around the edge of the door.

BB38. The screen is bolted back on, remembering to use more of that copper-impregnated grease on the threads so that the steel bolts are not prone to rusting inside the aluminium windscreen frame supports.

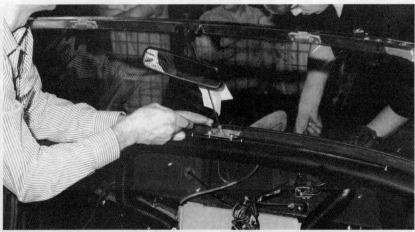

BB39. You may have to take care to fit the screen accurately, particularly since you will almost certainly be using new screen-to-body sealing rubbers. You will also have to ensure that the screen rake angle is precisely correct, setting it against the position of the quarterlights on the doors.

## Electrics & Brakes

E&B1. Unless the wiring loom on the donor car has been badly hacked into by ham-fisted electricians, or damaged in some other way, it can usually be reused. Wipe all of the plastic coating with white spirit on a rag to remove greasy dirt: wash the cloth covered type in hot soapy water. Carry out any repairs to the outer loom covering with an appropriate type of tape – plastic or cloth-type – and check all the endings and connectors. Corroded terminals or wire endings that have started to fray should be cut off and replaced with new: a fiddly job but one that will repay itself a thousand times over in terms of electrical reliability and, in addition, you'll save a lot of money over the cost of buying a new loom. You'll also save yourself the hassle of a loom that isn't exactly right for your car: a common occurrence

since the number of model changes is almost too great for the number of looms available and you almost always have to add bits on to a replacement loom, tape unwanted connections out of the way and take note of any possible alterations in colour coding.

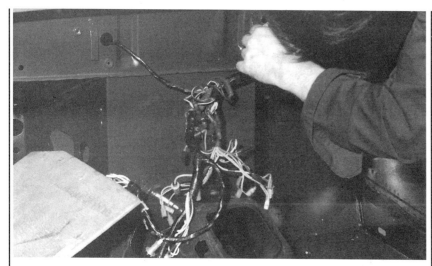

E&B2. Fitting the loom into the car can appear more daunting than it will prove to be in practice. All you need to do is work out where the major components of the loom have to go – it's here that any sketches and photographs that you should have made whilst taking apart the old car will prove to be invaluable – and a small but unfortunate side effect is that the wiring clips that are built into the car's bodywork will shed their paint when you bend them around the loom. It's always best when the bodyshell is painted to ask for an extra half litre of paint to be supplied because it is highly unlikely that these will be the only parts of the bodyshell that will need touching in after fitting in a complete car.

E&B3. In order to get the wires through some more complicated apertures, it's best to use a fish wire: a piece of stiff wire with a loop on the end which is passed through the wiring hole first, pulling the electrical cable through behind it.

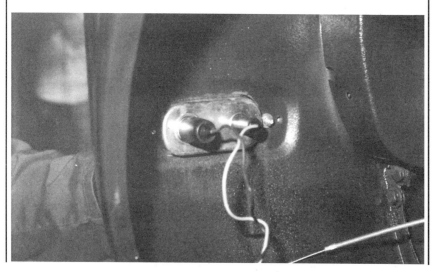

E&B4. Working out where all the connections go is not as difficult as you might at first think, since all of the wires are colour coded. Refer to your wiring diagram . . .

E&B5. . . . especially in the area of fuse box and voltage regulator where there is quite a knitting box of wires.

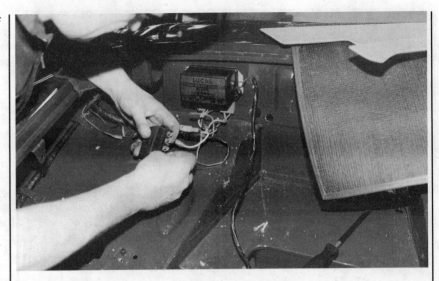

E&B6. Take some care to drape the wiring into smooth curves, with wires lying in neat groups, since this under-bonnet area is particularly visible. After cleaning up the fuse box and volt meter with white spirit, use black trim cleaner, preferably with silicone polish, to bring them up like new again. The plastic type of wiring harness can also be made to look like new by the same means.

E&B7. Before putting the wiper motor back into place, brush grease along the full length of the drive cable . . .

E&B8. . . . before reassembly. In this instance, the guide tube has been fitted back to the car before the wiper motor and drive cable were assembled, although it is probably simpler to reassemble all of the components before fitting them to the car.

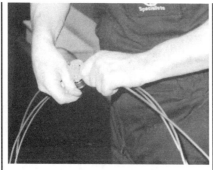

E&B10. For this job, Brown & Gammons chose to make up their own steel brake pipes, although many enthusiasts prefer to fit copper brake pipes such as those made by Automec which are ready-made-up to length with all the correct fittings and have the added advantage of never corroding away.

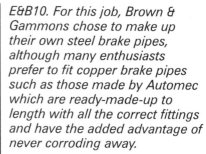

E&B11. Whichever system you use, make up the shape of the new brake pipes to match that of the old, which should have been preserved in their original form for this very purpose.

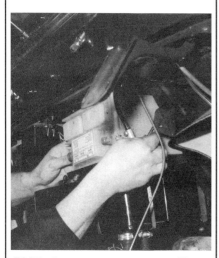

E&B9. At some stage, you will have to fit the battery or use a pair of jump leads to take power to the car so that you can check the operation of all of the electrical items. Don't reconnect the battery until everything is connected up, otherwise loose wire ends could easily short against the bodywork.

E&B12. Unfortunately, it's not unknown for even the Automec pipes to require the odd alteration to length or end fitting – perhaps it's something to do with all of those model changes mentioned earlier – in which case you'll need the use of a brake line flaring tool or to have brake line endings done for you by your local garage or local motor factor.

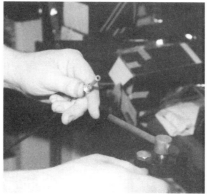

E&B13. It is crucially important that your brake lines have the correct endings, there being more than one type. The wrong ending will appear to screw into place but will not make a proper seal, and if your old brake lines don't give a 100% guide as to which type of ending your new brake lines should have, get your local MG specialist or Rover dealer to sort it out for you.

E&B14. The new brake lines should be given smooth runs along the route originally used by the manufacturer – another case where originality photographs will be necessary – and you must make absolutely certain that none of them can rub or foul on any mechanical equipment.

E&B16. You are very strongly recommended when carrying out a Midget/Sprite reshell to also fit brand new brake master cylinder and wheel cylinders. You are equally strongly recommended to have all of the braking system checked over by a qualified mechanic before using the car on the road.

E&B15. Along with new brake lines, you should also fit new flexible hoses. These are fitted to their brackets using the fitting nuts supplied, and then each flexible hose is held steady with a spanner while the brake line ending is screwed tightly into place. Make absolutely certain that there are no cross-threads and, throughout the whole process, be equally certain that no dirt is introduced into any of the system.

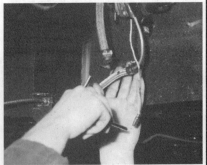

E&B17. Other flexible hoses and metal pipes are used to carry the petrol from the fuel tank to the carburettors via the fuel pump. Once again, copper pipes are available.

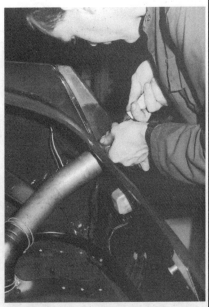

E&B18. Be sure to give the top of the fuel tank an extra coat of paint before Waxoyling it, thus extending its life considerably. All of the fuel tank fittings can normally be reused. This rubber elbow has been cleaned up with trim cleaner, while the metal fuel pipe has been given a spray coat of silver paint – it all helps to improve the appearance inside the boot.

E&B19. The front shock absorbers can easily be fitted at this stage – reconditioned replacements are not expensive. Note the way in which the brake line has to be run carefully in position, and also the fact that the engine chassis plate has already been swapped from the donor car.

E&B20. The front suspension wishbone pans are held to the body with a pair of bushed bolts, one of them seen being fitted here with its tab location washer from inside the engine bay.

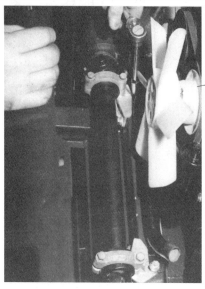

E&B22. The old steering rack was reused, although the sandblasted mounting brackets and bolts give a new appearance.

E&B23. The new anti-roll bar bushes are clipped over the anti-roll bar – one side of the bush is split – and the metal mounting strap pushed over the bush . . .

E&B21. We're going a little out of order here so that this picture sequence runs in a more logical progression, but the front suspension is best fitted with its coil spring when the weight of the engine is in place, otherwise the trolley jack has nothing to push up against, and the coil spring simply won't compress.

E&B24. . . . and in this case new bolts, washers and spring washers were used to screw the bushes up against the chassis frame.

E&B25. New brake discs were fitted to this car, and also new wheel bearings.

E&B27. . . . and you'll need to follow the instructions on fitting the hub correctly and safely.

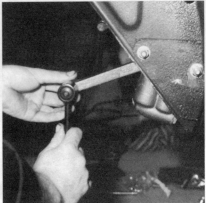

E&B28. Reconditioned shock absorbers are relatively inexpensive and worth using if your budget will stretch to it. The rears are easily fitted.

E&B26. Getting the washers and nut into place inside the splined hub on a wire-wheeled car can be a bit of a fiddle! . . .

## Major Mechanical Parts

MB1. The back axle should be built up as far as possible on the ground, off the car. This can include items such as the bump stops and rebound straps, the handbrake rods, hydraulic pipes and all of the drum brake assemblies. Note that the wheel spinners have been left on the axle in order to protect the threads, and so that they don't get lost while the end of the brake flexible hose is sealed off to prevent the ingress of dirt.

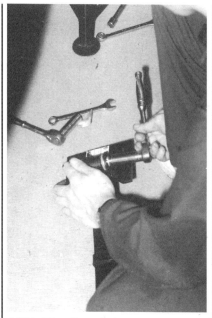

MB2. The (front) spring-to-floor pan shackle plates tend to rust out, but they are cheap to replace. Fit them with the springs off the car, then fit the springs to the axle.

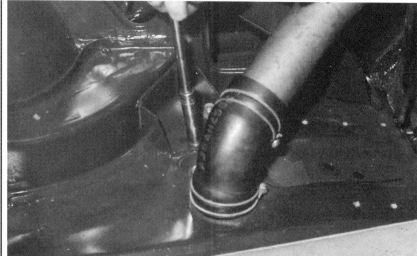

MB4. You have to fit the rear spring shackle plates to the rear floor of the car before the axle is fitted to it . . .

MB5. . . . and it is best to fit the front end of the springs to the car, bolting the shackle plates into their allotted places . . .

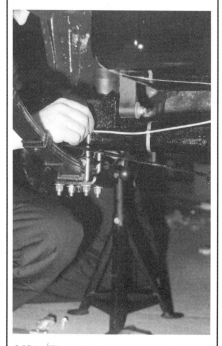

MB3. The whole spring and axle assembly can be manoeuvred beneath the car on a trolley jack, but because of the considerable weight involved it will take at least two of you to support the axle safely on the jack while it is being manoeuvred into position.

MB6. . . . before fitting the spring shackles to the spring ends and the shackle plates on the car. You almost never go this far – as far as replacing all the mounting plates on the car – unless you are carrying out a full bodyshell rebuild, but thanks to Heritage all of these items are available at distinctly modest cost.

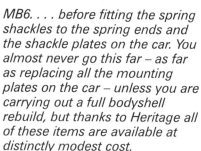

MB7. The rear axle assembly is finally fitted up by having the shock absorber link arms connected to it, and the rebound straps fitted to the bodywork, as well as connecting up the hydraulic and handbrake connections.

MB8. You may as well fit the rear wheels, at least hand tight, at this stage, to increase the safety factor when working on a car off the ground.

MB9. You may even wish to consider lowering the rear of the car to the ground and chocking the wheels. You will have to lift the rear of the car again later when you fit the engine, gearbox and prop shaft, but in the meantime, having the rear of the car down will help you to establish the right angle for entering the engine back into the car's bodywork as well as making the car more stable. This project car was fitted with new chrome plated wire wheels, but for anyone who is considering using their reshelled Midget on a regular basis, they are a distinctly bad idea since they need cleaning after almost every trip if they are to look their best.

MB10. Sometime earlier, the Brown & Gammons mechanics had painted the engine block in heat resistant engine paint before fitting a new clutch and refitting the gearbox.

MB11. Just as it's easier to get the engine out without the steering rack in place, so it's easier to fit the engine before fitting the steering rack. Note the sharp angle necessary to clear the car's bodywork . . .

MB12. . . . . whilst introducing the end of the gearbox into the transmission tunnel beneath the bulkhead. What you can't see here is that the prop shaft has been inserted into the transmission tunnel and slid onto the end of the gearbox by now. On original pre-1500 Midgets, there is no access plate in the gearbox tunnel to enable you to slide the drive shaft onto the end of the gearbox, so it has to be done at this stage with considerable difficulty!

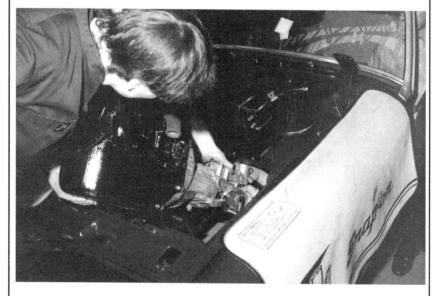

MB13. The engine hoist has been attached to the two BMC engine lifting straps on the top of the rocker box, and there is a suitable nylon rope passed between the two. This enables the engine to be tilted because the strap is allowed to slide through the hook on the lifting crane as the engine assumes the horizontal position. Note that the manifolds and fan have already been fitted at this stage.

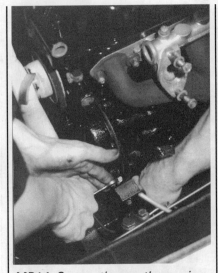

MB14. Connecting up the engine mountings is a matter of following the reverse procedure for taking them off. In other words, one of the engine mounting towers is left off the car while one is bolted to it, complete with engine mount. The engine is placed on that engine mounting, but none of the nuts is done up tight. On the other side of the car, the engine mounting and engine mounting tower can be introduced into place and the engine mounting tower bolted down tight to the car's bodywork. Then, finally, all the engine mounting nuts can be done up as the weight of the engine is lowered on to them.

MB15. The gearstick and gaiter can be refitted, and the rear end of the prop shaft connected to the differential unit.

MB16. Many hands make light work when it comes to connecting up all of an engine's ancillaries in a record amount of time!

MB17. And here's the fairly new exhaust system, taken from the donor vehicle and now laid out assembled beneath the car ready to go in place.

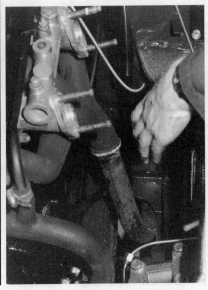

MB18. Obtaining a good seal between the exhaust pipe and manifold on an A-series engine is something of an acquired art. It's essential that the rear of the exhaust system has been lifted into approximate position by now and that the flange on the front of the exhaust pipe is of an even and consistent shape. Use exhaust jointing paste and lift the front of the pipe into position against the manifold, holding it there in contact by use of a trolley jack beneath, if necessary . . .

MB19. . . . before fitting a new exhaust pipe clamp, with another smear of exhaust pipe paste around the insides of the clamp. Don't be tempted to reuse the old clamp, since this is a notorious problem area, and also don't be tempted to grossly overtighten the clamp, as this only makes matters worse.

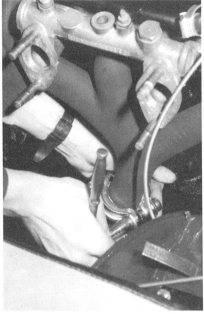

MB22. And be sure to loosely connect up all the exhaust pipe mountings before tightening any of them, otherwise you will be putting stresses on to the mountings that will cause premature failure.

MB20. The rear of the exhaust system should be made to fit correctly before fitting the clamp at the front of the car, because otherwise there's a strong risk of disturbing that critical joint. There must be good clearance between the bottom of the axle on full rebound and the top of the exhaust pipe. If you're fitting a new system and there's no way you can obtain this clearance, consider taking this system to an exhaust centre where they will have the appropriate bending equipment to put a bend in the pipe. If you attempt to do so yourself, you risk kinking the exhaust pipe tubing.

MB23. The old heat shield has been sandblasted and painted – don't leave it off, and also remember to use paper gaskets on either side of it and one on each face of any emulsion (spacing) block that goes between the heat shield and the carburettors.

MB21. Invest in new exhaust pipe mounting rubbers: they don't last as long as they should at the best of times.

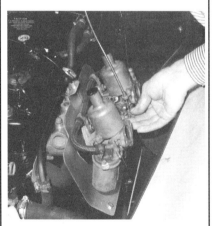

MB24. The show car's carburettors are connected up, their cleaned up appearance helping to make the engine bay look new again.

MB25. The oil cooler bolts down into the radiator intake aperture . . .

MB26. . . . and the old oil cooler pipes are reconnected, but once again remember to use a spanner on the hexagon on the top of the oil cooler to ensure that you don't twist the top of the oil cooler as you tighten down the oil cooler connections – and they have to be really tight since there's quite a bit of pressure there, and they are prone to leaking unless properly tightened.

MB27. With the engine in place, the bonnet release mechanism is connected up before refitting the bonnet – a wise move if you don't want to have to fool around trying to get the bonnet undone having suddenly discovered that you forgot to connect up the bonnet release pull!

## Seat Rebuilding

The seats taken from Stephen Guest's car were also rebuilt at the NEC show, and gave a timely reminder of the huge range of 'original' interior trim available for Midgets and Sprites. Newton Commercial have invested a large amount of money in putting this trim back into production, and it was they who carried out the work illustrated here.

SR1. In order to get the seats out of the car, you'll have to take out the two bolts at the rear, and the two at the front, of each seat runner.

SR2. The old seat trims have to be stripped off, starting with the back rest adjuster 'paddle' where fitted. This may take quite a bit of persuasion to lever off!

SR3. The seat base is held to the base frame with a series of horseshoe-shaped spring clips, which have to be levered off . . .

SR4. . . . following which the old seat base can just be lifted away.

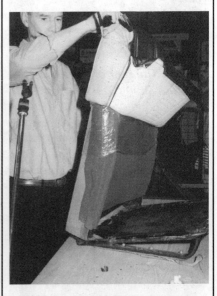

SR5. After removing the fixings holding the back-rest trim in place, that too can be lifted off, followed by all of the padding and trim structure beneath.

SR6. In almost all cases, the frame beneath is in excellent, reusable condition, and it's just a matter of cleaning off the surface rust and repainting. You'll probably find that the rubber diaphragm on which the seat base sits is perished or split, and now, of course, is the time to replace it. New ones are available.

SR7. The seat runners, however, are likely to be quite rusty, so now's the time to take them off, clean them down and repaint using a zinc-based primer.

SR8. The new seat base diaphragm is clipped back onto the frame which, as you can now see, has been rubbed down and repainted.

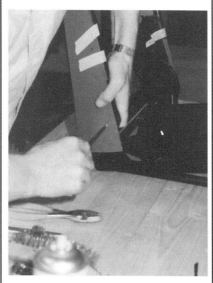

SR9. Newton Commercial also produce these new trim boards, to go around the back of the seat.

SR10. You should use thin foam over the 'shoulders' of the seat and down the sides, so that the retrimmed seats have a nice plump feel to them. Put a plastic bag over the whole thing . . .

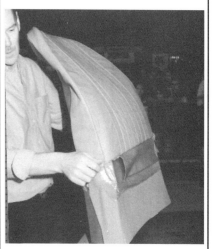

SR11. . . . so that the new seat back-rest cover slides smoothly into place.

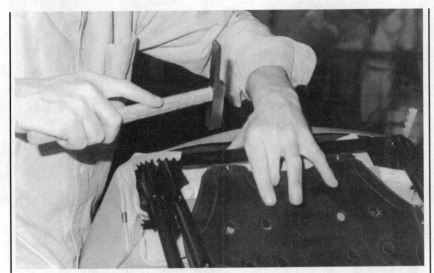

SR12. The bottom of the backrest trim is held in place with new, small spring clips, tapped into place as shown here. If you need replacement clips, new ones are available.

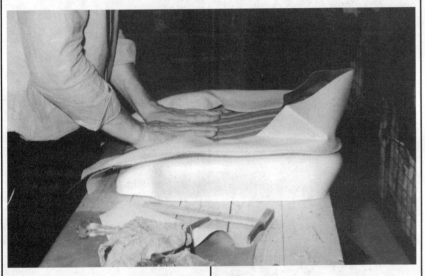

SR13. New seat foams are also available, and here the base trim is being glued down onto the top surface of the seat foam.

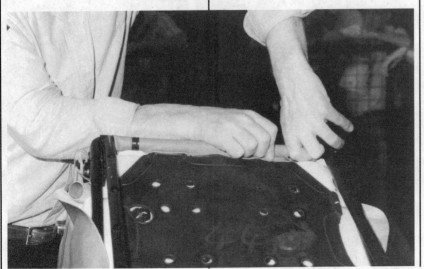

SR14. The whole thing is then just placed on the bottom of the seat, the seat is turned over and the base trim is loosely clipped down at the sides and front. It is then more carefully and accurately pulled down tight and clipped into place, starting with the back and working forwards.

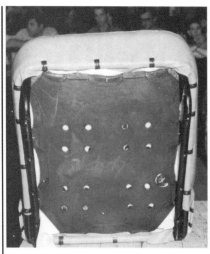

SR15. You must be prepared to remove and refit the trim clips several times if necessary . . .

SR16. . . . until all unwanted wrinkles in the seat base are pulled out and smoothed away.

## Trim Fitting & Finishing Off

TF1. How many enthusiasts over the years must have thought that a trim kit was as easily bolted into place as a new exhaust system? In fact, there's always a lot of fitting and fiddling to do, but all of it is within the scope of the careful DIYer. Here an extra cut is being made into a piece of carpet designed to fit the wheel arch . . .

TF2. . . . so that it follows the shape smoothly. If you have to leave any raw edges showing, make the overlap face the rear of the car so that it can't easily be seen. The easiest type of adhesive to use is that contained in an aerosol spray, although it's also the most expensive by far. Do ensure that you get hold of the modern type of adhesive that doesn't contain solvents that give off dangerous vapours – dangerous in the sense of being inflammable and also in the sense of being available for kids to use in glue sniffing experiments.

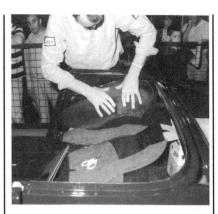

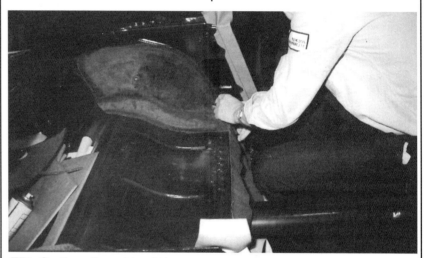

TF3. On the other side of the car, the wheel arch and rear chassis rail carpets are neatly glued into place . . .

TF4. . . . and more elements of the jigsaw go on to the car. Note that the larger floor and gearbox tunnel mats will cover many of these carpet edges. Note also that the carpet that fits over the rear bulkhead has a vinyl strip attached to its top and that this is glued down onto the car's bodywork. You will inevitably have to locate positions for safety-belt mountings and make careful cut-outs in the carpet as you go along.

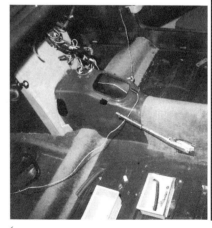

TF5. Trim boards are somewhat simpler to fit, being of the correct shape to start off with. You must refer to the old trim boards in order to establish exactly where the fixing screws need to go, and be sure to use fixing screws of the correct length and type. If your donor car had very messed-about-with interior trim panels, it is essential that you refer to an original looking car – check with someone else in your local branch of the MGOC or MGCC – so that you can ensure that everything goes in its correct location.

TF6. These B-post trim finishers are simple pieces of vinyl that have to be glued into place on the B-posts . . .

TF7. . . . before being trimmed off and glued down neatly at the top of the B-posts.

TF8. Matching door check straps are supplied as part of the kit, but be sure to purchase an adequate supply of self-tapping screws and cup washers for fitting all of these trim items to the car. The door check straps can't be screwed to the car until the footwell trim panels shown in TF10 have been fitted in place, since the mounting screws must pass right through the edges of the trim panels.

TF9. Door trim panels are now available with the exactly correct patterns reproduced on them. They are simplicity itself to fit, as they come with the correct fitting clips already supplied.

TF10. More footwell panels go into place. Be extremely careful not to drill through any wiring when drilling holes into which the self-tapping screws will go.

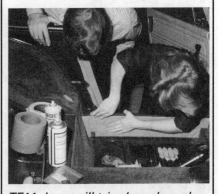

TF11. Inner sill trim boards make an extremely neat job of that area of the interior, while door seals push over the edges of the stuck-on trim panels that were shown earlier being glued to the B-posts.

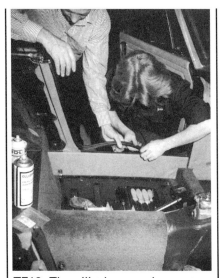

TF12. The sill trim panels must not be screwed into place until these door seals have been fitted, because it is only by offering them up that you can establish the exact correct position for the sill trim plates. Also note that the glued-on trims on the B-posts are finished at the top by the door seal trim finishers, the chrome clips that go over the ends of the door seals, and you must make note of that when deciding how to finish off the tops of these pieces of stuck-on trim. Note also that along the edges of the stuck-on trim, cut-outs have been made to expose captive nut positions.

TF13. Also part of the trim kit is the rear cockpit board, held on once again with lines of self-tapping screws and cup washers. The cockpit finisher strip, around the rear top edge of the cockpit, can usually be transferred from the donor vehicle, having been suitably cleaned up with trim finisher, or, if it is cracked and useless, a new one will have to be purchased, but do bear in mind that this is not part of the standard trim kit.

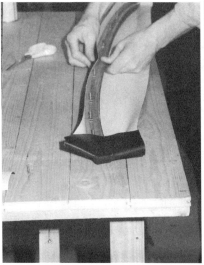

TF14. The padded crash rail that fits across the top of the dash-board is not actually something that you would want to crash into, but it is something that you may have to re-cover yourself. Start by gluing the two ends of the vinyl in place, ensuring that the trim is sufficiently stretched and taut, and that there is enough overlap on both sides for the trim cloth to be glued down.

TF15. The NEC crowd watches on as the Newton Commercial trimmer carefully glues down all along the outer edge of the back of the trim rail. Note that after gluing down, a knife has been used to cut the trim all the way around the fixing studs so that they are free to slide up and down when the crash rail is refitted to the dashboard. He is now applying aerosol adhesive to the back of the crash rail on the opposite side to that already stuck down, and to the back of the trim material . . .

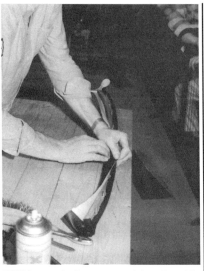

TF16. . . . before stretching it with great care, starting in the middle and working outwards, gluing it down as he goes along and ensuring that there are no creases appearing in the trim.

TF17. Once again, the excess material is cut away, and then the great flaps of material at the two ends have to be carefully trimmed down and glued flat, taking great care that (a) there are no raised ridges preventing the crash rail from pulling down flat against the dash board, and (b) that none of the cuts in the trim extends around to the sides or ends of the crash rail. You just have to experiment if you've never done it before, cutting away as little as possible and gluing down until its clear that the ends are smooth and neatly glued down.

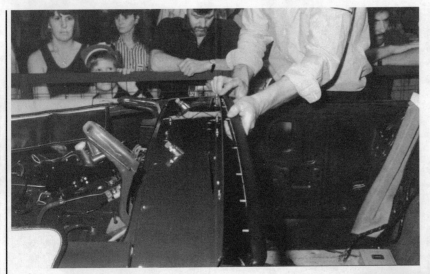

TF18. Then it's a simple matter to offer the crash rail to the bulkhead top, sliding those threaded screws one by one until they align with the holes in the bulkhead top. It's a slightly fiddly business to add the washers, spring washers and nuts on to the back of the bulkhead, and do take care not to overtighten the nuts because these studs are fairly lightweight and could quite easily shear.

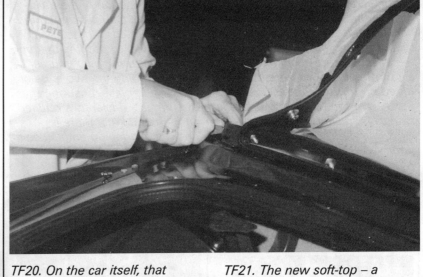

TF19. Meanwhile, back at the homestead, the exchange dashboard has been fitted up with all the cleaned up instruments and badges.

TF20. On the car itself, that cockpit trim is having to be cut so that soft-top mounting studs can be screwed into place.

TF21. The new soft-top – a Tickford-produced Original Equipment soft-top – is being accurately fitted to the car.

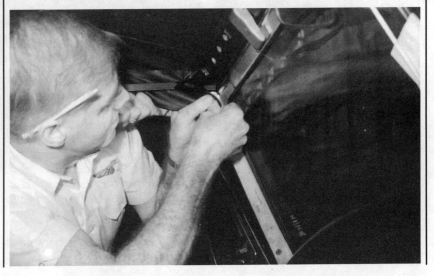

TF24. . . . and it will then be possible to fit the steering wheel for the first time, remembering to put the grommet onto the steering column before pushing it through the bulkhead and connecting up the end of the steering column.

TF22. In order to fit the dashboard, you'll have to make a whole host of electrical and mechanical connections. Be sure that the battery is disconnected at this stage, unless you are particularly keen on putting on a firework display!

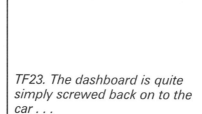

TF23. The dashboard is quite simply screwed back on to the car . . .

Although all new trim and soft-top have been fitted to this particular car, a more economical way of carrying out a reshell is to steel yourself to use all of the old trim, and then to replace it later when you can afford it. That way, you get yourself a perfectly sound car which may not look as wonderful as it would if you fitted all new trim, but trim is purely cosmetic and is something that you could add later on.

TF25. With the team of willing hands from Moss, Newton Commercial, Brown & Gammons and Heritage in the background, Ron Gammons hands the keys of PPO 1K over to its owner Steven Guest at the completion of the rebuild.

TF26. As the key is turned in the ignition for the first time, is that apprehension on Steven's face? The engine burst into life as sweetly as ever, and Steven had the pleasure of driving out of the NEC Exhibition Hall a 'new' version of the rusty MG Midget that Stirling Moss had driven in not all that many hours previously.

# 4 Interior & Hood

The interior of a Midget or Sprite's cockpit is important from many angles. A tidy interior adds greatly to the value of a car, it makes it feel more comfortable for driver and passenger and, at more rarified levels, it adds to a concours entrant's chances of winning a prize.

The cost of having such work carried out professionally is very high and most of it is eminently D.I.Y.-able, which is certainly not the case with more exotic and sophisticated automobiles. Yet another reason for owning a Spridget!

## Fitting a New Hood

As so many proprietary replacement hoods are available, it is impossible to give detailed fitting instructions which would be applicable to all. Any good quality replacement hood should come complete with detailed

fitting instructions – a point to check when buying.

The following sequence, compiled with the assistance of Spridgebits Ltd, should give the reader some idea of what is involved.

Always drape the new hood loosely over the old one before

commencing work. The author has, in the past, been sent dreadful hoods that were impossible to fit. It's best to find out now!

*HF1.    Unclip the hood, fold it back and peel out the rubber sealing strip from the channel on the base of the cant rail.*

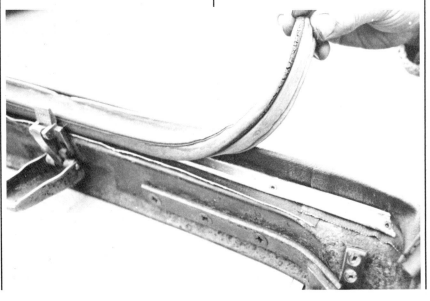

HF2. Drill the rivets out, releasing the channel.

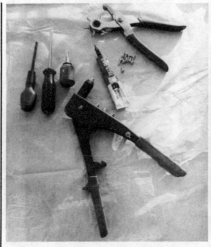

HF5. Tool Box. A range of screwdrivers; pop rivets and gun; 'snap' for fixing hood clips in place (although they can be riveted in place by less sophisticated means using a pair of hammers — one as an anvil) and a punch; hood clips.

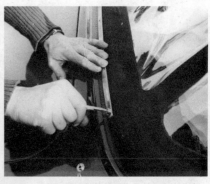

HF8. Position the rear of the hood precisely and screw on the rear support exactly as it came off the old hood.

HF3. Take off the channel and pull back the fabric from around the cant rail. Remove the rest of the hood material from the car in the usual way.

HF6. Place the new hood in place over the hood frame.

HF9. Tap through the hood to establish the exact position of the fixing stud . . .

HF4. Clip the cant rail back in place on the screen.

HF7. Make sure that both 'corners' of the hood are correctly positioned and symmetrical.

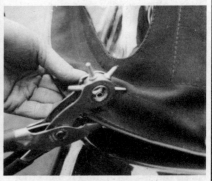

HF10. . . . punch a hole in the correct position.

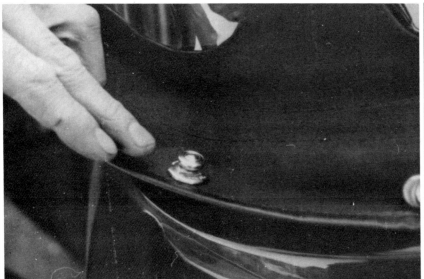

HF11.   Push the Tenax fastener through a hole made in the place indicated.

HF12.   Secure the base of the Tenax fastener over the protruding top portion.

HF13.   If necessary, renew any body clips or studs that are broken or missing.

HF14.   Pull the hood forwards stretching it lightly and working it forwards over the hood stays. This should not be attempted in cold weather as there is then not enough 'stretch' in the material. In winter carry out the operation in a heated garage.

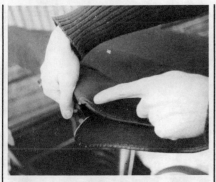

HF15.   Ensure that the hood is level on both sides, unclip the cant rail and fold the front flap under to test the fit.

HF16.   Spread contact adhesive onto the cant rail and onto the front of the hood fabric. Use a slow setting adhesive such as Thixofix to allow some adjustment time.

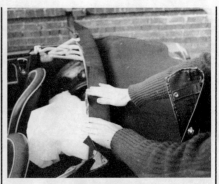

HF17.   Fold the hood over and glue it down – but do check that the tension is still there by popping the cant rail back into place.

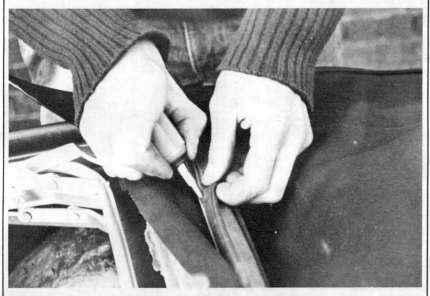

HF18.   Pop rivet the channel back into place and refit the sealing rubber with the aid of a screwdriver.

HF19.   A taut fitting new hood gives a touch of extra elegance to any sports car.

# Door Mechanism Strip

## Tool Box

A ⅜ inch drive A.F. socket set would be useful here as it can reach into more confined spaces; long-nosed and engineers' pliers; cross- and straight-point screwdrivers.

Before any significant work can be carried out on a door, it must be stripped of all its door gear. Door internals look, at first glance, rather more frightening than they really are, particularly in the case of Sprites and Midgets where the interior lock mechanism is an integral part of the catch and doesn't have any complex linkages weaving their way through the door casing.

Removing and stripping out a door is precisely the sort of operation that even the most limited of home restorers can carry out and thus save themselves a fair proportion of the cost of having a door re-skinned. Most restoration firms would be only too happy to recondition a door on this basis.

Doors from earlier cars, lacking internal mechanism, are of course far easier to strip out than the door shown here. Apart from the simple catch, whose removal is perfectly straightforward, the ribbed rubber glued to the inside of the door skin is the only other part requiring removal. If it is to be retained it has to be removed with the greatest care otherwise it will tear.

DS2.    At this stage, a small cross-point screwdriver (No 1 point) has to be used (the usual size, that used for the previous task, is known as a No 2 point). The screws holding the recessed plate into place are removed with the No 1 point screwdriver.

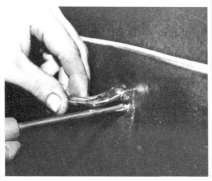

DS3.    The chrome door pull is held in place by two screws found beneath the pull handle when it is lifted upwards. Back to a No 2 point screwdriver, here.

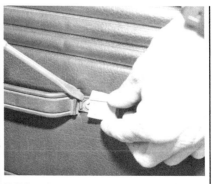

DS4.    Later cars have door pulls with no obvious method of removal. Start by pushing the finishes off the edges of the door pull with a flat screwdriver.

DS5.    This exposes the fixing screws which are removed with a cross-head screwdriver.

DS1.    With a cross-point screwdriver, remove the door catch internal handle. After removing the screw, pulll the chrome handle towards you and off its square shaft.

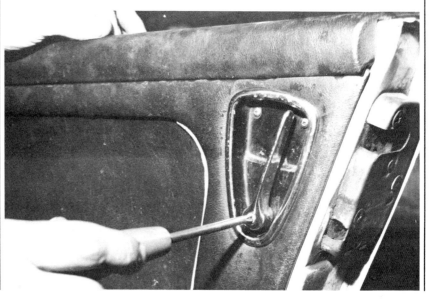

DS6. Window winder handle removal — at first an apparent mystery — is really quite simple. Push back the chrome bezel with a screwdriver against its spring loading. In the normally concealed handle shank will be found two holes running right through the shank, set at right angles to one another. A pin will be located in one of the holes and also through the square shaft inside the winder handle shank. Push the pin out with a piece of welding rod or something similar. Catch the pin (with your third hand!) and the handle and bezel will pull right off.

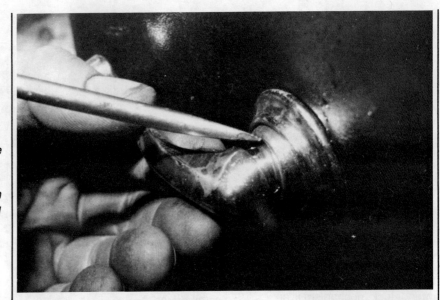

DS7. The door casing is held in place by a series of spring clips which are situated around the bottom and two vertical edges of the door. A screwdriver carefully slid between the trim and door can be used to lever the casing clips out of their holes. BEWARE — on an older door, it is all too easy to pull the clip out of the hardboard door casing because the hardboard will probably have deteriorated with age. Take care to slide the screwdriver right up to a clip and to pull the trim forwards evenly.

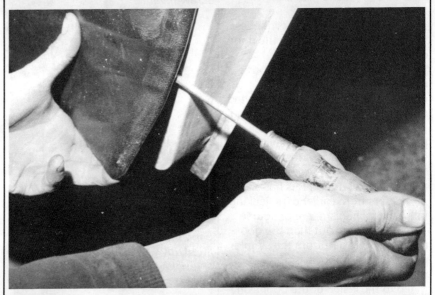

DS8. Pull the trim panel forwards to clear the winder shaft and then downwards; the top of the casing is held lightly behind the top rail.

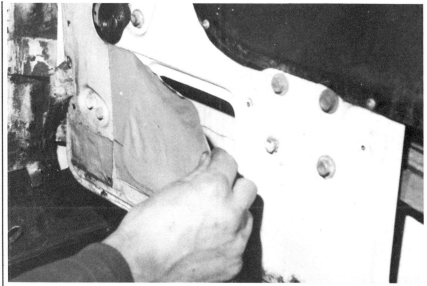

DS9.    Remove, and carefully preserve, the sticky-backed door aperture covers. These help to keep water, which does find its way into the door aperture, away from the hardboard door casing.

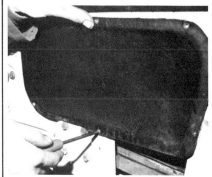

DS10.    Unscrew the centre trim panel . . .

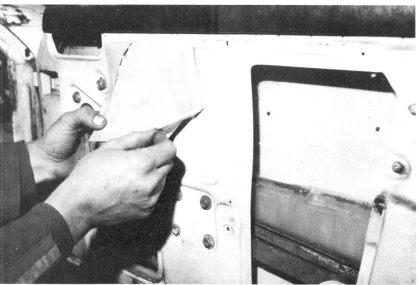

DS11.    . . . and remove the sticky-backed cover found beneath it.

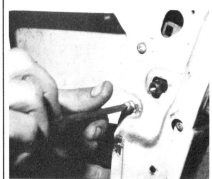

DS12.    Now it's the turn of the ironmongery! Take out the two screws adjacent to the door aperture . . .

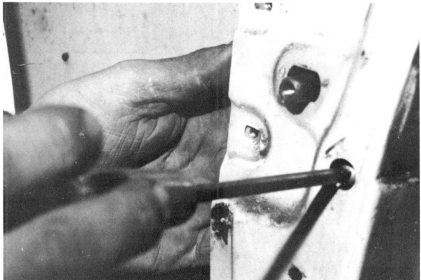

DS13.    . . . and a third screw situated behind a hole in the door frame.

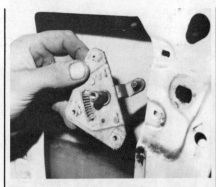

DS14. The door handle shaft has an arm with a peg which locates into the catch mechanism. Push the peg out of location and lift the shaft assembly away.

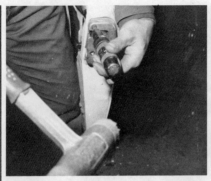

DS15. The catch mechanism is held in place by three cross-point screws. They are usually very tight and are best started off with an impact screwdriver.

DS16. After loosening, remove all three screws with a conventional screwdriver . . .

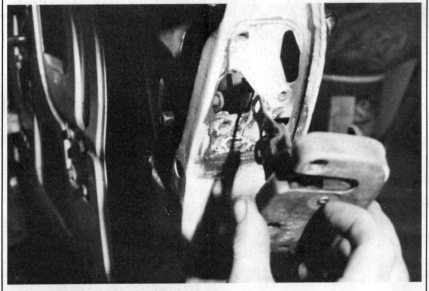

DS17. . . . then lift the mechanism out of the way. Note that in this instance, the catch mechanism is being removed before the door handle shaft assembly. In this case, push the handle shaft locating pin out of the lever arm shown here before attempting to pull the mechanism out.

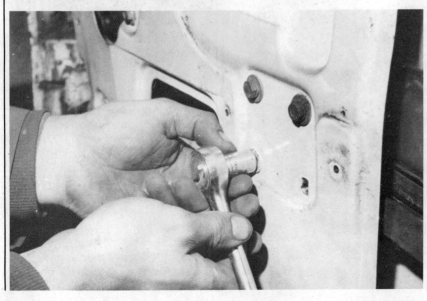

DS18. The window winder mechanism has to apply a great deal of leverage and so it is strongly located in a couple of different places. First, remove the four bolts at the centre of the door . . .

DS19. . . . then remove the four bolts around the winder mechanism. Don't try to remove the mechanism at this stage — it is best left until there is more room for manoeuvrability.

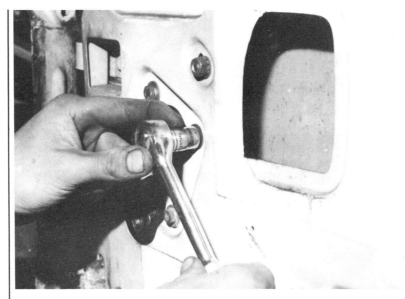

DS20. The front glass guide (actually an extension of the quarter light rear upright) is held at the top by a nut and spring washer. . .

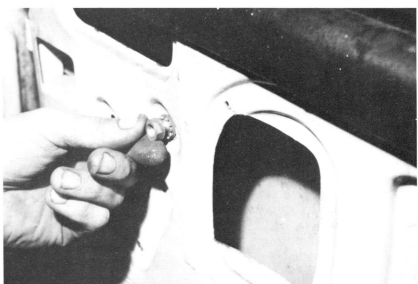

DS21. . . . and at the bottom by a pair of bolts which screw into captive nuts on the bottom of the guide.

DS22. The front of the quarter light is held in place by a bolt found underneath a grommet in the front of the door.

DS23. Next, the top trim rail must come off. The front securing nut screws onto a bolt which protrudes horizontally. Follow that finger!

DS24. The rear bolt will be found behind one of the holes seen here across the top of the door frame. The two bolts can slide the length of the trim rail and so, in theory, could be fitted through any of these holes. It depends who fitted it last!

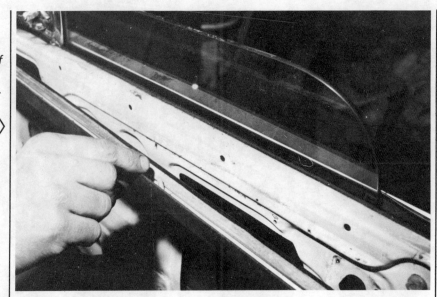

DS25. Behind the rail is the bolt which holds the rear glass guide in place.

DS26. The bottom of the guide is held in place with two bolts.

DS27. Ease the rear guide off the glass and take it out of the door. Push the winder mechanism back into the door and slide the wheels at the end of the raise/lower arm out of the runner fixed to the bottom of the glass. The assistance of an extra bod to hold the glass will make things easier and could save trapped, sore fingers.

DS28. It will be necessary to remove the bracket on the bottom of the front slide . . .

DS29. . . . so that the bottom of the slide will go through the aperture in the top of the door. Note that the slide and glass are now separate items. Removing the glass itself is best left until the slide/quarter light assembly is out of the way.

DS30. The push-button door handle is bolted and clipped to the door skin . . .

DS31. . . . and the door frame is conveniently fitted with an aperture giving access to these fixings.

DS32. The lock mechanism is held in place with a clip found at the back of the panel.

"I 'fink they go better wiv' the square arches"

CF3. . . . so that the claws protrude through from beneath.

## Carpet Fitting

It really isn't worth buying carpet and cutting it up when ready-made carpets can be bought at reasonable cost. On the other hand, it isn't worth buying cheap carpets because they usually only fit where they touch (which isn't everywhere!) and they are often of poor quality. So try to take a good look at replacement carpets before you buy.

CF1. *Unless carpets are clipped down to the studs provided, they will slip about, look untidy and make a thorough nuisance of themselves. If new panels have been fitted, screw new studs down with self-tapping screws. If extra sound-deadening felt has been laid, the studs will need to be packed out with packing pieces — marine grade plywood is fine.*

CF2. *When you receive your new carpets, start by placing them in the car, feeling for the position of the stud and marking it with chalk. Press the clawed ring down onto the top of the carpet . . .*

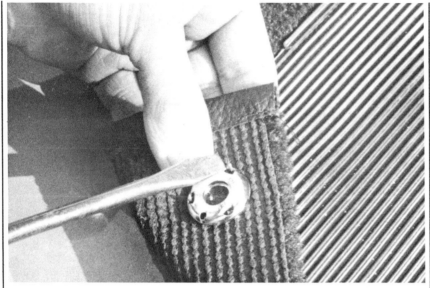

CF4.   *Place the clip over the claws and fold them inwards with a screwdriver.* Simple!

## Seat Re-Covering

### Tool Box

A pair of scissors; small very sharp knife; specialist hammer as shown or lightweight, woodworker's cross-pein hammer; Dunlop S758 adhesive or other contact adhesive with "shuffling-time" (i.e. slow set); glue spreader.

### Safety

**Do not work in a confined space. Adhesive fumes can be dangerous and are highly flammable.**

One of The Classic Restoration Centre's customers wanted his Frogeye seats re-covered so we took them out of the car and over to Spridgebits where Mr. Lewis, a man who trimmed seats for B.M.C. at the time when Frogeyes were being built, re-covered them using one of Spridgebits sear re-covering kits.

SR1.   *First, the seat base is lifted out. It is not held in place by anything except gravity and the seat base frame shape.*

SR3.   *Tipping the backrest forwards exposes the two rear mountings. These fixings were seized solid with rust and it was necessary to drill the heads off.*

SR2.   *This exposes the nuts and bolts which hold the seat base frame to the floor mounting brackets. The nut at the bottom was held with an 'open-ender' while the socket spanner undid the bolt from above.*

SR4.   *After lifting the seat away, the backrest pivot bolts were taken out and the seat frame left behind.*

SR5. Later type seats also have re-covering kits made for them. They are somewhat different in construction but, if anything, rather easier than the Frogeye's to replace. To be on the safe side, only strip one seat at a time, retaining the other as a reference in case you forget how the covers fit back together.

SR6. This is the aimed-for result. On the left, a thoroughly delapidated cover. On the right a Spridgebits/Mr. Lewis creation. Why was this shot taken in a domestic kitchen? Read on, and all will be clear!

SR7. Mr. Lewis stripped the old cover off the seat base and retained all the clips. Then he peeled off the foam rubber base.

SR8. It is impossible to buy new foam rubber bases of the correct shape and type but, by now, most have sagged horribly. Mr. Lewis gets over the problem by stuffing rolled-up pieces of rubber carpet underfelt into all the holes.

SR9. Using Dunlop S758, he wiped a coat of adhesive all the way roung the outer edge of the seat base.

SR10. A similar coat was wiped all the way round the outer edge of the seat base. If this trade adhesive cannot be obtained, try any contact adhesive which allows some shuffling-time (i.e. time to move one piece over the other before it finally becomes immovable). Thixofix is one such adhesive.

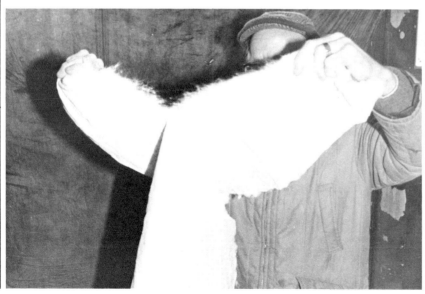

SR11. The foam rubber base is carefully placed upon the steel base. Incidentally, seat bases have often rotted out by now. Allow time to repair it or have it repaired if necessary.

SR12. Obtain some wadding from an upholsterer's or even a dressmaker's shop and tear it to about the width shown here.

SR13.    Mr. Lewis applied adhesive to the front and sides of the seat base . . .

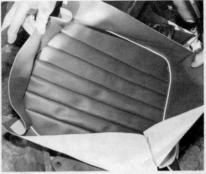

SR16.    Next, he took the seat base cover and turned it inside-out, so that the side flaps stuck upwards.

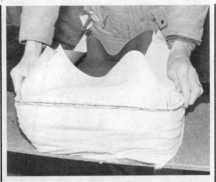

SR19.    The base cover was placed accurately on the top of the seat base . . .

SR14.    . . . and to the back of the wadding and then he wrapped it around the front of the seat . . .

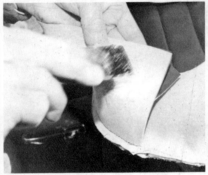

SR17.    After glueing around the insides of the rear flaps . . .

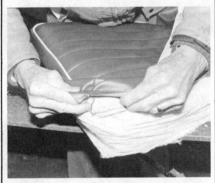

SR20.    . . . and the side flaps folded down at the corners . . .

SR15.    . . . and tucked it in neatly. This has the effect of allowing for the settlement of the old upholstery and pulls the new covers nice and taut.

SR18.    . . . he glued the rear underside of the seat base.

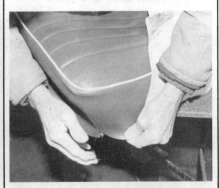

SR21.    . . . before being pulled taut at every corner.

SR22.　The seat base was turned over and the front flap pulled well down.

SR23.　It was wrapped around the bottom edge of the frame and then clipped into place (use the clips that were taken off, if no new ones are available).

SR24.　With the front clipped down, Mr. Lewis moved his attention to the side flaps. These were clipped down, working from front to back . . .

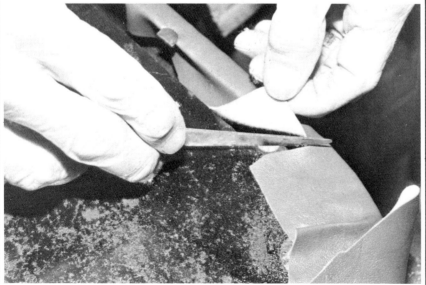

SR25.　. . . until the point where the flange on the base peters out and becomes part of the flat seat base. There, the fabric was cut with a sharp knife.

SR26. The further along the sides you go, the less room there is to use the hammer. Mr. Lewis pressed the clip on as far as it would go with a piece of wood.

SR28. At the end of the valley between flange and seat base, there is just enough room for one more clip, at 90° to all the others along the side.

SR30. At the corners, where the wrinkles were too great to be smoothed out, the fabric was cut, lifted and glued down again in an overlap.

SR27. Then he hammered the piece of wood until the clip went fully home.

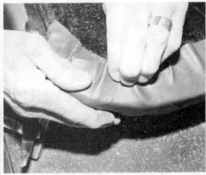

SR29. By now, the back flap which had been folded down, approximately in place, had begun to dry in place. Mr. Lewis pulled it taut, smoothing out the wrinkles where possible.

SR31. The finished seat base! And now — the reason why the cover was fitted in a domestic kitchen. In the winter (when this job was carried out) it is too cold to fit a new cover outside or in a normal garage. The plastic fabric of which the cover is made has to be stretched into shape and, in order to be stretched, the temperature needs to be upwards of the high sixties Fahrenheit (20°C).

SR32. Next, the backrest was tackled. First the old fabric was ripped off the horns on each side.

SR33. The the old clips were removed from the backrest base.

SR34. If you do intend looking for new clips, this is the type to look out for. Any good upholsterer or upholsterer's supplier should be able to help.

SR35. With the clips out of the way, the old fabric tears easily down the seam. Obviously, this part of the work can just as easily be carried out outdoors, especially if you don't want too much dust and mess in the kitchen. Mr. Lewis didn't fancy going out into the cold again!

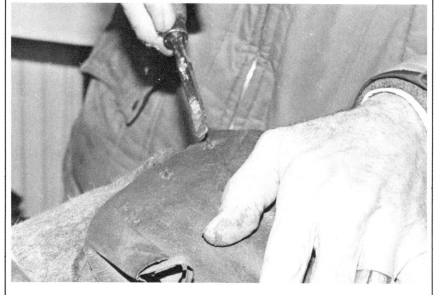

SR36. Mr. Lewis used an old chisel to bend up the pointed tabs which held the back of the fabric down before tearing the back off.

SR37. The inside of the seat back is covered in a rubberised matting which must be retained for future use; it's virtually irreplaceable.

SR38.    The stripped seat back should look like this with all of its padding intact. If any is missing, patch it up with whatever suitable alternative is available — consult your trim supplier.

SR41.    He wrapped the plastic strip around the end of the seat back horn. If you have difficulty getting it to stay on try using a rubber band.

SR42.    The Spridgebits trim kit includes the two pieces for this part of the seat. Mr. Lewis took one of them and folded a collar at the open end.

SR39.    Mr. Lewis put a coat of adhesive on the bare patch, where the sharp tabs are situated.

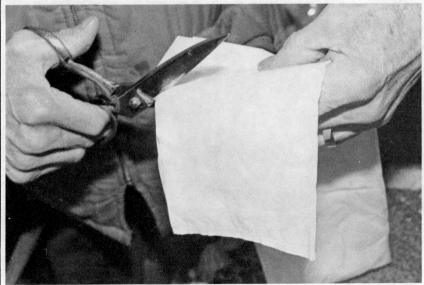

SR40.    He then took the open end of a plastic bin liner and cut 15cm (6 inches) or so off the end, giving him a longish continuous strip of plastic.

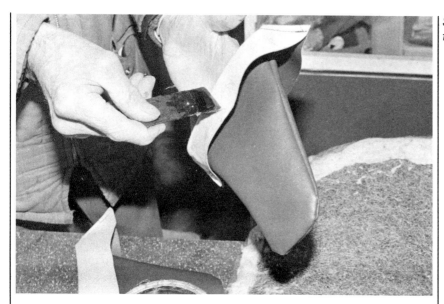

SR43. And applied a smear of glue to the folded back collar.

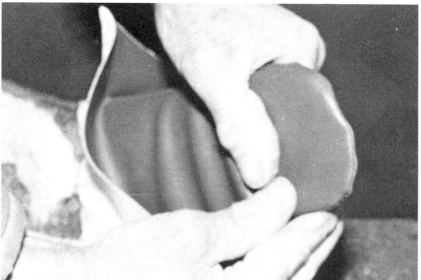

SR44. He then pulled the re-covering piece tightly onto the end of the horn, the plastic allowing the trim to slip smoothly onto the seat back.

SR45. At the other end, the collar was folded down and glued to the metal. After another check that the trim was fairly tightly stretched back (don't overdo it, of course!) the pointed tabs were pushed through the fabric using the flat of a knife . . .

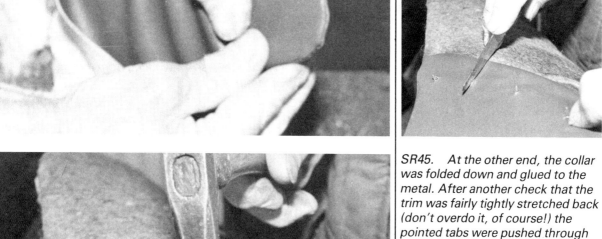

SR46. . . . and then hammered over.

SR47. Mr. Lewis draped another piece of wadding over the shoulders of the seat back . . .

SR50. . . . and all surplus fabric trimmed from the stitched seam with a pair of sharp scissors. This was to ensure that the seat back would lie as flat as possible.

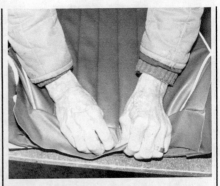

SR53. He then turned his attention to the front of the cover. In the centre, beneath his finger, he is locating a clip on the bottom flange while keeping the cover taut with his other hand.

SR48. . . . and covered it with another piece from the plastic bin liner.

SR51. The cover was pulled down over the backrest from the inside-out position, rather like the reverse of pulling off a jumper from the bottom.

SR54. The first clip is hammered into place, followed by the others, working from the middle, outwards.

SR49. The backrest cover was then turned completely inside out . . .

SR52. Mr. Lewis then spent several minutes pulling the cover down evenly and tightly all the way around.

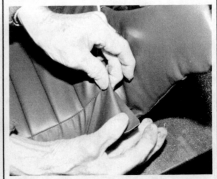

SR55. He tucked the outer edges under, to make a neat edge . . .

SR56.  . . . and then clipped them down, in turn.

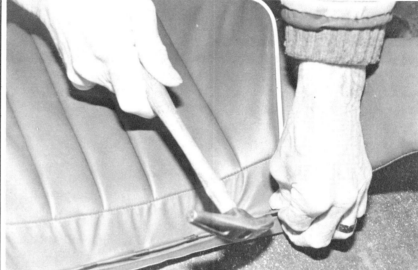

SR57.  The centre of the rear of the cover was then folded forwards and clipped down.

SR58.  No, it's not a relic from the bad old days of dentistry! It's for gripping fabric tightly and stretching it. It should be possible to copy its effectiveness (albeit much more slowly) with a pair of pincers and two strips of thin, smooth plywood.

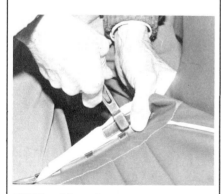

SR59.  The grippers were used to grasp the loose fabric from the rear of the cover and then, from the position shown here, they were rocked forwards, pulling the material tight.

SR60.  The last remaining job is to pierce the bolt hole for the backrest pivot.

SR61.  The finished article — as good as new and a credit to any Frogeye Sprite. All the original trim colours are available from Spridgebits and, for the later cars, the range of re-covering kits is growing all the time.

# Dashboard Repair (Frogeye)

## Tool Box

Typical bodyshop equipment – see Bodywork chapter for details.

## Safety

**Apart from normal bodyshop safety points, remember to disconnect the battery before attempting to remove the dashboard.**

Mk I Sprite's dashboards are plain, simple, no-frills affairs, which have made them perfect for people to add all sorts of extra gadgets over the years, at a time when originality mattered little. Attaining an uncluttered, original looking dash is vitally important if a restored car is to look right.

*FD1.   This dash looked tidier than some but there were lots of extra holes in it and beneath the vinyl, on the left-hand side, the radio opening had been crudely mis-shaped.*

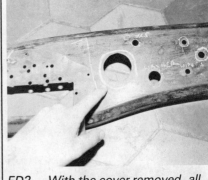

*FD2.   With the cover removed, all the unwanted holes were marked up with chalk. The left-hand side makes you wonder whether the car once belonged to Al Capone! This large hole was carefully patched.*

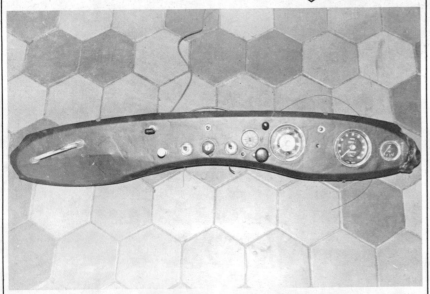

*FD3.   We tried several techniques for filling up the old holes. First, soft soldering was tried. A small hole was thoroughly cleaned up . . .*

*FD4.   . . . and solder was applied by heating the workpiece until it was just hot enough to melt a blob of solder placed on it. Then more solder was fed in. Verdict: a tricky operation. Could be useful for very small holes up to ⅛ inch and gives little distortion.*

FD5.    Secondly, we tried brazing holes up in the normal way. Verdict: much easier to carry out than soldering but creates a great deal of heat distortion which would cruelly twist a dash in need of much patching.

FD6.    The third system tried was MIG welding. You fill a hole by "pulsing" the trigger so that, in effect, you are dabbing in the weld a blob at a time. More sophisticated MIGs than ours, which is an SIP Ideal 120N, incorporate an automatic pulsing arrangement in them which turns the current on and off in short bursts while allowing the wire to feed in continuously.

FD7.    After welding, the front face of the dash had to be ground flat . . .

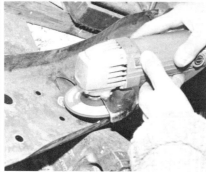

FD8.    . . . and then the rear. Verdict: there was still a little distortion but far less than with any other method. A bullseye, in more ways than one!

FD9.    A larger hole like this one is much too big to fill up with weld. We cut out a small rectangle of steel . . .

FD10. . . . placed it under the hole and marked it out.

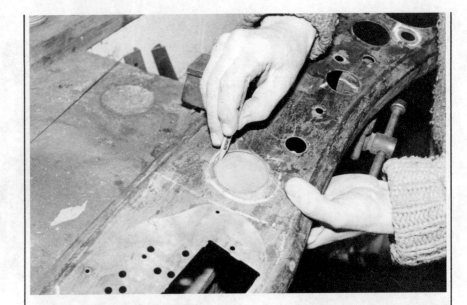

FD11. One leg of the tin snips was gripped in the vice, one hand worked the other leg of the snips while the other hand steadily turned the workpiece.

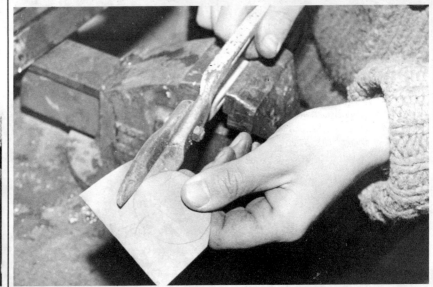

FD12. The MIG was used to make two light tacks opposite one another, the patch was tapped perfectly flat and welded all the way round.

FD13. After linishing it flat with the mini-grinder, the repair looked perfect.

# 5 Mechanical Components

## Front Suspension Strip/Rebuild

It is very common for Sprites and Midgets to fail the MOT because of front suspension problems. These are variously described by the tester as problems with "trunnions", "king pins", "swivel pins", "fulcrum pins", "A-frames", etc., when almost always the troubles are with both wishbones and kingpins/stub axles and requiring replacement of both. Note all references are to Figure 1.

### Tool Box

Most people acquire equipment suitable for working on a car's 'mechanics' as they go along. The publishers of this book have compiled a thorough selection of tools suitable for workshop use in the areas covered by the following sections of this book and in the *Haynes M.G. Midget and A-H*

*Sprite Owners' Workshop Manual*. (The Manual is highly recommended by the author as a companion to this book, incidentally.) Their suggested tool kit is found in an appendix. If a new clutch is to be fitted, a clutch alignment tool will be required – see text for details.

### Safety

**The greatest dangers in carrying out mechanical work stem from the fire risk inherent in working on fuel systems (don't smoke, obviously) and the dangers of working with heavy weights. Ensure that engine lifting equipment *and the framework supporting it* are in first-class condition, beware of trapped fingers and be careful when moving heavy engine and engine/gearbox units about, otherwise there are risks of back and other injuries. Read the appropriate appendix in this book.**

FS1. *We supported the bodyframe on axle stands then compressed the wishbone upwards against the spring to compress it. Spridgebits assure us that with "top trunnion, steering arm, callipers, etc. disconnected", you can push the wishbone down, taking the force out of the spring so that no form of compression is needed. Here, the steering arm and track rod end were split, using a proprietary splitting tool and the shocker arm disconnected from the trunnion.*

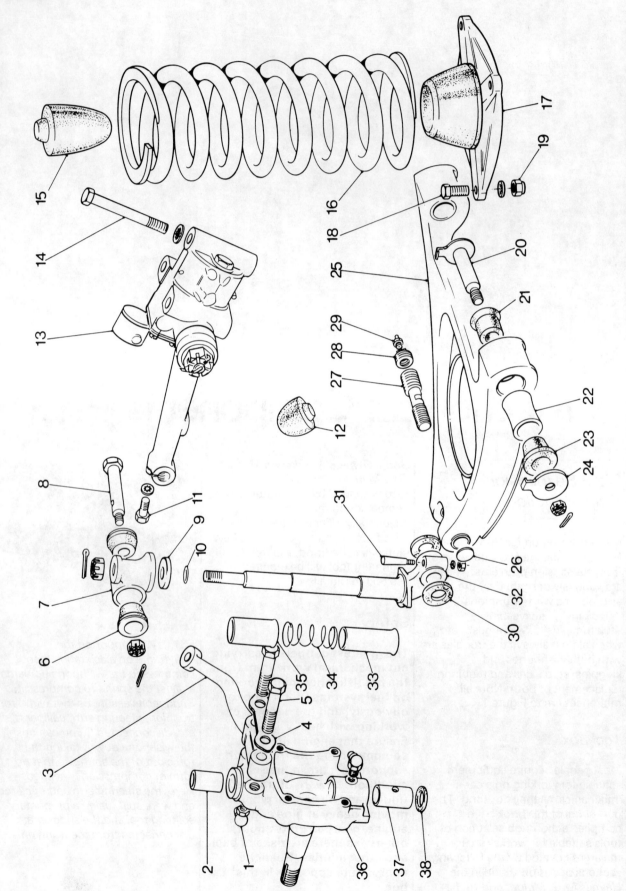

**FS2.** *The stub axle can be tilted sideways; this is a good opportunity to check the fulcrum pin (27) and kingpin bottom trunnion (32) for wear.*

 *Figure 1:* *The component parts of the front suspension*

1 Lubricator
2 King pin bush
3 steering arm
4 Lockwasher
5 Set screw
6 Trunnion bush (bearing)
7 Trunnion link
8 Trunnion fulcrum pin
9 Oilite thrust washer
10 Adjustment shim
11 Clamp bolt
12 Rebound buffer
13 Damper
14 Set bolts
15 Rebound rubber bumper
16 Coil spring
17 Spring seat
18 Bolts
19 Simmonds nut
20 Fulcrum pin
21 Rubber bush (bearings)
22 Lower link bush (inner)
23 Rubber bush (bearing)
24 Special washer
25 Lower link
26 Welch plug
27 Fulcrum pin (outer)
28 Screwed plug
29 Lubricator
30 Cork rings
31 Cotter
32 King pin
33 Dust excluder (bottom)
34 Spring
35 Dust excluder (top)
36 Stub axle
37 King pin bush
38 Cork sealing ring

**FS3.** *With the jack lowered, the coil spring can be easily removed. You can also check the A-bracket fulcrum pins (20) for wear.*

**FS4.** *"Unbolt the A-bracket from the chassis", say most manuals. It's not that easy! The pin (20) seizes into the bushes (21, 23) making dismantling very difficult. You can use a strong drift, as shown here . . .*

FS5. . . . or try this Spridgebits tip: "Use a wedge-type ball-joint splitter; insert the wedge under the flanged head of the inner pin and 'belt-it' very hard — it usually works".

Theoretically, the next job is to unscrew the fulcrum pin (27) but in at least 90% of cases things are so badly worn that the cotter pin will not knock out, and even if it does there is little chance of unscrewing the fulcrum pin.

Spridgebits recommend that, since if one part is worn, the rest is almost certain to be worn too, it is best to leave the kingpin attached to the A-bracket (or "lower link" as it is properly called) and to exchange it for a complete, reconditioned unit with the kingpin bushes pressed home and reamed and the threaded bushes brazed into place. Incidentally, the Spridgebits kit has a grease nipple at both ends of the kingpin trunnion — the original has only one and so one end of the trunnion becomes starved of grease.

If an anti-roll bar is fitted, renew the metalastic bushes at each end and the mounting rubbers.

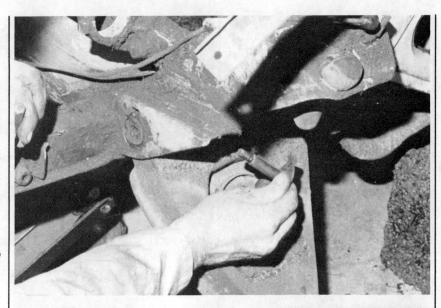

FS6. The lever arm shock absorbers are simply bolted to the plate shown here. It's well worth replacing them if they are suspected of being worn. Be sure to purchase a reputable brand — there are some very poor offerings on the market.

Tip 1): lubricate the dust excluder tubes (33) extensively before attempting to dismantle. They can usually be saved and are surprisingly expensive to replace.

FS7. Tip 2): the top trunnion (7) can be fitted back to front. This makes the kingpin lean out giving an 'interesting' degree of positive camber. They are not handed; it's simply a matter of ensuring that the trunnion fulcrum pin (8) is always OUTSIDE the line of the kingpin (32).

## Engine/Gearbox Removal

Frogeyes and Spridget engines all come out in much the same way, although in the case of the Mk I Sprite, it is advisable to remove the bonnet first (although raising the bonnet alone gives ample access, it will be found impossible to use a hoist with the bonnet in place). It is also sensible to remove the bonnet from later cars if only to improve access and prevent damage.

Unfortunately, there is less room inside the bonnet of a Midget than in, say, a Morris Minor, which used virtually the same engine and gearbox. It is therefore almost impossible to photograph many of the stages involved in engine removal. The first stage should, actually, take place at the rear of the car — if the engine and gearbox are to be removed together. It is impossible to remove the propshaft from the gearbox rear flange because of the construction of the body, so begin by jacking-up the rear of the car and placing it on axle stands, then unbolt the rear of the propshaft from the rear axle (four ⁹/₁₆ inch A.F. bolts and lock nuts).

ER1. Paul Skilleter, Managing Editor of Practical Classics magazine takes a look at the big hole where the engine used to be. Points to note here are that the gearbox mounting has been left attached to the gearbox and unbolted from the 'chassis' rails that run each side of it; and that a lifting bracket — crude, perhaps, but effective — had been welded up out of 1 ½ × 1 ½ inch angle iron and bolted down to the rocker cover using the existing rocker cover studs to provide a safe means of lifting the engine. Factory lifting brackets are often found fitted to

Minors and these do the job just as well, naturally. Ropes are often used between engine and hoist but they can give problems. First there is the problem of tying knots that won't come undone under the great weight of the engine and yet can be untied after the lifting is over. Second, there is the problem of actually finding somewhere to attach the ropes (most people end up passing them under the sump) and third, the problem that it is very difficult to gain the right centre of balance for lifting the engine out of the car. This last difficulty is usually compounded by the rope slipping as the pressure is applied.

ER2. Frogeye and Spridget bonnet hinge arrangements are very similar. Start by scribing around the hinge mounting plate so that the bonnet can be put back accurately in exactly the same place. It is not uncommon for the bolts to shear off, in which case the remainder of the bolt will have to be drilled out of the bonnet mounting later on. It takes two people to lift the bonnet away, if you are to be certain of not causing any damage. Remember to disconnect and label the wiring from the Frogeye bonnet and also that the two telescopic stays have to be disconnected.

ER3. Inside the engine bay now, drain the water out of the radiator and engine block both of which are fitted with drain taps. (The 1500 model is not fitted with drain taps at all; instead disconnect the bottom hose). While the water is draining away — and remember to remove the radiator filler cap to speed the water flow — disconnect and remove the battery. Drain the oil from the engine sump and gearbox and then replace both plugs to avoid mislaying them and also to prevent messy and potentially dangerous oil drips when the engine is being removed.

ER4. If the radiator hoses are good enough to be used again, disconnect them. If they are showing signs of wear, or if any of the hoses have almost welded themselves to the inlet/outlet stubs, saw the hoses in two with a hacksaw to save time. The radiator shroud contains eight captive nuts: remove the six retaining bolts and two screws and lift the assembly away, remembering to disconnect the pipe from the expansion chamber, if fitted. To get at the screws, the car's radiator grille has to be removed. Earlier cars than the one stripped here have a smaller shroud, held in place rather more simply by four bolts and captive nuts. Remember to disconnect the bulb type water temperature gauge from these models and to undo the electrical connection to the water temperature gauge on later models. Take off the exhaust pipe at the manifold by disconnecting the pinch clamp found there, and also disconnect the throttle and choke connections at the engine end of the cables.

ER5. From underneath the car, unscrew the knurled cap holding the speedometer cable to the gearbox (it may be necessary to start it off with pliers or a self-grip wrench). On Frogeyes and early Spridgets fitted with a mechanical rev counter drive at the rear of the dynamo, take off the cable from the dynamo drive in the same way. Also on earlier cars, unscrew the oil pressure sender unit from the block at the very rear on the right-hand side. Later cars have an electrical version: take off the wire from the sender unit on the right-rear of the block. Also disconnect the low tension lead from the distributor and the leads from the dynamo or alternator and from the starter motor. Take off the earth strap which runs from one of the bellhousing bolts to the body frame of the car. Take out the bolts holding the clutch slave cylinder to the gearbox and let it hang free beneath the car.

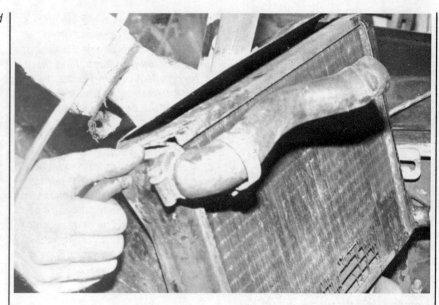

ER6. It can be difficult to gain access to the right-hand engine mounting with the dynamo in place. We found it easier to take it off first. The dynamo is held in place by the two bolts easily visible at the top and by a sliding adjuster bolt which connects to a sliding bracket at the bottom. All three must be removed before the fan belt and then the dynamo are removed. In our case the coil was strapped to the dynamo and so the wires to the ''SW'' (switch) and ''CB'' (contact breaker) terminals (or '' + '' and '' – '' on some coils) were marked by wrapping a tag of masking tape around each, writing on it which

connection it came from and then removing it. Take off the gearstick tunnel cover, put the gearstick into neutral and take out the three bolts holding the gearstick in place. Take out the gearstick.

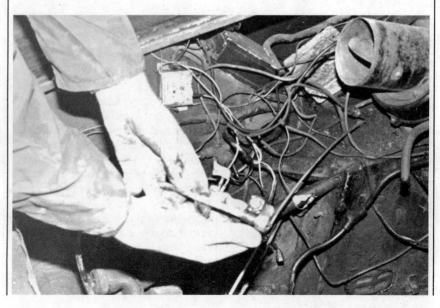

ER7. If the engine is to be removed without the gearbox, then it will also be necessary to take off the starter motor as it is held in place by two bolts which double as bellhousing bolts. On the other hand, it is not necessary to undo the propshaft or to take off the speedo connection, of course. Virtually all that remains to be done is to take out the ring of nuts and bolts that hold the gearbox to the engine backplate. Take care not to rest the weight of the rear of the engine upon the first motion shaft of the gearbox (the shaft that is inserted through the clutch into the rear of the engine).

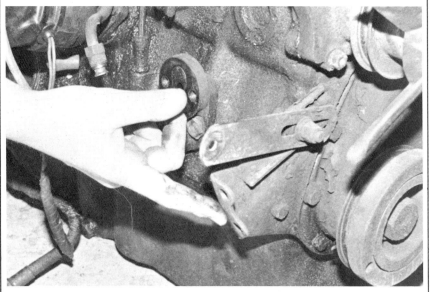

ER8. On the right-hand side of the engine, take off the nuts and spring washers that hold the engine front-plate to the engine mounting and also undo – but don't remove – the nut at the base of the engine mounting (this gives the mounting some extra movement and flexibility as the engine is removed).

ER9. On the left of the engine take out the four nuts, bolts and spring washers that hold the engine mounting to the chassis-frame, thus allowing the engine the little bit of upwards and sideways movement necessary to get it off the sloping rubber engine mounting block on the right-hand side.

ER10.   Removing the heater ducting gives a little more room for manoeuvrability. Lift the engine at the front, allowing the rear of the gearbox to drop down. The gearchange extension housing tends to foul on the car's bodywork as the engine is removed. Use a large lever to hold it out of the way as the engine is lifted and drawn forwards.

ER11.   If you use this type of free-standing hoist with castors, the engine or engine/gearbox can be rolled away from the car. If an immobile lift or overhead gantry is used, make sure before you start that there is room to push the car backwards from under the engine. If this is impossible, lean a wide plank against the front of the car and lower the engine, sliding it down the plank as you go. At LEAST two people will be needed for this little exercise.

ER12.   When refitting the engine and gearbox as a unit, getting the gearchange extension in place while stopping the bellhousing from fouling the bulkhead can be the biggest problem.

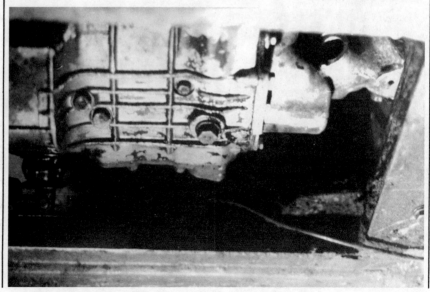

ER13. Note how the Frogeye steering rack also contrives to get in the way. If you hang an engine hoist from the garage roof, make absolutely certain that the roof is strong enough to take strain. To make certain, try placing a pair of vertical baulks of timber (4 × 4 inch fencing posts are ideal) each side of the car, to act as a pair of temporary pillars supporting the beam from which the hoist is to be hung.

A footnote for those taking out the engine alone, in order to replace the clutch: all gearboxes fitted the pre-Marina A-series engines use the same first motion shaft. So, if you want a perfect clutch alignment tool, go to the local scrapyard and find a scrap A-series-type gearbox (Minors, A30/A35, A40's as well as Spridgets all used the same box). Take off the nuts holding the front cover from inside the bellhousing and knock out the complete first motion shaft. This makes a cheap — and, of course, perfect guide for aligning the new clutch and so avoids a lot of trouble when sliding the engine back onto the first motion shaft of the gearbox in the car.

## Engine Strip

See "Tool Box" and "Safety" at start of chapter.

One of the advantages of owning a Midget or a Sprite is that so many of these cars' mechanical components were shared with saloons built in large quantities, that parts are likely to be available for some time to come. An even more important quality is that all Sprite and Midget engines were developed from simply-designed, soundly-constructed little engines which were first used in the 1950s, before the common use of overhead camshafts and special tools for such units. In other words, the D.I.Y. restorer should find it quite simple

to remove and rebuild any Sprite or Midget engine.

A fuller history of the engines used in these cars is found in the appropriate section of this book but a brief résumé would be useful here. First came the Frogeye engine which was virtually indistinguishable from the Morris Minor unit except, of course, that it was fitted with twin carburettors. There were minor differences (if you'll forgive the pun) but they were few. As engines grew from 947cc to 1098cc and then 1275cc differences between the lowest tune and the Midget/Sprite level of tune grew. 1275cc engines became marginally less "get-at-able" as engine side plates were dispensed with, making cam follower removal rather more difficult.

When the Triumph 1500cc engine was fitted, a logical decision was made by the B.L. management. Instead of having to prepare two engines for U.S. Emission Regulations it meant that only one engine had to be developed and then shared between the Midget and the Spitfire. In fact, the Triumph engine's historical pattern was almost identical to that of the B.M.C. unit; they both started life at 803cc and were first introduced within a year of each other. Consequently, as the following picture sequences show, there is nothing to fear from having to strip either of them. In fact, lessons learned from one can be applied in very many areas to the other engine as they're basically quite similar — and basically quite basic!

## Cylinder Head Removal

ES1.   The 1275cc Midget engine, as it looks after it has been taken from the car. Note that the starter motor has to be taken off in order to split the engine from the gearbox. (It fits in the large hole seen here on the engine backplate.) The carbs have already been removed complete with both manifolds.

ES2.   Start by undoing the chromed special nuts which hold the rocker cover down. The oil seal washers have, as so often happens, stuck lightly to the rocker cover top. Be careful that they don't drop off and get lost.

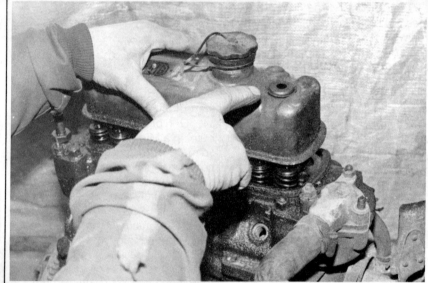

ES3.   It is almost certain that the rocker cover gasket will require renewal.

ES4.   The cylinder head is held down with, in some cases, studs which pass through the rocker shaft trunnions — the blocks through which the shaft passes. These trunnions are also held down by smaller studs in the middle of the head. Remove these first.

ES5.    Next remove the head nuts, including those on the dynamo/alternator side of the head. Follow the workshop manual order of removal but, broadly, start from the outside and work in – removing diagonally opposite nuts in turn.

ES6.    Have a large box ready in which to place the bits as they are removed. This is the rocker shaft assembly.

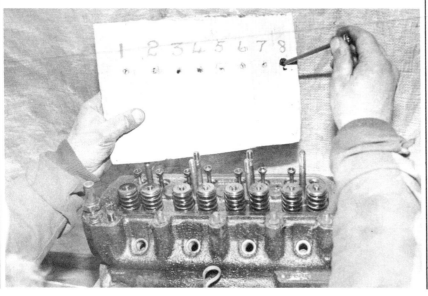

ES7.    The pushrods lift upwards out of the engine. On an old engine, some may be a bit difficult to pull out (which is some measure of how much gunge has been deposited in there) but they will come eventually. If they are to be reused, make up a piece of card in which they can be kept in the correct order.

*ES8.* Heads usually stick to the block to a lesser — or greater — degree. Resist the temptation to drive a screwdriver between the two which would be sure to damage both faces. Instead, tap upwards at the projection in the head casting at each end, using a soft-faced mallet.

*ES9.* The head will come off eventually. Use the end of a steel rule to scrape both faces free of any stuck-on gasket.

*ES10.* Remove the nuts holding down the thermostat housing. It's almost certain to be stuck! Tap it loose with a soft-faced mallet or, under extreme circumstances (and running the real risk of destroying it), take off the top hose and insert a bar into the stub and work it up and down.

ES11. It only remains to remove the valves and studs. Use a proprietary valve spring compressor on the valves and, with the springs closed up, take out the cotters found at the top of each valve stem. Then, as the compressor is freed, the spring assembly comes free. To remove the studs, run a pair of nuts down the top of the stud, tighten them against each other with a pair of spanners, then turn the bottom nut anti-clockwise. Instead of the nuts turning, the whole stud should come out. If the nuts move, they haven't been tightened sufficiently against each other.

## Carburettor Removal and Strip

ES12. Both exhaust and inlet manifolds are held to the head by brass nuts run onto the six studs shown here. Missing from this picture are the sprung rings slipped into the mouths of the inlet manifolds. These give the manifold a positive location in the head.

ES13. These pancake air filters are often fitted in place of the original Coopers paper element type. Remove the domed nuts, take out the sponge rubber filter and unbolt each filter from its carb.

*ES14. These springs close throttles and choke. Unclip them from the carbs and from the bottom of the heat shield.*

*ES15. Carburettors are held to the manifold by two nuts which tighten against the carburettor flange. Slacken off each nut a little at a time, removing all risk of distortion at the alloy flanges.*

*ES16. As the carbs are pulled off the manifold studs, make a note of how the throttle and choke linkage bars are fitted. They are simply pushed into loose bushes on both carbs.*

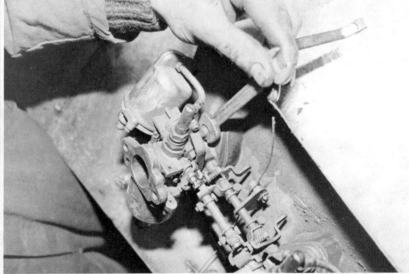

*ES17. After the carbs, the emulsion blocks then the heat shield slide off the manifold studs. Keep all the old, sound gaskets for emergency re-use. The assembly takes ten of them in all!*

ES18. Start stripping the carbs by removing the float bowl top; three screws hold it down.

ES19. Lift off the top and the float which is hinged to it.

ES20. The float works by pushing the valve, shown here lying on the bench, into the seating indicated by the pointing screwdriver. In case of doubt, the seat can be removed with a small socket spanner and replaced along with the valve. A leaking float is replaced by drawing out the hinge pin and replacing it.

ES21. Next, unscrew and remove the dashpot damper and drain out any oil found inside the dashpot by tipping the carb upside-down.

*ES22. Two screws hold the dashpot down. Remove them and lift off the dashpot exposing the piston and spring.*

*ES23. Lift out the piston from the carb body. The needle at its base is critical to economy and smooth running. If it is worn at the base, or bent, renew it.*

*ES24. The needle is held in the bottom of the piston by means of a grub screw which fits in the hole shown. Later models incorporate a spring here too. When refitting, use the edge of a steel rule to align the shoulder at the top of the needle with the bottom face of the piston.*

ES25. To remove the butterfly spindle which, if worn, can allow air leaks into the carb and induce poor running, start by pushing the locking washer tabs over at the end of the butterfly spindle.

ES26. With the lock washer tabs back, the retaining nut and other fittings shown are removed.

ES27. Now, with a fine bladed screwdriver, the two screws holding the butterfly to the spindle are removed . . .

ES28. . . . and the butterfly slid out of the slotted spindle.

ES29. And then the spindle, with nothing retaining it, can be slid out of the carb body.

ES30. The jet into which the metering needle mates is removed in three moves: First unscrew the choke arm from the block at the base of the jet . . .

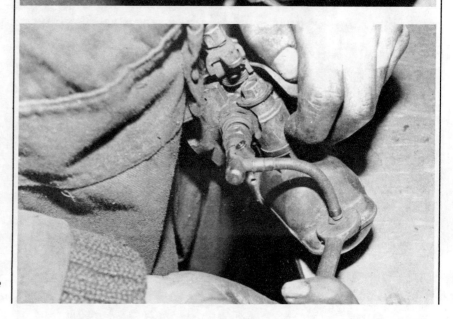

ES31. . . . next, undo the petrol feed pipe from the base of the float chamber body and carefully pull the tube and retaining nut out . . .

*ES32. . . . finally, the jet simply slides out of the base of the carb.*

Earlier Frogeye-type carbs are basically similar except that the petrol feed is internal instead of via the external pipe shown in the photo sequence, and the choke lever assembly is completely different. Be certain that the correct carb type is specified when buying parts. Refer to Figure 2 when stripping early-type carbs.

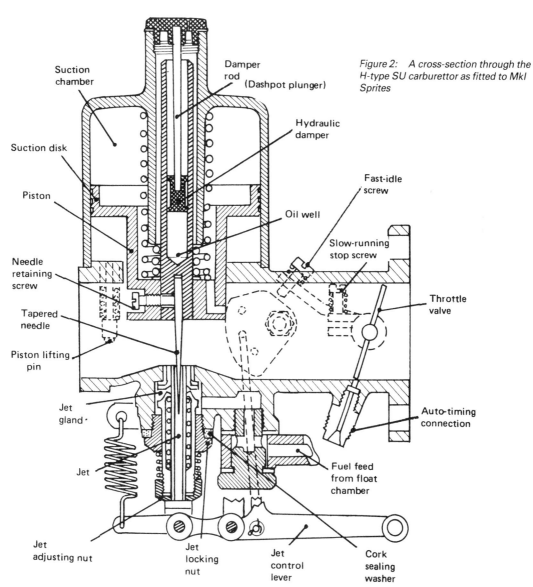

*Figure 2: A cross-section through the H-type SU carburettor as fitted to MkI Sprites*

## Engine Block Stripdown (Except 1500)

When an engine is badly worn, it often makes good economic sense to exchange it for a fully reconditioned unit — but before doing so, DO check the credentials of the firm you are using and also ask for a list of all parts renewed. As in most things, you only get what you pay for and it could be that one firm is cheaper than another only because they recondition or renew fewer parts. One back-street trader who sold extremely low-priced engines carried out the disgraceful practice of selling "reconditioned" exchange units, the restoration of which amounted to steam cleaning and a coat of shiny paint. If a customer brought an engine back with a complaint, *then* he fitted the cheapest reconditioned unit he could buy. If not . . . However, this man was an exception and it is reasonable to assume that all the larger firms are far more reputable. They, after all, have a lot to lose.

The trouble with buying an exchange engine, is that if the original engine is in the car, a useful piece of originality has been lost. There are two ways around this problem. The first is to ask the reconditioner to rebuild your own unit and nearly all will happily oblige. The second is to strip the components yourself, have them reconditioned by an engineering firm and then rebuild the engine yourself.

Whichever course of action you choose to take, all involve at least some degree of block stripping. The following sequence shows how it's done.

ES34.    Lift the unit complete with adjusting bracket from the block and remove the fan belt.

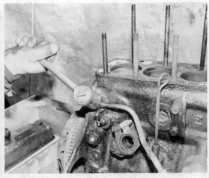

ES36.    . . . and the banjo bolt which holds the oil feeder pipe in place.

ES35.    Undo the two bolts which hold the oil filter cannister in place . . .

ES37.    The whole oil filter assembly now simply lifts off. Drain it by tipping it upside-down over a suitable receptacle.

ES33.    Remove the three bolts holding the dynamo or alternator to the block. The nuts are locknuts and it will be necessary to use another spanner to grip the bolt head while the nut is turned.

ES38. Two more bolts secure the filter bowl mounting to the block . . .

ES39. . . . allowing the mounting to be lifted away.

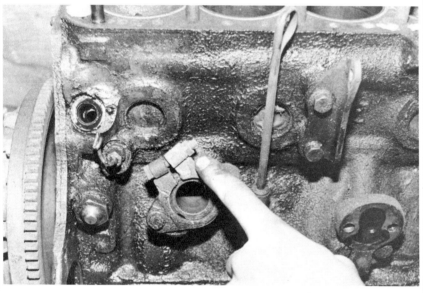

ES40. The distributor goes in here; it had already been removed from this engine. It comes off in one of two ways: either by slackening the pinch bolt shown here, in which case the timing will be totally lost (but does that matter? Do you intend to totally strip the engine?) . . .

ES41. . . . or by taking out the two bolts which hold the clamp-plate in place.

ES42.   Underneath the clamp-plate, the distributor housing is held by one bolt.

ES43.   After its removal, the housing pulls out of the block.

ES44.   The distributor drive is beneath it. It has to be removed with a slight clockwise twist − use either a large screwdriver in the slotted top face or screw a $^5/_{16}$ inch bolt into the threaded top plate of the drive (between the two slots).

ES45.   At the rear of the block, the oil pressure release valve and spring are removed after undoing the domed nut. Above and to the right of the oil pressure release valve can be seen the oil pressure gauge sender mounting. This is removed by using the hexagonal nut built into it − usually almost concealed by dirt and oil.

ES46.    Any remaining mounting brackets and ancillaries, such as the fuel pump on the left-hand side of the earliest cars' blocks, the water drain tap and, as shown here, the dynamo mounting bracket, should also be removed and stored carefully.

ES47.    Before any of the heavy components can be reached, you have to start at the outside and work in. Begin by knocking back the tab washers holding the cooling fan bolts in place.

ES48.    Hold the fan with one hand and remove the retaining bolts.

ES49.    If the tab washers are re-usable, store them carefully with the bolts. The fan and the pulley section pull forwards off the water pump nose.

ES50.   The water pump itself is bolted through to the block with four long bolts (or studs and nuts on some earlier cars).

ES51.   The water pump is usually another of those sticky customers that doesn't want to be taken off. Tap the dynamo mounting with a soft-faced mallet to break the bond, then remove the water pump.

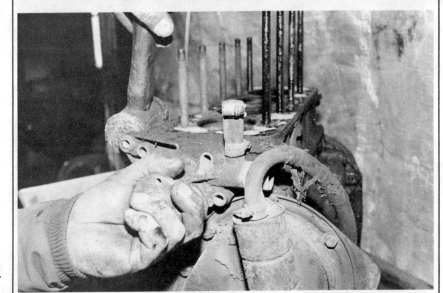

ES52.   Use a cold chisel to knock back the large tab washer holding the crankshaft pulley retaining bolt in place.

ES53. DON'T use the ½ inch drive ratchet here; hammering it will probably break it. Use a tommy bar instead. If the bolt refuses to free, nil desperandum! Go on to the stage where you remove the sump and place a large block of wood between one of the crankshaft webs and the side of the block, preventing the crank from turning. Then, thump happily at the tommy bar until the bolt shifts — but ensure that the tab washer is right back out of the way.

ES54. Tap the pulley off the end of the crank. Earlier pulleys are not damped and are lighter, pressed-steel affairs.

ES55. Take out the ring of bolts holding the timing chain cover in place and remove it. Again, it may well stick and require tapping to encourage it to come loose. DON'T be tempted to prise it with a screwdriver blade.

ES56. Lift the cover off. Note how, on this model with early type of emission control system, the valve has first to be removed from the inlet manifold if, for some reason, the timing chain cover is being removed with the manifold in place. Later models have a breather pipe which connects to the carburettors via a vee-connection.

ES57. Take off the oil thrower (a loose push fit) from the end of the crankshaft. Note which way round it fits.

ES58. Knock back the tab washer holding the timing chain sprocket to the camshaft . . .

ES59. . . . lock the engine as shown, and take off the camshaft sprocket nut.

ES60. Carefully ease the sprocket forwards with a lever, pulling the smaller crankshaft sprocket at the same time.

ES61.    Slide both sprockets and the chain off together. It is essential, when reassembling the engine, that these sprockets are replaced in the correct position with regard to one-another. See the Haynes Workshop Manual *for further details.* Note that the crankshaft pulley floats and is not held in place other than by the timing chain itself.

ES62.    Remove the three bolts holding the camshaft end plate in place . . .

ES63.    . . . remove the end plate . . .

ES64.    . . . and pull out the camshaft. This will require considerable twisting, turning and pulling to enable the cam lobes to clear the obstacle course of the cam followers still inside the block – this task is easier if the block is inverted. This may damage the camshaft bearings so take great care. If they are not to be replaced, leave the camshaft in place until the cam followers have been removed through the block side covers fitted to earlier engines (See Figure 3, 129 and 179) but of course it is impossible to remove them in this way from later engines without side covers.

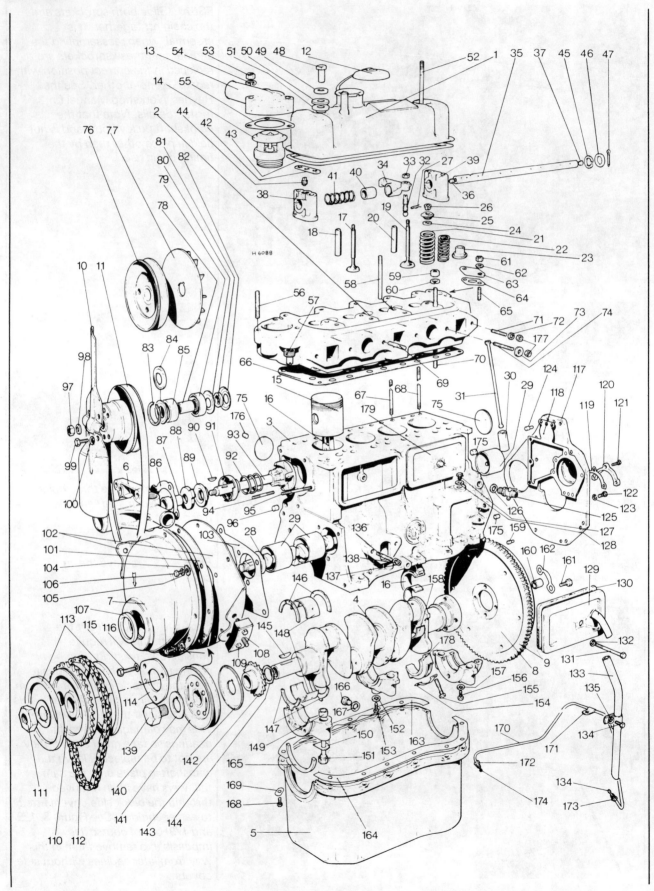

H 6088

Figure 3  Exploded view of 'A' series engine  (typical)

1 Cover – rocker gear
2 Cylinder block
3 Block – head
4 Crankshaft
5 Sump
6 Water pump body
7 Cover – cylinder block front
8 Flywheel
9 Starter ring
10 Fan blade
11 Fan belt
12 Oil filler cap
13 Elbow – water outlet
14 Thermostat
15 Piston assembly
16 Connecting rod
17 Exhaust valve
18 Exhaust valve guide
19 Inlet valve
20 Inlet valve guide
21 Outer valve spring
22 Inner valve spring
23 Shroud for valve guide
24 Valve packing ring
25 Valve spring cup
26 Valve cotter
27 Valve cotter circlip
28 Camshaft
29 Camshaft bearing liners
30 Tappet
31 Pushrod
32 Tappet adjusting screw
33 Locknut
34 Rocker (bushed)
35 Valve rocker shaft (plugged)
36 Rocker shaft plug (screwed)
37 Rocker shaft plug (plain)
38 Rocker shaft bracket (tapped)
39 Rocker shaft bracket (plain)
40 Rocker bush
41 Rocker spacing spring
42 Rocker shaft bracket plate
43 Cover joint gasket
44 Rocker shaft locating screw
45 Spring washer

46 Washer
47 Split pin
48 Nut
49 Cup washer
50 Distance piece
51 Cover bush
52 Rocker bracket long stud
53 Nut
54 Spring washer
55 Elbow joint gasket
56 Water outlet elbow stud
57 By-pass adaptor
58 Rocker bracket stud (short)
59 Cylinder head nut
60 Washer
61 Cover nut
62 Spring washer
63 Cover plate
64 Cover plate joint gasket
65 Cover plate stud
66 Cylinder head gasket
67 Cylinder head stud (short)
68 Cylinder head stud (long)
69 Exhaust manifold stud (medium)
70 Cylinder head stud (long)
71 Exhaust manifold stud (short)
72 Small washer
73 Large clamping washer
74 Exhaust manifold stud (long)
75 Core plug
76 Dynamo pulley
77 Dynamo fan
78 Bearing distance piece
79 Bearing
80 Outer retainer for felt
81 Felt
82 Inner retainer for felt
83 Retainer circlip
84 Bearing grease retainer
85 Bearing
86 Water pump gasket
87 Distance piece
88 Seal
89 Seal rubber
90 Pulley key
91 Spring locating cup

92 Spring
93 Spindle with vane
94 Water pump body stud (short)
95 Water pump body stud (long)
96 Oil gallery plug
97 Spindle nut
98 Spindle washer
99 Screw to pulley
100 Spring washer
101 Cover gasket
102 Front bearer plate
103 Bearer plate joint gasket
104 Plain washer
105 Spring washer
106 Front bearer plate screw
107 Cover felt
108 Rubber front mounting block
109 Block attachment bolt
110 Camshaft sprocket (upper)
111 Sprocket nut
112 Camshaft drive chain
113 Tensioner rings
114 Locking plate
115 Plate to crankcase screw
116 Shakeproof washer
117 Gearbox bearer plate
118 Joint gasket to plate
119 Cover joint washer
120 Rear cover
121 Cover screw
122 Screw to block
123 Spring washer
124 Dowel (top) to block
125 Drain tap (water)
126 Tap washer
127 Oil priming plug
128 Copper washer
129 Block front side cover (with elbow)
130 Side cover gasket
131 Screw to block
132 Fibre washer
133 Fume vent pipe (with clip)
134 Clip screw
135 Spring washer
136 Stud (blanking plate)

137 Nut
138 Washer
139 Pulley retaining bolt
140 Lockwasher
141 Crankshaft pulley
142 Oil thrower
143 Crankshaft sprocket
144 Packing washer
145 Crankshaft key
146 Upper thrust washers
147 Lower thrust washers
148 Main bearing
149 Main bearing cap dowel
150 Lockwasher
151 Bearing cap bolt
152 Shakeproof washer
153 Bearing cap screw
154 Lockwasher for bolts
155 Cap bolt
156 Bearing cap screw
157 Shakeproof washer
158 Big end bearing
159 Dowel
160 First motion shaft bush
161 Flywheel to crankshaft screw
162 Lockwasher
163 Sump right-hand gasket
164 Sump left-hand gasket
165 Main bearing cap seal
166 Sump drain plug
167 Drain plug washer
168 Screw
169 Washer
170 Ignition control pipe
171 Pipe clip
172 Pipe nut (distributor end)
173 Pipe nut (carburettor end)
174 Pipe olive
175 Oil gallery plug
176 Oil pressure relief-valve passage plug
177 Stud nuts
178 Big end cap
179 Block rear side cover

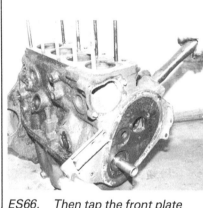

ES65.  Use an Allen key to remove the machine screws now holding the engine front plate in place (bolts on earlier cars).

ES66.  Then tap the front plate from the block using a soft-faced mallet.

ES67.  Next, start working inwards from the other end of the engine. Take off the clutch, remembering that it is sprung and bolts should be freed a turn at a time in sequence to avoid stressing and distorting the cover plate.

ES68.   Beneath the clutch cover and driven plates is a rather artistic looking tab washer holding the six bolts in place (earlier cars have two pair-of-spectacles-shaped tab washers and only four bolts), remove the bolts and take off the flywheel. It can be surprisingly heavy, so be careful that it doesn't drop off suddenly and pinch unwary fingers!

ES69.   An array of bolts holds the engine backplate into place. After it has been tapped away from the block, the oil pump can be taken out from the back of the block (this fitting, incidentally, being one of the few areas that are substantially different from the layout of the 1500 engine).

ES69A.   Before turning the engine over, if not already done, take out the head studs from the top of the block. Lock two nuts onto each stud in turn, as shown, then turn the bottom nut, taking the stud with it.

ES69B. Turn the engine over, take out the sump bolts and tap the sump free with the soft-faced mallet.

ES70. Remove the sump. Take out the cam followers which will have fallen — or can be pushed with a pushrod — down into the sump.

ES71. Unbolt the bracket holding the oil pump pick-up gauze filter in place . . .

ES72. . . . unbolt the feeder pipe and take off the complete assembly.

ES73. Take off the locknuts holding the big-end bearing caps in place (earlier cars are fitted with plain nuts and tab washers which will have to be knocked back first).

ES74. Rotate the crank so that the big end is at the bottom of its stroke and tap the cap upwards and off with a soft-faced hammer.

ES75. Main bearing cap retaining bolts are held in place by tab washers. Knock them back, take out the retaining bolts . . .

ES76. . . . take off the three caps and lift out the crank.

ES77.   Push the pistons and conrods up through the bores . . .

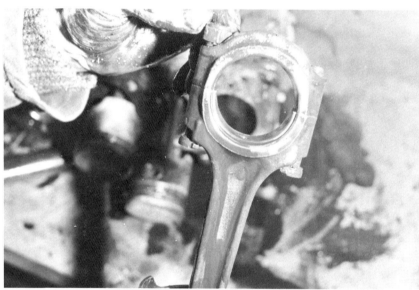

ES78.   . . . and replace the big end caps onto the correct conrods straightaway, so that there is no chance of their becoming confused.

ES79.   The crank rear oil seal simply unbolts from the back of the block.

ES80.   The dipstick tube is a tight push fit in the block. It can be tapped out from beneath but take great care as it is easily damaged during removal .

227

## Engine Block Stripdown (1500)

In many ways the same principles apply in stripping both Austin and Triumph-type engines. For that reason, the following section is shorter than the previous one; it deals largely with areas which are different to those of the Austin-derived unit.

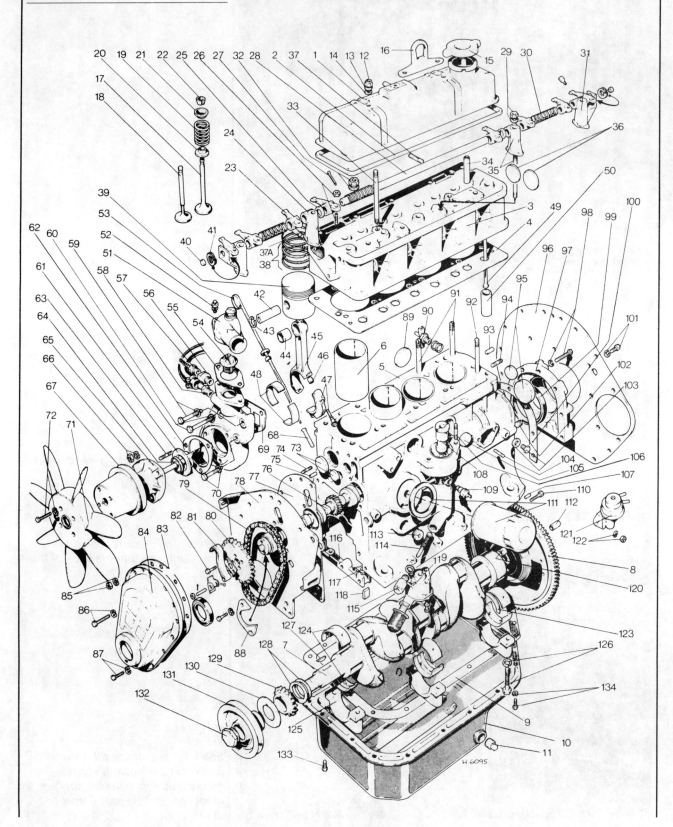

Figure 4    Exploded view of 1500 engine (typical)

 1 Cover – rocker gear
 2 Cover – joint gasket
 3 Cylinder head
 4 Cylinder head gasket
 5 Cylinder block
 6 Cylinder liner
 7 Crankshaft
 8 Starting ring and flywheel
 9 Sump gasket
10 Sump
11 Sump drain plug
12 Self locking nut
13 Washer
14 Fibre washer
15 Oil filler cap
16 Lifting bracket
17 Exhaust valve
18 Inlet valve
19 Valve spring
20 Shroud for valve guide
21 Valve spring cup
22 Valve cotter
23 Rocker
24 Rocker shaft bracket
25 Spacer
26 Tappet adjusting screw and locknut
27 Split pin
28 Rocker shaft
29 Nut and washer – rocker shaft bracket
30 Rocker spacing spring
31 Rocker shaft bracket
32 Head securing nut and washer
33 Rocker cover securing stud
34 Valve guide
35 Rocker shaft bracket and stud
36 Core plugs
37 Induction manifold stud
37a Exhaust manifold stud
38 Piston rings
39 Piston
40 Plug
41 Spring washer
42 Gudgeon pin
43 Circlip
44 Small end bush
45 Connecting rod
46 Sleeve
47 Big end cap and bolt
48 Big end bearing shells
49 Pushrod
50 Tappet

51 Water pump elbow
52 Elbow securing stud, nut and lockwasher
53 Dipstick
54 Thermostat
55 Top gasket – water pump
56 Adaptor for temperature sensor
57 Temperature sensor unit
58 Hose adaptor
59 Water pump securing bolt (medium) and washer
60 Water pump securing bolt (long) and washer
61 Spindle and vane
62 Spindle housing gasket
63 Spindle housing plug (securing)
64 Seal
65 Spindle and bearing housing
66 Spindle housing nut and lockwasher
67 Fan pulley and hub
68 Dipstick guide
69 Water pump housing gasket
70 Water pump securing bolt (short) and washer
71 Fan
72 Fan securing bolt and lockwasher
73 Core plugs
74 Stud
75 Dowel
76 Camshaft
77 Gasket
78 Front engine plate
79 Timing chain
80 Camshaft sprocket
81 Chain tensioner
82 Sprocket bolt
83 Chaincase gasket
84 Chaincase
85 Chaincase securing nut and lockwasher
86 Chaincase securing bolt and lockwasher (long)
87 Chaincase securing bolt and lockwasher (short)

 88 Camshaft locating plate
 89 Core plug
 90 Drain tap (water)
 91 Head securing studs (grooved)
 92 Head securing stud (standard)
 93 Dowel
 94 Stud
 95 Core plugs
 96 Gearbox bearer plate
 97 Rear oil seal housing
 98 Seal housing bolt and lockwasher
 99 Rear oil seal
100 Oil seal housing gasket
101 Bolt and lockwasher (bearer plate)
102 Oil gallery plug
103 Drain plug and washer
104 Securing plug for fuel pump
105 Core plug
106 Securing plug for distributor housing
107 Dowel
108 Distributor drive adaptor
109 Oil pressure sensing unit
110 Flywheel bolt

111 Oil filter and joint washer
112 Sleeve
113 Plug
114 Oil pressure relief valve
115 Relief valve nut
116 Crossmember
117 Gasket
118 Seal
119 Oil pump
120 Sleeve (flywheel to crankshaft)
121 Fuel pump
122 Fuel pump securing nut and lockwasher
123 Rear main bearing thrust washer
124 Main bearing shells
125 Main bearing cap
126 Bearing cap bolt and lockwasher
127 Crankshaft key
128 Thrust washers
129 Crankshaft sprocket
130 Oil thrower
131 Crankshaft pulley
132 Pulley retaining bolt
133 Sump securing bolt
134 Securing bolt and lockwasher

ES81.    The engine which Spridgebits stripped for us had suffered the fate of a number of neglected and over-revved 1500 engines – an engine blow up. Perhaps taking an engine that began life at 803cc and stretching it to almost twice the capacity was asking a bit much! The point for owners is that these engines should be maintained carefully and driven with just a touch of care in the lower gears.

ES82.    It is sometimes said that the 1500's crank journals are not up to the job. But on the evidence of what was to be found in this engine's sump, did the pistons seize first, or did the conrod break where the cap fits? Obviously, this engine was scrap, but we stripped it down all the same to see what a worn old engine would look like.

ES83. With the oil filter, distributor (two vertical studs), fuel pump (two horizontal studs) and alternator already out of the way, we removed another couple of ancillaries: the oil pressure sender unit and water jacket drain plug.

ES84. The distributor drive can clearly be seen through the distributor mounting aperture. Place a screwdriver in one of the slots in the top face.

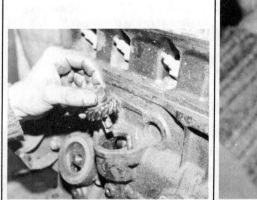

ES85. Unlike the A-series engine, this should be twisted (and lifted) anti-*clockwise*.

ES86. The cylinder head comes off in the same way as the A-series head, with the exception that the water pump is bolted to the front face of the cylinder head.

ES87.    Cam followers can be lifted out through the pockets in the top of the block. Try pushing a (relatively?) grease-free finger into each cam follower, rather like inserting the finger into a thimble, and lifting upwards.

ES88.    Take off the front crank nut, pulley and timing chain cover. See the appropriate section in the A-series engine strip for details.

ES89.    Timing chain tension is provided by this replaceable spring fitted to the inside of the timing chain cover.

ES90.    Remove the oil thrower from the crankshaft nose.

*ES91. Knock back the tab washers holding the camshaft sprocket bolts in place.*

*ES92. Remove the two securing bolts.*

*ES93. Then lift off the sprockets and timing chain (this time single, not double) in much the same way as for the earlier engine.*

*ES94. Tap out the Woodruff key that holds the crankshaft sprocket in place and take off the spacer washer found behind it.*

ES95.    The camshaft is located by a plate which slides into a groove behind the camshaft nose. Take out the two bolts holding the plate in place and slide it away.

ES96.    The engine front plate is now held in place by a series of slotted machine screws.

ES97.    Once they have been taken out, the front plate can be removed from the block.

ES98.    Next, the camshaft is removed by pulling and turning, so that the cam lobes clear the camshaft bearings inside the block. Take care not to damage them.

ES99.   At the rear of the engine, remove the clutch and flywheel using the same methods as those employed for the A-series unit.

ES100.   And again, in the same way, the backplate is removed. (The starter motor mounting shouldn't be bent into the shape shown here. This engine had sustained more than one lot of damage.)

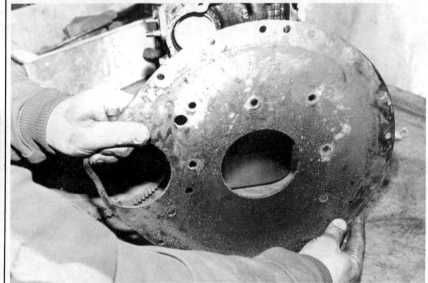

ES101.   With the engine on its side, the sump bolts can be removed and the sump tapped free with a soft-faced mallet.

ES102.   Three bolts hold the oil pump pick-up and gauze filter in place . . .

ES103. . . . and the same bolts pass straight through the oil pump body, so their removal allows the oil pump to be lifted away, too.

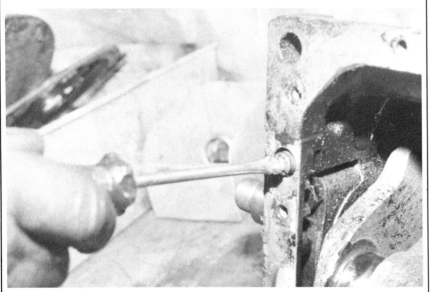

ES104. Bridging the gap across the top of the front main bearing is a cross-member which is unscrewed . . .

ES105. . . . and lifted away.

ES106. At the back of the engine, the rear oil seal housing is removed after removing the seven bolts holding it in place.

ES107. Access can now be gained to the main bearing caps which are removed in a similar way to those on the A-series engine.

ES108. The three remaining (!) big end caps on this car were removed, as shown in the A-series sequence and, again, the pistons pushed upwards through the bores. If the bores are worn, the piston rings tend to stick at the ridges left by bore wear at the top of the bores. Use the handle of a hammer inserted from below to tap the piston upwards and out.

ES109. The crank is then lifted off the main bearings.

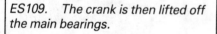

ES110. Finally, any plugs or ancillaries such as this oil pressure relief valve, which have not yet been removed are taken off the engine so that all oilways and water passages can be fully cleared when the block is reconditioned.

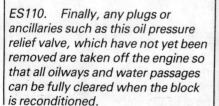

## Single Zenith/Stromberg Carb Cleaning & Adjustment (USA models only) *with John H. Twist of University Motors, Michigan*

It is recommended that this section is used in conjunction with Haynes M.G. Midget Owners Workshop Manual.

### Tool Box

½ and ⅝ inch AF wrench; straight and crosspoint screwdrivers; needle-nosed pliers; aerosol carb cleaner; light lubricating oil; grease.

### Safety

**Gasoline is highly volatile, highly flammable – DON'T SMOKE!**

*Z1.    Remove the air cleaner with a ½ inch wrench. Be certain to disconnect the spring between the rear of the air cleaner can and the throttle return cam at the right side of the carb (not shown).*

⇩

*Z2.    Before removing the cam from the engine compartment, it will be necessary to release the wing nut holding the air filter in place. Inspect the filter and note that the filter gets dirty from the inside out. If there is any question about the filter, replace it with the correct filter.*

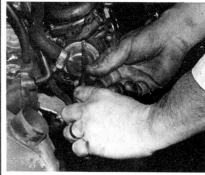

*Z3.    Remove the three screws holding the water jacket and bi-metal spring assembly to the auto choke. These are fine thread screws and can be easily stripped! Loosen the hose clamp at the top of the water jacket, allowing the hose to rotate freely.*

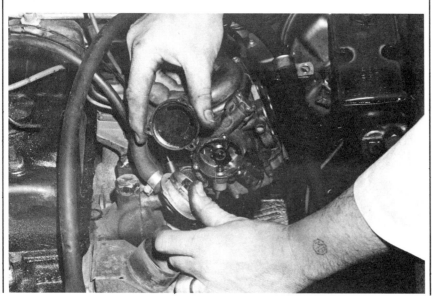

*Z4.    Then withdraw the jacket and carefully remove the black bakelite insulator from the choke assembly.*

**Z5.** Using a pair of needle nosed pliers, remove the small rubber plug immediately above the outside screw, holding the choke assembly to the carb body. This makes access to the choke easier.

**Z6.** In this picture, the water jacket/bi-metal spring has been tied back with a piece of mechanics' wire so that it will not interfere with the rest of the process. Remove the three screws holding the choke assembly to the carb body. These have a $^{10}/_{32}$ or 2 BA thread, but if one is lost, $^{10}/_{32}$ will act as a suitable replacement.

**Z7.** Withdraw the choke assembly and the orange gasket holding it to the carb body. Be certain NOT to tear the gasket. A new one is not easily obtainable!

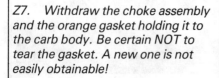

**Z8.** Carefully inspect the base of the choke assembly. The brass plug sealing the mixture valve is often loose. When loose, or when the plug has dropped away, fuel can drip onto the catalytic converter – and if the converter is red hot as it often is while on a cold start, a FIRE can result.

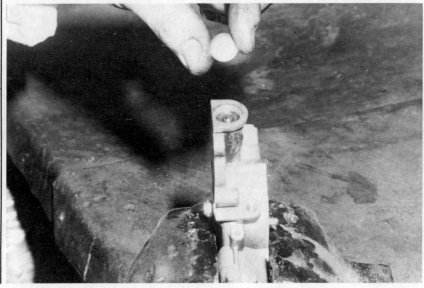

Z9.    If the brass plug is loose, tap it into place with a small hammer. If the plug is missing altogether, inspect the left frame rail, as it is sometimes found there, after dropping out.

Z10.    Spray the choke assembly well with carb cleaner, working the "finger" on the choke mechanism all the time.

Z11.    Then lubricate the assembly with very light lubricating oil, or silicone based lubricant.

Z12.    Replace the choke assembly onto the carb body after lightly greasing the orange gasket. Get the screws TIGHT. Remember to replace the small black rubber plug. It will be necessary to hold the throttle part-way open while fitting the choke assembly to the body. Then again open the throttle, position the "finger" at about a 2:00 position (as shown) and rotate the black insulator anti-clockwise by about 60 degrees — so that the finger can be seen from above.

Z13.    CAREFULLY, refit the water jacket/bi-metal spring onto the choke assembly ensuring that the finger is inserted into the hook on the bi-metal spring. Rotate the plastic insulator clockwise and align the three marks — on the choke housing, the insulator and on the water jacket (as shown). In colder climates rotate the water jacket slightly clockwise to richen the starting mixture.

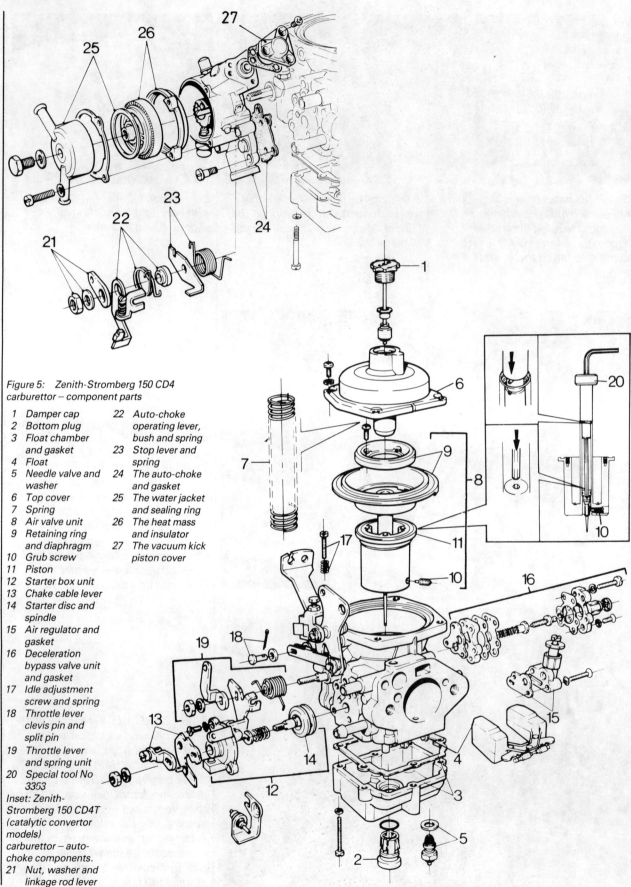

Figure 5: Zenith-Stromberg 150 CD4 carburettor – component parts

1  Damper cap
2  Bottom plug
3  Float chamber and gasket
4  Float
5  Needle valve and washer
6  Top cover
7  Spring
8  Air valve unit
9  Retaining ring and diaphragm
10 Grub screw
11 Piston
12 Starter box unit
13 Chake cable lever
14 Starter disc and spindle
15 Air regulator and gasket
16 Deceleration bypass valve unit and gasket
17 Idle adjustment screw and spring
18 Throttle lever clevis pin and split pin
19 Throttle lever and spring unit
20 Special tool No 3353

Inset: Zenith-Stromberg 150 CD4T (catalytic convertor models) carburettor – auto-choke components.

21 Nut, washer and linkage rod lever
22 Auto-choke operating lever, bush and spring
23 Stop lever and spring
24 The auto-choke and gasket
25 The water jacket and sealing ring
26 The heat mass and insulator
27 The vacuum kick piston cover

Z14. Remove the two screws holding the air regulator valve to the right side of the carb. Take care with the orange gasket.

See Fig 5. Dissemble and clean all idle air regulator parts (item 15). Then screw the ⅝ inch hex white plastic adjusting nut into its housing until it bottoms. Unscrew the nut then by two turns. Then screw the brass adjusting pin into the white plastic nut until it bottoms out, then unscrew it by two-and-a-half turns. Grease the gasket, and reinstall the bleed valve to the side of the carb.

Z15. Remove the dashpot (Fig 5 item 7) (or suction chamber as it's called by the Stromberg people). Often the crosshead screws are too tight to allow easy removal. Tap lightly on the end of the screwdriver and they'll loosen easily.

Z16. Remove the cover, spring, piston and diaphragm. Note the tag on the left of the diaphragm and its corresponding relief in the carb body.

Z17. Remove the diaphragm from the piston prior to cleaning. Remove the 4 crosshead screws. Use spray carb cleaner and a rag to wipe the varnish and soot from the carb. This process may take quite a time as the carb is usually very, very dirty. Similarly clean the piston, cover, spring etc. – but do NOT allow the carb cleaner to contact the diaphragm – or the diaphragm will expand and a new one will be needed. Additionally, inspect the diaphragm for perforation. A new diaphragm is available as BLM 225 480.

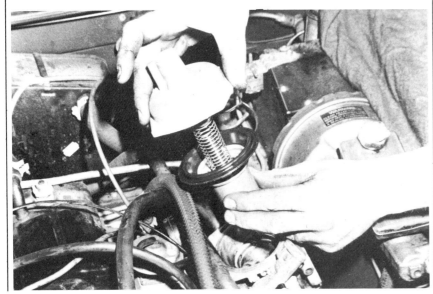

Z18. Replace the components into the carb body, again ensuring that the tags on the diaphragm are in their respective slots and that the two vacuum holes at the base of the piston are at the rear of the carb throat.

241

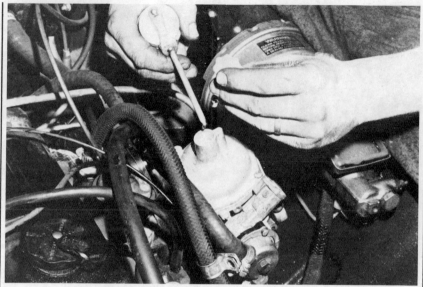

Z19.    Fill the dashpot with oil (any excess will quickly be pushed out).

Z20.    Start the engine and allow it to come to operating temperature. The idle should be set at about 800rpm and the mixture adjusted as for an SU carb, i.e. raise the piston slightly. If the idle speed increases dramatically, the mixture is too rich. If the idle speed drops, the mixture is too weak. There should be a slight increase, then steadying (or slightly dropping back) of the idle speed, if the mixture is correct. To make the

mixture adjustment, a special adjusting tool is necessary, available in the USA as BLT 0020100. If the tool is not available, then a ⅛ inch Allen wrench can be used, but the piston MUST be kept from turning (or a torn diaphragm will result). Sometimes a thumb, placed against the piston wil prevent rotation. Sometimes it is necessary to remove the suction chamber top, remove the piston, hold it in hand, make the adjustment, then replace it. If the air pump is in place, the catalytic converter MUST NOT glow red hot at idle − if it does, the mixture is too rich. If in spite of re-adjustment the mixture remains too rich, replace the needle.

## Rear Axle/Suspension Removal (Frogeye)

See "Tool Box" and "Safety" at start of chapter.

Removal of the Frogeye's rear axle complete with suspension can be necessary for a number of reasons. The most common are that the springs sag through old age and need replacing or that the spring boxes and the surrounding area have corroded and are in need of repair.

A point worth making here is that corroded spring mountings are all too frequently bodged by plating around the visible outer areas, from beneath the car, or even by welding the reinforcement plates onto the surrounding floor. Not only are these repairs unoriginal, they are also distinctly unsafe. The only way to repair this area properly is to strip out the rear suspension, and do the job properly.

RS1.    After removing the fuel tank, the first job is to hold the rear of the car high off the ground on a pair of strong axle stands. Remember to chock the front wheels. Place a baulk of timber across the front of the boot floor, where it bends upwards to form the rear axle tunnel.

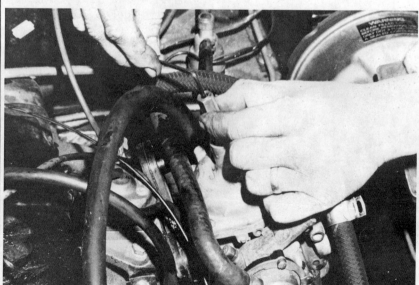

RS2.	If the flexible brake hose is in need of renewal, save time by cutting it through with a junior hacksaw or snips. Otherwise, disconnect it at the bulkhead end. Disconnect the propshaft using a pair of spanners as shown. Note that the trolley jack has been placed under the axle housing with only the slightest amount of upwards pressure upon the jack.

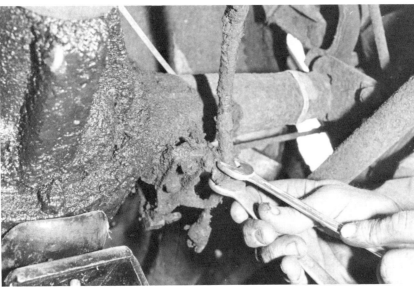

RS3.	Undo the handbrake cable outer using a pair of spanners as shown. One holds the flats on the end of the cable outer while the other slackens the fixing nut, which only has to be slackened a few turns — the cable is slotted into its bracket.

RS4.	The cable inner is held to the mechanism by a pin which is in turn held by a split-pin which must first be pulled out.

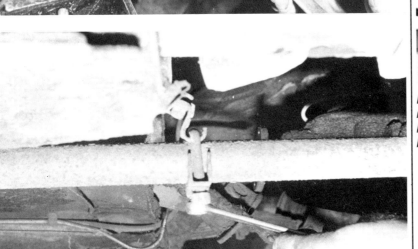

RS5.	Remove the exhaust pipe — at the engine manifold (unbolt the pinch clamp) and at the flexible mountings, as shown.

RS6.   Remove the shock absorbers, or disconnect them from the axle. Getting at the shock absorber to body bolts can be a little difficult.

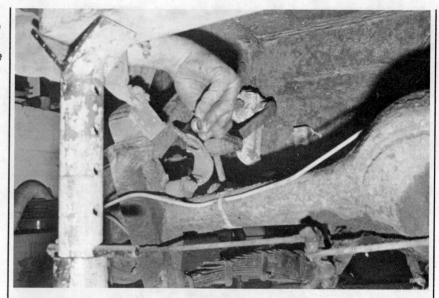

RS7.   Check-straps are all but impossible to remove without shearing their retaining bolts. It can be done, but is best attempted with the axle off the car so that nothing can get in the way of the application of heat, releasing fluid and the necessary curses. So, cut through them to save time.

RS8.   Remove the nuts from the bolts which hold the springs to the floorpan/spring boxes, and to the U-bolts at the rear of the reinforcement plates.

RS9. It will be almost essential to apply heat to the nuts — it may even be necessary to cut them off.

RS10. Try drilling through the side of the nut, in the same direction as the line of the bolt, before chiselling through what is left of the wall of the nut.

RS11. Remove the reinforcement plate. It may very well be that an "artful bodger" will have welded the plate into place in the past making it necessary to cut through the weld.

RS12.    If the radius arm brackets are to be removed, take off the retaining nuts.

RS13.    The bolt which holds the radius arm can be a bit of a pig to remove. Apply lots of heat to the bush mounting (have some water ready to put out the inevitable small, but smelly, rubber fire) and use a large drift, a large hammer and a big dose of persistence.

RS14.    Finally, with everything disconnected, lower the axle to the ground, refit the road wheels and wheel it away.

#  Electrical Components

This section, in being aimed at the restorer, complements the relevant repair section of *Haynes Midget and Sprite Owners' Workshop Manual.*

## Tool Box

In addition to the basic tool kit, some odd sized spanners are sometimes needed (see text for details). Engineers' and long-nosed pliers. Heavy duty soldering iron.

## Safety

**ALWAYS disconnect the battery before working on any electrical part of the car. A short can destroy parts of the wiring system in a second or even start a car-wrecking fire.**

## Heater Overhaul

Heaters fitted to Sprites and Midgets can be notably efficient at their best, especially when bearing in mind the dates at which they were first fitted. However, when they do stop working efficiently, the causes are usually numerous. The heater radiator can be blocked; the heater tap can be badly adjusted so that it does not open fully; the heater tap cable can be seized in the "off" position; the heater flaps can be jammed shut; the heater tap on the engine can fill with deposits (especially in a hard water area) or simply, the engine is running too cool. Putting most of these problems to rights is simplicity itself.

Another potential trouble-spot is the heater motor which can break down or simply become tired and slow, reducing the volume of warm (or cold) air available to feet or screen. The following sequence shows how to remove the heater radiator for flushing and how to overhaul the blower unit. See "Tool Box" and "Safety" at start of chapter.

*HM1.  Take off the front of the box in which the heater radiator (or matrix) is fitted by taking off the clips holding it in place (Figure 6, items 3 and 4).*

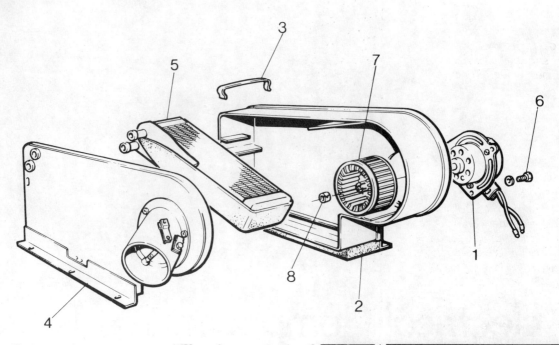

*Figure 6.    The heater unit component parts*
  *1  Fan motor*        *5  Heater matrix*
  *2  Heater cover*     *6  Securing screw*
  *3  Spring clip*      *7  Fan*
  *4  Heater cover*     *8  Clip*

HM3.    Take out the motor (6) and hold the body carefully in the vice and on earlier models, remove the nut holding the fan to the fan motor armature.

HM5.    Lubricate the shaft with penetrating oil, hold the armature with vice-grips between the fan and motor and work the fan loose from the shaft. Then, tap the shaft through the fan as shown.

HM2.    Remove the heater radiator (5) flush it through in both directions using a hose and a strong flow of water. Tap it on a hard surface to help remove the hard scale encrusted inside.

HM4.    On later models (fitted with a plastic fan) prise off the slip ring with a thin screwdriver poked between the fan blades.

HM6.    Loosen the 2BA nuts at the back of the motor then tap the body apart and withdraw the armature.

*HM7. Spin the commutator by holding it in the chuck of an electric drill, as shown, cleaning it with fine glasspaper. Undercut the insulators.*

*HM8. Solder new brushes onto the plate. Older units use a ¼ × ¼ inch brush, while newer units (those fitted with plastic fans) use a $^5/_{16}$ inch brush. Reassemble the unit having placed several drops of oil in the front and rear bearing. AFTER the unit has been re-installed, try the wiring on both of the alternative combinations and select the one offering the greatest air movement.*

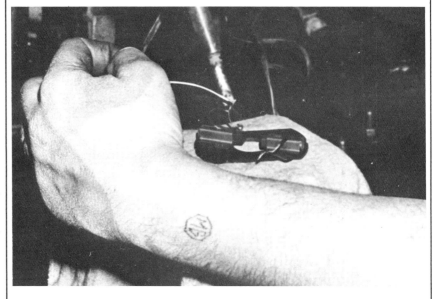

## Distributor − general

Many parts of the distributor wear and malfunction. In particular the following points should be checked:

1) The vacuum unit perforates and no longer functions.
2) The plates holding the points wear, allowing the points to contact the distributor cam on an angle − and causing the vacuum unit to work in jerky motions.
3) The mechanical advance seizes (freezes).
4) The cam develops freeplay (sideways) on the distributor shaft.
5) The distributor shaft wears in the bushing of the body.
6) The points and condenser fail.

All these items conspire to create a spark at the wrong time, or to give the spark to each cylinder at a different degree (the sparks should be separated by 90°).

### Lucas Parts List

Bush (421 998)
Top plate (422 318): This plate has a vertical brass shaft for holding points.
Top plate (54 412 154): This has only a short shaft for holding the Quickafits.
Base plate (54 419 792): This wears in the curved slot.
LT lead (54 413 549): An excellent low tension connection is essential.
Cap (54 412 472 DC1) − early models − uses screw in distributor terminals.
Cap (54 417 214 DC6) − later models − uses push on terminals.
Rotor (400 051 RA1)

Points/Cond. (600 41 004 TK50)
Spacer (1G 2673): This keeps the wires apart on the DC1 cap but is no longer available.
Suppressors (60 460 666): The present Lucas supressors are made in Italy.
Vacuum Unit: These are differentiated mainly by "carb vacuum" or "manifold vacuum", depending on their connection on the left side of the engine. Early models will have carb type (54 411 985) and later models manifold type (54 425 359). There are, however, about ten different vacuum units, depending on the year and model. Consult the local Lucas dealer for the proper listing.

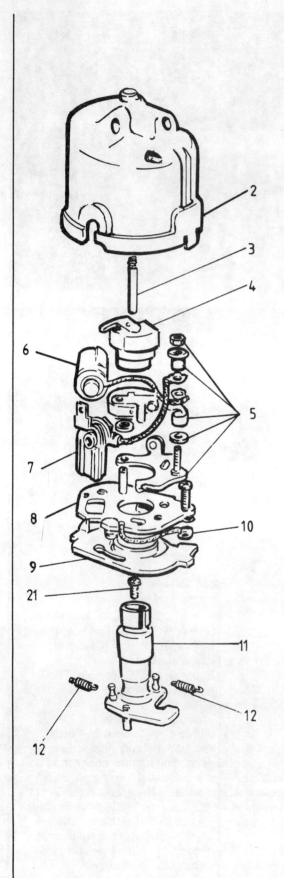

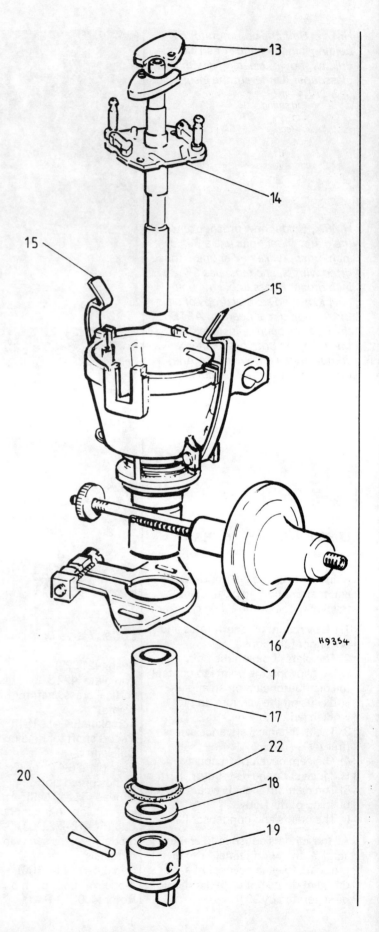

H9354

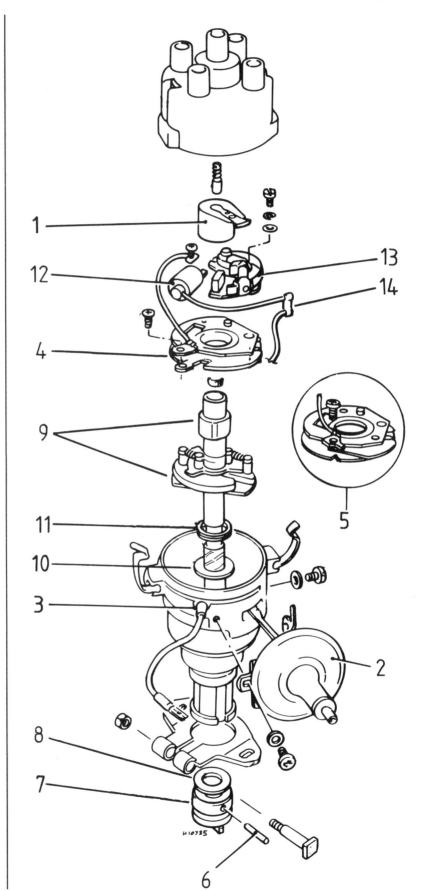

Figure 7.    Lucas 25D4 Distributor
 1  Clamping plate
 2  Moulded cap
 3  Brush and spring
 4  Rotor arm
 5  Contacts (set)
 6  Capacitor
 7  Terminal and lead
    (low tension)
 8  Moving contact
    breaker plate
 9  Contact breaker
    baseplate
10  Earth lead
11  Cam
12  Automatic
    advance springs
13  Weight assembly
14  Shaft and action
    plate
15  Cap retaining
    clips
16  Vacuum unit
17  Bush
18  Thrust washer
19  Driving dog
20  Parallel pin
21  Cam screw
24  O-ring oil seal

Figure 8.    Lucas 45D4 Distributor
 1  Rotor arm
 2  Vacuum unit
 3  Low tension lead
 4  Baseplate
 5  Baseplate (early
    cars)
 6  Retaining
    pin – drive dog
 7  Drive dog
 8  Thrust washer
 9  Cam spindle and
    automatic
    advance weights
    assembly
10  Steel washer
11  Spacer
12  Capacitor
13  Contact set
14  Low tension lead
    connector

Figure 9. The component parts of the
electronic ignition distributor

| | | | |
|---|---|---|---|
| 1 | Rotor arm | 9 | Baseplate |
| 2 | Anti-flash shield | 10 | Roll pin |
| 3 | Felt pad | 11 | Drive dog and |
| 4 | Pick up unit | | thrust washer |
| 5 | Amplifier module | 12 | Spindle |
| 6 | Roll pin | 13 | Shim |
| 7 | Circlip and | 14 | Return spring |
| | washer | 15 | Vacuum retard |
| 8 | Timing rotor and | | unit |
| | 'O' ring | | |

1

2

7

8

4

9

12

14

3

5

6

14

13

11

15

10

H.6077

## Lucas Horn overhaul

### Tool Box

Bench vice; $^3/_{16}$ inch drill; screwdrivers; wire brush.

### Safety

**Refer to the notes on "Safety" at the start of this chapter.**

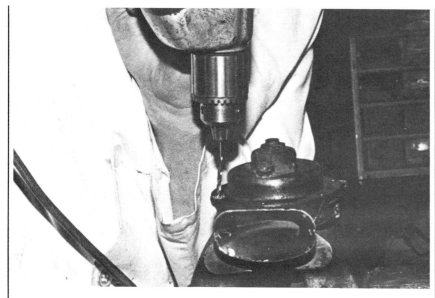

*EH1.*   *Hold the horn in the vice as shown, and drill off the six rivet heads with a $^3/_{16}$ inch drill.*

*EH2. Separate the diaphragm and base from the top.*

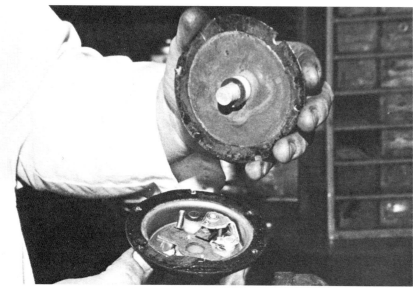

*EH3.*   *Free up the 2BA basic adjusting screw (Note – It has a LEFT HAND THREAD and unscrews clockwise).*

*EH4.*   *Free the locknut and remove it and the tone adjusting screw. Wire brush the screw so that it will work freely in the assembly.*

EH5.    Clean the contact points
with fine sandpaper.

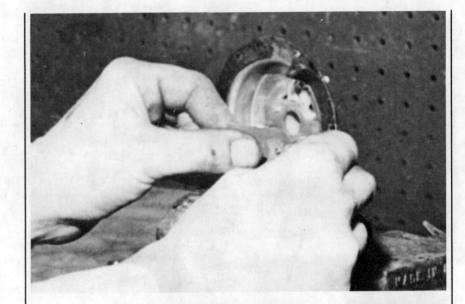

EH6.    With a ³/₁₆ inch bit, drill out
the insulators holding the electrical
spade terminals to the body.

EH7.    Replace the spade terminals
with a 2BA crosshead screw, or its
metric equivalent.

EH8.    Ensure that the end of the
screw is well insulated from the
horn body by using new insulating
washers or portions of the old
spade-terminal base.

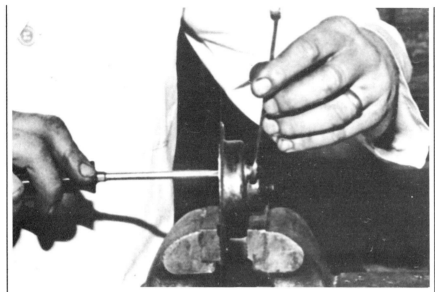

EH9. Tighten the screw and nut assembly, making absolutely certain that, when tight, there is NOT A SHORT between the post and the horn body. A double spade terminal, such as that fitted to a Lucas coil, can be added later.

EH10. Reassemble the diaphragm and cover to the base.

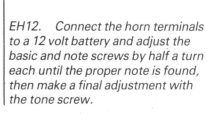

EH11. Replace the rivets with 2BA screws and nuts, or their metric equivalent. Sometimes one side of the nut has to be filed down so that it clears the body of the horn.

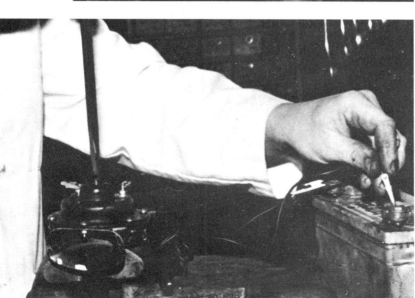

EH12. Connect the horn terminals to a 12 volt battery and adjust the basic and note screws by half a turn each until the proper note is found, then make a final adjustment with the tone screw.

## Wiring Loom – general and Courtesy Light Switches

### Tool Box

Small open-ended spanners; crosshead screwdriver; wire brush; hammered-finish paint; small paint brush; 2 pairs of pliers for separating stubborn bullet connectors.

### Safety
**Refer to the notes on "Safety" at the start of this chapter.**

With care an older cloth covered loom can be cleaned to make it appear new and fresh. CAREFULLY remove the loom, noting the location of the clamps which hold it in place and, to speed up renewal, fold a piece of masking tape double leaving an inch at the end single and sticky. Wrap this around the end of a wire as it is disconnected and write its location on the masking tape. Wire brush the clamps and repaint them with a hammered metal finish paint. Coil the wiring loom and place it into a shallow pan with warm soapy water. SQUEEZE, BUT DO NOT SCRUB the loom until it is as clean as it will get before it begins to unravel, then hang it in the garage to dry. The PVC wires can be cleaned to almost new lustre by spraying a rag and the wires with aerosol carb cleaner, and wiping the sludge and grease from the wires. The newer looms, incidentally, are wrapped in a light blue PVC tape.

As a rule, the wires themselves do not fail. The ends may lose contact with the wires but the wires themselves rarely break. Any splicing or correction to the loom should be made outside the wrapping. There should be no connections within the loom itself. If changes are made in the loom, solder Lucas bullet connectors to the wires and use the black female

connectors of the type used with the rest of the system.

NOTE: Prior to removing the loom from the car, remove ALL the black female connectors as they impede the free movement of the loom through the bulkhead, boot etc. Prior to replacing the loom in the car, clean each bullet connector with fine sandpaper to ensure a good connection.

The interior light switches in the door pillars become bent and corrode so that they do not work. Remove them from the pillar and from the purple/white wire. Wire brush them so that they will make good contact to the pillar and to themselves. Straighten a bent plunger with pliers.

## Lighting Circuit Fault Finding

After rewiring the lights following a rebuild or after renewing the wiring loom, or simply after a period of neglect, the lights can begin to give problems. John Twist of University Motors, Michigan, shows how to solve some of them.

*When a car stands, its battery can quickly go flat which is irritating and shortens a battery's life. The Exide 12V Charger Battery Saver Plus provides a constant trickle charge from the sun – free and continuous!*

### Headlights:

*Glowing or very dim – faulty earth connection.
*No illumination BUT bright light indicator is on for both highs and dims – faulty earth.
*High or low beam not working on one side – faulty bulb or faulty connection (BLUE/WHITE = Bright; BLUE/RED = dims).
*Bright light flashers not working – BROWN/PURPLE fuse.

### Parking Lights:

*One side (left or right) not working – red fuse.
*One light not working – probably the bulb.
*Diagonal not working (e.g., front left, right rear) – red fuse.

### Turn Signals:

*Neither dash nor lights illuminate – faulty HAZARD switch. (Snap the HAZARD switch OFF and try again.)
*Lights and indicators illuminate but don't flash or flash very slowly – faulty flasher.
*One side flashes properly, one side doesn't – faulty bulb front or rear.

*These are quite different from conventional batteries. The plates are coiled and the acid is sealed-in-gel. As a result, an Optima battery is smaller, more powerful and can be recharged in an hour without damaging it. It can be mounted at any angle – even upside down!*

# 7 Modifications

Information on tuning and modifying the Spridget could easily fill a book in itself! This section offers advice to U.S. owners who would like their cars to go as fast as its designers intended, information on converting earlier cars to negative earth (ground) so that modern radios, cassette players and alternators can be fitted and then a general section on go-faster tuning and performance accessories.

## De-toxing USA Midget (except 1500)

This section was compiled from information and material supplied by John Twist of University Motors, Michigan.

    North American Midgets were fitted with progressively more strangulatory exhaust emission control regulations which, though initiated for the most commendable of motives, did nothing for the sporting character of the Midget. The North American owner who wishes to "de-tox" his or her car may gain the following advantages (although nothing can be guaranteed): mileage may be better; acceleration can improve; deceleration too, should be sharper (there will be generally more positive throttle response); there'll be no more "popping" or red hot converters; the engine looks "cleaner"; the front spark plug will no longer be hidden from view.

    NOTE: de-toxing in some states may be illegal. Responsibility for compliance with the law must rest with the individual owner.

    Throughout this section procedures are illustrated by work on an MGB — in practice these are virtually identical for the Midget.

## Tool Box

$5/16$ inch combination spanner; $3/8$ inch drive ratchet; $3/8 \times 6$ inch extension; Allen wrench for pipe plug; $1/2$ inch socket; $5/8$ inch deep socket (for injector bolts); $1/2$ inch open-end wrench; $7/16$ open-end wrench; $1/4$ NPT tap and tap wrench; four $7/16$ inch bolts; one $1/4$ inch (Allen driven) NPT pipe plug.

## Safety

**Remember when working on or around fuel systems that gasoline is volatile and highly flammable. DON'T SMOKE!**

DT1(A). "Tool Box" illustrated.

DT1(B). Before starting, the bonnet (hood) must be removed or held aloft with a stick as the factory slide is too short and both fenders should be covered with large cloths or old blankets.

DT2. Remove the two hoses to the air pump. Remove the long bolt (½ inch wrench) holding the air pump to the thermostat cover and remove the bolt from the adjusting strap (½ inch).

DT3. Remove the pump and the fanbelt.

DT4. Remove the four air injectors with a 7/16 inch wrench. If the injectors will not unscrew, cut the tubing at the injector and use a 7/16 inch socket. Remove the bolt holding the injector to the rear right head nut.

*DT5.  Remove the air pump adjuster bracket. If this is left in place, and if it should loosen, it could foul the alternator fan. Use a ½ inch wrench.*

*DT6.  Replace the air injectors with ⁷⁄₁₆ inch fine bolts or Allen screws, and tighten snugly.*

*DT7.  Hold the tall nut at the thermostat cover with a ½ inch wrench to keep it from spinning and remove the bolt at the top.*

*DT8.  Remove the thin black vacuum line from the manifold to the TCSA switch on the master cylinder box.*

DT9. Remove the two bolts holding the gulp valve to its bracket (⁷/₁₆ inch wrench and socket).

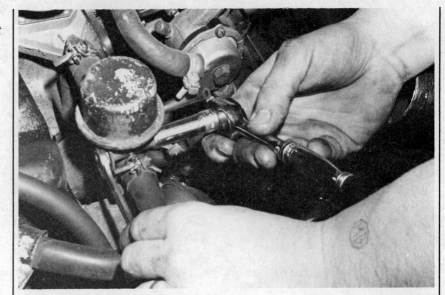

DT10. Lift the gulp valve 90° fitting and hoses away. It may be necessary to twist the 90° fitting to facilitate removal.

DT11. Remove the bolt holding the gulp valve bracket (¹⁵/₁₆ inch socket) discard the bracket and the thinnest of the two copper washers. Then replace the bolt and one washer snugly.

DT12. Tap the hole from the 90° fitting ¼ NPT. There will be metal shavings and it's best to grease the tap before cutting the threads so that the chafings will remain on the tap, or better still, to remove the manifold first.

DT13. Fit a ¼ NPT plug or Allen screw to the hole. To stop possible vacuum leaks, wrap the threads with teflon tape, or use jointing compound.

DT14. Move the vacuum advance line from the TCSA switch directly to the intake manifold. Midgets fitted with the TCSA switch allow the distributor vacuum advance to work only in fourth gear.

DT15. The detox is now completed. At University Motors, John Twist says, "We find that setting the timing at factory specs allows good acceleration without further pinging". John carries on, "Further steps, which we don't do, could include removing the EGR line from the EGR valve (top of the manifold) and plugging it. The catalytic converter could be removed but that's best left for an exhaust job in the future.

Some cars were fitted with the following equipment. Where appropriate proceed as follows.

*DT16. The manifold with the gulp valve and piping are removed.*

*DT17. Replace the vacuum fitting with a $^5/_{16} \times \frac{1}{2}$ inch bolt (fine) which can be found holding the air manifold to the head, or the air hose clamp to the thermostat cover nut.*

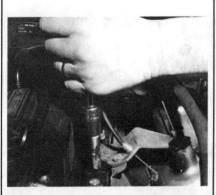

*DT18. Tap the centre hole ¼ NPT. Use grease on the tap to hold the shavings, or remove the manifold to be absolutely sure.*

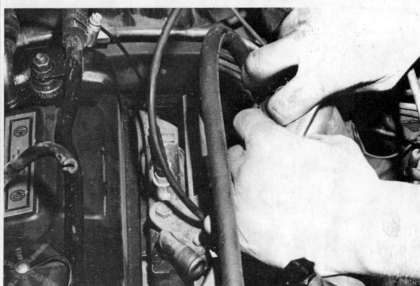

*DT19. Use a $^{15}/_{16}$ inch wrench to remove the nut from the gulp valve bracket. Replace the nut and the largest copper washer.*

DT20.    The final view of the carb side. DO NOT remove or block the hoses to the carbs from the front tappet inspection cover.

The detox on the 1968 Midget is the same as for 69-74, except that the 90° fitting in the centre of the intake manifold cannot be blocked, as a Smith's PCV valve is fitted there. Two options: leave a piece of hose on the T-fitting and block the hose

with a bolt and hose clamp or, tap the manifold as suggested and instead of blocking it with a pipe plug, fit a ¼ NPT nipple, about 1 ½ inch long and reconnect the PCV valve.

## De-toxing USA Midgets (1500)

The ex-Triumph 1500cc engine has a very different emission control set-up fitted to it, but the principles of removal are pretty much the same as the 1275-style system. The most notable exception is that the 1500 engine is not fitted with air injectors and so there is less to remove in this area. The hose leading from rocker box to carb should be retained, but blank off the branch leading to the charcoal absorption canister. It may

be necessary to decide whether to retain the restricted connection (Figure 10, item 4) by experimentation.

Figure 10.    Emmission control components (1500 cc model)
 1  Charcoal absorption canister
 2  Vapour lines
 3  Purge line
 4  Restricted connection
 5  Sealed oil filler cap
 6  Oil separator/ flame trap (arrester)
 7  Fuel pipe
 8  Fuel pump
 9  Running-on control valve
10  Running-on control pipe
11  Air manifold
12  Air pump
13  Diverter valve
14  Check valve
15  Diverter valve pipe
16  Air temperature control valve
17  Hot air hose
18  Exhaust gas/recirculation valve
19  EGR valve flame trap
20  EGR valve line to carburettor choke cam
21  EGR valve pipe
22  Distributor flame trap
23  Distributor flame trap line carburettor
24  Flame trap line to distributor vacuum unit

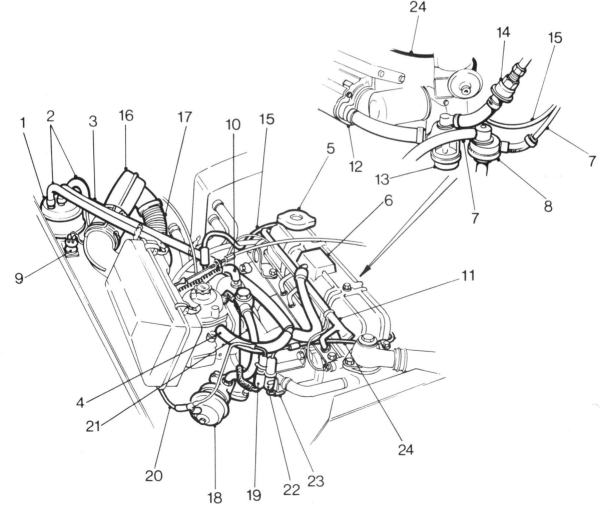

## Negative Earth Conversion (1963-1967 models) With John Twist of University Motors, Michigan

Earlier Sprites and Midgets were supplied from the factory with a positive earth (ground) electrical system. The system was reversed with the introduction of the alternator rather than a dynamo type generator and which continued until 1979 with the negative earth system. A modern approach to ownership often includes the fitting of a radio or tape player, both of which are difficult and cumbersome to wire with the existing system. Wired negative earth, the earlier Spridgets continue to function properly.

### Tool Box

AF Spanners; engineers' pliers (use two pairs for parting stubborn bullet connectors); jumper wire; wire strippers; soldering equipment.

### Safety

**Refer to notes at start of chapter.**

1) Disconnect the batteries, remove them from position, clean all posts and clamps and renew the connection from the earth strap to the body (left/nearside).

*NE1. While the batteries are removed, replace the Lucas "cap" style terminal ends with "wrap around" American style clamps. The Lucas terminal ends are sized to fit the battery posts, and since the positive is larger than the negative, these clamps will no longer be satisfactory for use.*

*DO NOT CUT the old terminal ends from the wire, but melt them off with a small propane torch. Cutting the wiring, especially the cable from the batteries to the solenoid shortens it needlessly, and it may not reach the new battery position. Be certain to add the proper battery fixtures (clamp – AHH 6353; bolt – AHH 6750; rubber pad – AHH 6351), as excessive bouncing and shaking will take years off battery life.*

Replace the batteries 180° from their old alignment, and connect the major power cable (solenoid to battery) to the positive post, then connect the intermediate cable (negative post of right battery to the positive post of the other battery). Finally, reconnect the earth cable to the negative post of the left battery.

2) Examine the ignition coil. The WHITE wire must be connected to the "+" or "CB" terminal; the WHITE & BLACK wire (distributor to coil) must be connected to the "−" or "SW" terminal. ("CB" = contact breakers; "SW" = switch; reversed in this application since the batteries are now reversed.).

3) Polarize the generator. Remove the BROWN/GREEN wire from the "F" (Field) terminal on the generator (the smaller spade). Use a jumper wire and make a momentary connection between this spade terminal and the live post of the starter solenoid (post with the BROWN wire).

A spark will occur as the connection is made. This procedure reverses the magnetic field in the generator. Reconnect the BROWN/GREEN wire to the generator and start up the engine. The ignition light should act as before − (ON when the ignition is ON, ON at very low RPM, OFF above about 1000 and OFF when the ignition is OFF). WARNING: If the ignition light remains ON when the ignition is OFF, IMMEDIATELY disconnect the BROWN wires from the starter solenoid and check your work!

4) Check the heater blower operation. With the ignition ON, turn on the heater blower and judge the amount of air which is being blown into the footwells. Then reverse the wires at the heater motor (bullet connectors) and again judge the amount of air being blown. Use whichever connection affords the greatest air movement.

5) Converting the Tachometer to Negative Earth.

*NE2. Remove the tachometer from the car by undoing the two knurled nuts and taking off the lock washers and clips.*

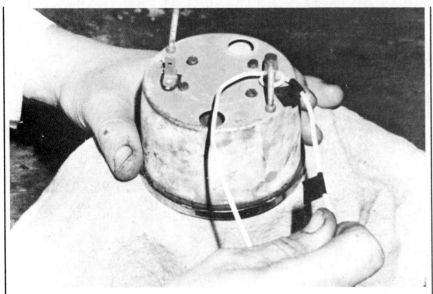

NE3. In this illustration one leg of the white wire loop is tagged with two pieces of electrical tape. This operation cannot be carried out as shown, as the white wire is part of the wiring loom — this is for illustration only.

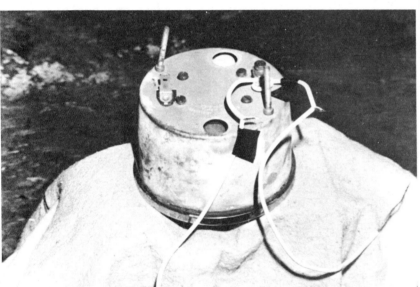

NE4. The white wires are now cut through and a section of insulation removed, and then reconnected to the OTHER white wires. The connections should be soldered, or Lucas bullet connectors soldered to all four ends and connectors used.

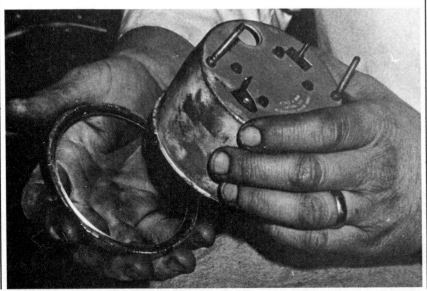

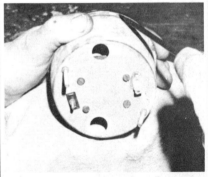

NE5. The chrome bezel is now loosened along its circumference.

NE6. Once loosened, the chrome ring can be turned and removed.

NE7. The two screws holding the unit's internals (there are washers under the cheese head screws) can be removed and the internal working assembly will drop out.

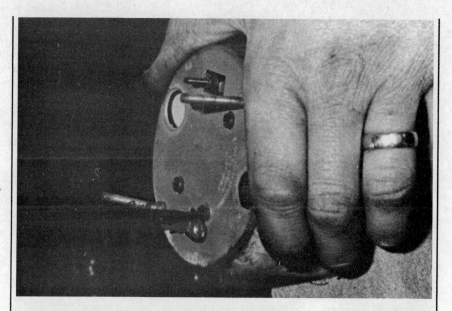

NE8. The power and earth wires must be cut and connected to the opposite terminals in much the same way that the white wires were cut and reversed. The resistor connected to the spade terminal must be unsoldered and connected to the post immediately to its left (pointer). At the same time the wire connected to the left terminal must be soldered to the right terminal. This illustration shows the wiring PRIOR to reversal.

6) From a newer MGB or Midget, or by hand lettering your own, place a warning label under the bonnet and on the battery cover: "WARNING — This vehicle wired negative earth".

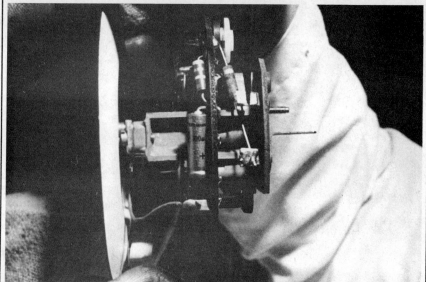

## Wire Wheel Conversion

In spite of all the problems associated with wire wheels — difficult to keep clean, need maintenance/repair, the splines can wear and require renewal — the romantic appeal of wire wheels still persists. On the other hand some owners, from the purely practical point of view, are keen to swap their wire wheel set up for disc wheels. Either swap is possible.

WW1. At the rear, the wire wheel splines are attached to the half shafts and these must be changed complete. At the front, the splines are a component of the front hub assembly. At the rear of the front hub in this picture (the brake disc is shown still attached) is a new brake disc while at the front is a new hub spinner which holds the wheel in place.

## Lenham Le Mans Coupe

The Lenham Motor Company's rear body conversion for Sprites and Midgets is one of the most attractive and useful bodywork conversions available. It is a fibreglass Kamm-tailed rear end, based on the Warwick-built racing Sprites' bodywork and is a link with a time when, in the early sixties, Sprites were putting up remarkable giant-killing performances at Le Mans.

The first Lenham GT body was built in aluminium and when it was complete, GRP moulds were taken from it and the "Lenham Le Mans Coupe" was born.

It was found that Lenham had not only copied the Healey Company in terms of aesthetics, but also in terms of greater overall efficiency; the Lenham Healey gives improved fuel economy and all of 9mph on top speed as spinoffs of its low weight and improved aerodynamics.

The Le Mans Coupe has been raced ever since its inception and is still eligible in ModSports.

See Bodywork Chapter for 'Tool Box' and 'Safety', also appendix.

LC1.    Detail styling and mould quality has been improved over the years with respect to changes in the cars' basic shape. One disadvantage of the conversion is that none of the rear glass can be opened, making things a bit sticky in hot weather.

LC2.    First job, of course, is to strip bootlid, soft top and lights from the rear end of the car. This is a rubber bumpered car and is as easy to convert as the chrome bumpered cars.

LC3.    With courage taken in both hands, make a cut all around the rear wing. Cut along the line of the wing top beading, through the light apertures and a couple of inches up from the bottom of the rear wing. Continue the cut around the wheel arch (leaving the flared portion in place) and cut forwards a couple of inches from the top of the sill and the same distance from the door pillar. Use a non-distorting cutter such as a Monodex.

**LC4.** Take the cut out piece of rear wing away – and be prepared to carry out repairs to inner wings, rear box sections and reinforcement plates. Integral soundness and strength in these areas is vital.

**LC5.** Next step is to cut the entire bulkhead away as well as the boot lid surround and rear apron. It is recommended that a lateral strut is fitted to tie the door pillars together, and that this area is made sufficiently rigid when the GRP bodywork is fitted.

**LC6.** The Lenham body is offered into place, clipped onto the windscreen header rail and very accurately and carefully positioned. All GRP to steel joints must be thoroughly bonded on before any filler is applied.

LC7. All steel to which fibreglass is bonded must be very thoroughly cleaned and degreased. Unless the job has been carried out before, some degree of improvisation is inevitable. Make sure that the wiring loom has been carefully removed or taped into a neat roll well out of the way, or popped into a plastic bag so that the fibreglass does not make a mess of it.

LC8. As already pointed out, strength of fitting at the door pillars is crucial, especially if the car is to see road use. A high quality of fitting and finishing is also crucial if the fibreglass is not to be stressed and wrinkled and if professional looking profiles are to be obtained.

LC9. Lenham also make a one-piece, hinge-forward bonnet to match the body conversion, called the ''Superfast'' bonnet. Together they certainly give the Spridget a distinctive look!

It must be remembered that the Le Mans conversion is not, by itself, an answer to rotten bodywork. The Spridget's outer panels provide only a relatively small part of the cars' strength and a badly corroded car would require at least as much work doing to it for a Le Mans conversion as for a conventional rebuild.

## Spridget Tuning

To give a full account of the number of tuning options available to the Midget and Sprite owner is beyond the scope of this book, but the following is intended as a brief look at what it is possible to do to produce a vehicle with more road performance.

First of all, however, a word from the Leyland Special Tuning handbook: "Before carrying out any tuning on these cars, it is essential to ensure that both the engine and chassis components are in good mechanical condition. Obviously some of these cars have now had a considerable amount of use and it is important to ensure that the whole car is in a safe and satisfactory condition before carrying out any work."

In general, although some are now to be seen on the race tracks, 1500-engined cars are far less tuneable than their earlier counterparts. Without carrying out considerable work to their bottom ends (the crank and bearings) they are not considered capable of standing up to the extra strains imposed by engine tuning.

### 948cc engine (9C Frogeye type, 9CG early Spridget)

There is not a great deal to be done with this engine and in any case most owners of original engines will probably wish to retain their originality. It is possible to gain a few bhp by polishing the combustion chambers while removing as little material as possible, and matching the inlet ports on the head with the manifold, after grinding out the inlet ports as shown in Figure 11. 1¼ inch carburettors can be fitted in place of the brass topped 1⅛ inch variety, in which case V3 needles (Part No. AUD 1411) or richer V2 needles (AUD 1410) should be fitted.

The easiest way to improve performance with these early cars is to fit later engine units. A 1098cc

engine and gearbox can be fitted to a 948cc car as long as the engine backplate from a 1098cc engine, along with its flywheel and clutch, are fitted. It is possible to fit a 1275 engine and gearbox but there may be a problem with the fan fouling the radiator in which case the radiator could be repositioned or an electric fan fitted.

When these sort of modifications are carried out, it is vital to uprate other areas too. Fit disc brakes to a drum braked car and fit a front anti-roll bar where none is fitted as standard. Take great care to check that the front brake flexible hoses do not chafe when the wheels are moved from lock-to-lock and under all suspension conditions from full bump to full rebound.

### 1098cc engines

Earlier engines (prefix 10 CG), have a weaker crankshaft than later cars and are not suitable for a great deal of tuning. Later engines (prefix 10 CC) have a stiffer bottom end which is far more durable.

Again, the quickest and easiest way to uprate these cars is to slot in a later 1275 engine.

However, if it is desired to tune the 1098cc engine, replace the exhaust valves with Stellite-faced valves (Part No. KE 965). The compression ratio can be raised by degrees to give the power output shown in the table below.

Note that this table incorporates the benefits gained by fitting camshaft number 88G 229, suitable for road/rally use. A

| Comp. Ratio | Machine Head | Combustion Chamber cc | Ignition Setting B.T.D.C. & B.H.P. @ 6000RPM Std. Camshaft | Camshaft 88G 229 |
|---|---|---|---|---|
| 8.9:1 | NIL | 28.2cc | 5°, 60BHP | 2°, 63BHP |
| 9.5:1 | 0.035" | 26.5cc | 3°, 62BHP | 1°, 65BHP |
| 10:1 | 0.060" | 24.7cc | 3°, 62.5BHP | 0°, 67BHP |
| 10.5:1 | 0.080" | 23.2cc | 2°, 64.5BHP | 0°, 68.6BHP |

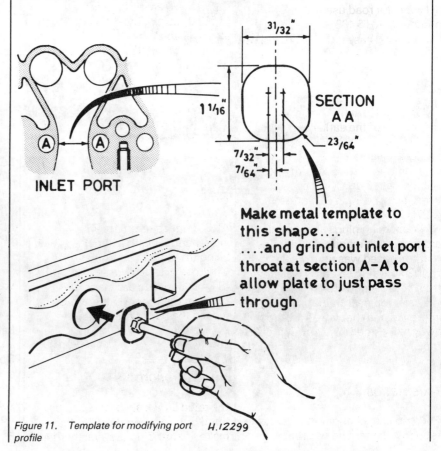

Make metal template to this shape....
....and grind out inlet port throat at section A–A to allow plate to just pass through

Figure 11.    Template for modifying port profile        H.12299

270

competition distributor, part number C-27H 7766 is available for use with Road/Rally engines and the correct timing will be found to lie between 3° B.T.D.C. and T.D.C. Where a high lift camshaft is fitted, the single row timing chain will wear out very quickly. A Duplex (twin row) chain can be fitted using Duplex Chain Kit C-AJJ 3325. If this kit should prove impossible to obtain and a DIY-kit is made up, remember to countersink the engine front plate and fit countersunk head machine screws in place of the original bolts which would otherwise foul on the sprockets.

## 1275cc engines

Raise the compression ratio by machining the head face: 0.012 inch is approximately equal to a 1cc reduction in combustion chamber volume. A ready to fit modified head was available under part number C-AHT 134 with 19cc combustion chambers and thus a 9.5:1 compression ratio. Also available for road use was head number C-AHT 463 with larger valves. In all cases, use head gasket C-AHT 188. Larger diameter inlet valves are available for those who wish to have their own cylinder heads machined, but note that the 1275cc's valve stems are longer than those of the earlier engines and the Cooper S, so they are not interchangeable.

Motor has road tested a 1275cc Midget with C-AHT 463 cylinder head, twin 1½ inch carburettors, C-27H 7766 distributor, Champion N64Y sparking plugs and longer centre branch manifold and found that top speed was up from 95mph to 102mph, the 0-60 time was down from 13.5 seconds to 10.0 and even the car's top gear tractability was improved and that it was able to pull away fairly smoothly from 20mph in top.

## Axle Ratios

For road use, changing the rear axle ratio to a higher one can bring

useful benefits in diminished engine noise/wear and lower fuel consumption.

Three different ratios were used, as shown in the table:

| From | To | Ratio | Diff. Assy. Part No. |
|---|---|---|---|
| Intro Intro | H-AN7 24731 (Sprite) G-AN2 16183 (Midget) | 4.22 | ATA 7326 |
| | H-AN9 66226 (Sprite) G-AN4 77591 (Midget) | 4.22 | BTA 550 |
| Start of Midget 1500 engine | | 3.9 | BTA 1222 |
| | End of production | 3.727 | BTA 551 |

All of the complete differential assemblies are interchangeable and the Riley 1.5 assembly (3.727) is also interchangeable. However, the earliest Spridget crownwheel and pinion (ATA 7266) is only interchangeable with the crownwheel and pinion from the early Riley 1.5 (ATA 7240: later Riley 1.5 crownwheel and pinion is number BTA 535) but it is more likely that only the differential assembly complete would be changed.

An extremely high ratio (3.55:1), part number STR 0520 is also available. When compared with the 'standard' 1500 ratio it gives the following:

| | Standard (3.9:1) | 3.55:1 |
|---|---|---|
| Mph/1000rpm | 16.4 | 18.1 |
| Rpm @ 70mph | 4270 | 3870 |

## Drive shafts

All Spridget axle shafts are interchangeable. If a larger engine is being fitted to an earlier car, it would be wise to fit later axle shafts (BTA 806) which are made of stronger material and therefore reduce the risk of breakage.

## Shock Absorbers

Up-rated shock absorbers can be fitted but, for everyday use, they make a firm-riding car even harder.

In addition, shock absorber reconditioning firms report that stiffer shock absorbers have a higher failure rate then standard items.

## Anti-roll Bar

On 948cc models it is necessary to drill the A-brackets to accept anti-roll bar mountings or to fit later A-brackets, if indeed they have not already been fitted as part of an earlier reconditioning exercise. Thicker anti-roll bars are available and fit as a straight swap to cars already fitted with an anti-roll bar and this is perhaps a better way of uprating the front suspension, if it needs it at all.

M1. For the ultimate in engine tuning, twin Weber carbs look after the breathing department, but it takes the sort of extremes in performance sought by the likes of James Thacker to make it worthwhile.

# Appendices

# 1 Workshop Procedures – Safety First

Professional motor mechanics are trained in safe working procedures, whereas the onus is on you, the home mechanic, to find them out for yourself and act upon them. However enthusiastic you may be about getting on with the job in hand, do take the time to ensure that your safety is not put at risk. A moment's lack of attention can result in an accident, as can failure to observe certain elementary precautions.

There will always be new ways of having accidents, and the following points do not pretend to be a comprehensive list of all dangers; they are intended rather to make you aware of the risks and to encourage a safety-conscious approach to all work you carry out on your vehicle.

Be sure to consult the suppliers of any materials and equipment you may use, and to obtain and read carefully operating and health and safety instructions that they may supply.

## Essential DOs and DON'Ts

**DON'T** rely on a single jack when working underneath the vehicle. Always use reliable additional means of support, such as axle stands, securely placed under a part of the vehicle that you know will not give way.

**DON'T** attempt to loosen or tighten high-torque nuts (e.g. wheel hub nuts) while the vehicle is on a jack; it may be pulled off.

**DON'T** start the engine without first ascertaining that the transmission is in neutral (or 'Park' where applicable) and the parking brake applied.

**DON'T** suddenly remove the filler cap from a hot cooling system – cover it with a cloth and release the pressure gradually first, or you may get scalded by escaping coolant.

**DON'T** attempt to drain oil, automatic transmission fluid, or coolant until you are sure it has cooled sufficiently to avoid scalding you.

**DON'T** grasp any part of the engine, exhaust or catalytic converter without first ascertaining that it is sufficiently cool to avoid burning you.

**DON'T** allow brake fluid or antifreeze to contact vehicle paintwork.

**DON'T** syphon toxic liquids such as fuel, brake fluid or antifreeze by mouth, or allow them to remain on your skin.

**DON'T** inhale dust – it may be injurious to health (see Asbestos below).

**DON'T** allow any spilt oil or grease to remain on the floor – wipe it up straight away, before someone slips on it.

**DON'T** use ill-fitting spanners or other tools which may slip and cause injury.

**DON'T** attempt to lift a heavy component which may be beyond your capability – get assistance.

**DON'T** rush to finish a job, or take unverified short cuts.

**DON'T** allow children or animals in or around an unattended vehicle.

**DON'T** park vehicles with catalytic converters over combustible materials such as dry grass, oil rags, etc., if the engine has recently been run. As catalytic converters reach extremely high temperatures, any such materials in close proximity may ignite.

**DON'T** run vehicles equipped with catalytic converters without the exhaust system heat shields fitted.

**DO** wear eye protection when using power tools such as an electric drill, sander, bench grinder, etc., and when working under the vehicle.

**DO** use a barrier cream on your hands prior to undertaking dirty jobs – it will protect your skin from infection as well as making the dirt easier to remove afterwards; but make sure your hands aren't left slippery. Note

that long-term contact with used engine oil can be a health hazard.

**DO** keep loose clothing (cuffs, tie, etc.) and long hair well out of the way of moving mechanical parts.

**DO** remove rings, wrist watch, etc., before working on the vehicle – especially the electrical system.

**DO** ensure that any lifting tackle used has a safe working load rating adequate for the job, and is used precisely as recommended by the manufacturer.

**DO** keep your work area tidy – it is only too easy to fall over articles left lying around.

**DO** get someone to check periodically that all is well, when working alone on the vehicle.

**DO** carry out work in a logical sequence and check that everything is correctly assembled and tightened afterwards.

**DO** remember that your vehicle's safety affects that of yourself and others. If in doubt on any point, get specialist advice.

**IF**, in spite of following these precautions, you are unfortunate enough to injure yourself, seek medical attention as soon as possible.

## Fire

Remember at all times that petrol (gasoline) is highly inflammable. Never smoke, or have any kind of naked flame around, when working on the vehicle. But the risk does not end there – a spark caused by an electrical short-circuit, by two metal surfaces contacting each other, by a central heating boiler in the garage 'firing up', or even by static electricity built up in your body under certain conditions, can ignite petrol vapour, which in a confined space is highly explosive.

Always disconnect the battery earth (ground) terminal before working on any part of the fuel system, and never risk

spilling fuel on to a hot engine or exhaust.

It is recommended that a fire extinguisher of a type suitable for fuel and electrical fires is kept handy in the garage or workplace at all times. Never try to extinguish a fuel or electrical fire with water.

## Fumes

Certain fumes are highly toxic and can quickly cause unconsciousness and even death if inhaled to any extent. Petrol (gasoline) vapour comes into this category, as do the vapours from certain solvents such as trichloroethylene and those from many adhesives. Any draining or pouring of such volatile fluids should be done in a well-ventilated area.

When using cleaning fluids and solvents, read the instructions carefully. Never use any materials from unmarked containers – they may give off poisonous vapours.

Never run the engine of a motor vehicle in an enclosed space such as a garage. Exhaust fumes contain carbon monoxide which is extremely poisonous. If you need to run the engine, always do so in the open air or at least have the rear of the vehicle outside the workplace.

If you are fortunate enough to have the use of an inspection pit, never drain or pour petrol, and never run the engine, while the vehicle is standing over it; the fumes, being heavier than air, will concentrate in the pit with possibly lethal results.

## The battery

Never cause a spark, or allow a naked light, near the vehicle battery. It will normally be giving off a certain amount of hydrogen gas, which is highly explosive.

Always disconnect the battery earth (ground) terminal before

working on the fuel or electrical systems.

If possible, loosen the filler plugs or cover when charging the battery from an external source. Do not charge at an excessive rate or the battery may burst.

Take care when topping up and when carrying the battery. The acid electrolyte, even when diluted, is very corrosive and should not be allowed to contact the eyes or skin.

If you ever need to prepare electrolyte yourself, always add the acid slowly to the water, and never the other way round. Protect against splashes by wearing rubber gloves and goggles.

## Mains electricity

When using an electric power tool, inspection light, etc., which works from the mains, always ensure that the appliance is correctly connected to its plug and that, where necessary, it is properly earthed (grounded). Do not use such appliances in damp conditions and, again, beware of creating a spark or applying excessive heat in the vicinity of fuel or fuel vapour.

Also, before using any mains powered electrical equipment, take one more simple precaution – use an RCD (Residual Current Device) circuit breaker. Then, if there is a short, the RCD circuit breaker minimises the risk of electrocution by instantly cutting the power supply. Buy from any electrical store or DIY centre. RCDs fit simply into your electrical socket before plugging in your electrical equipment.

## Ignition HT voltage

A severe electric shock can result from touching certain parts of the ignition system, such as the HT leads, when the engine is running or being cranked, particularly if components are damp or the insulation is defective. Where an electronic ignition system is fitted, the HT voltage is much higher and could prove fatal. Consult your handbook or main dealer if in any doubt. Risk of injury while working on running engines, e.g. adjusting the timing, can arise if the operator touches a high voltage lead and pulls his hand away on to a projection or revolving part. On some vehicles the voltage used in the ignition system is so high that it can cause injury or death by electrocution.

## Welding and bodywork repairs

It is so useful to be able to weld when carrying out restoration work, and yet there is a good deal that could go dangerously wrong for the uninformed – in fact more than could be covered here. **For safety's sake** you are strongly recommended to seek tuition, in whatever branch of welding you wish to use, from your local evening institute or adult education classes. In addition, all of the information and instructional material produced by the suppliers of materials and equipment you will be using must be studied carefully. You may have to ask your stockist for some of this printed material if it is not made available at the time of purchase.

In addition, it is strongly recommended that *The Car Bodywork Repair Manual*, published by Haynes, is purchased and studied before carrying out any welding or bodywork repairs. Consisting of 292 pages, around 1,000 illustrations and written by Lindsay Porter, the author of this book, *The Car Bodywork Repair Manual* picks the brains of specialists from a variety of fields, and covers arc, MIG and 'gas' welding, panel beating and

accident repair, rust repair and treatment, paint spraying, glass-fibre work, filler, lead loading, interiors and much more besides. Alongside a number of projects, the book describes in detail how to carry out each of the techniques involved in car bodywork repair, with safety notes where necessary. As such, it is the ideal complement to this book.

## Compressed gas cylinders

There are serious hazards associated with the storage and handling of gas cylinders and fittings, and standard precautions should be strictly observed in dealing with them. Ensure that cylinders are stored in safe conditions, properly maintained and always handled with special care, and make constant efforts to eliminate the possibility of leakage, fire and explosion.

The cylinder gases that are commonly used are oxygen, acetylene and liquid petroleum gas (LPG). Safety requirements for all three gases are: Cylinders must be stored in a fire resistant, dry and well-ventilated space, away from any source of heat or ignition and protected from ice, snow or direct sunlight. Valves of cylinders in store must always be kept uppermost and closed, even when the cylinder is empty. Cylinders should be handled with care and only by personnel who are reliable, adequately informed and fully aware of all associated hazards. Damaged or leaking cylinders should be promptly taken outside into the open air, and the supplier and fire authorities should be notified immediately. No one should approach a gas cylinder store with a naked light or cigarette. Care should be taken to avoid striking or dropping cylinders, or knocking them together. Cylinders should never be used as rollers. One cylinder should

never be filled from another. Every care must be taken to avoid accidental damage to cylinder valves. Valves must be operated without haste, never fully opened hard back against the back stop (so that other users know the valve is open) and never wrenched shut but turned just securely enough to stop the gas. Before removing or loosening any outlet connections, caps or plugs, a check should be made that the valves are closed. When carrying cylinders, close all valves and appliance taps, and extinguish naked flames, including pilot jets, before disconnecting them. When reconnecting, ensure that all connections and washers are clean and in good condition, and do not overtighten them. Immediately a cylinder becomes empty, close its valve.

Safety requirements for acetylene: Cylinders must always be stored and used in the upright position. If a cylinder becomes heated accidentally or becomes hot because of excessive backfiring, immediately shut the valve, detach the regulator, take the cylinder out of doors well away from the building, immerse it in, or continuously spray it with, water, open the valve and allow the gas to escape until the cylinder is empty. If necessary, notify the emergency fire service without delay.

Safety requirements for oxygen are: No oil or grease should be used on valves or fittings. Cylinders with convex bases should be used in a stand or held securely to a wall.

Safety requirements for LPG are: The store must be kept free of combustible material, corrosive material and cylinders of oxygen.

Cylinders should only ever be carried upright, securely strapped down, preferably in an open vehicle or with windows open. Carry the suppliers' safety data with you. In the event of an

accident, notify the Police and Fire Services and hand the safety data to them.

## Dangerous liquids and gases

Because of inflammable gas given off by batteries when on charge, care should be taken to avoid sparking by switching off the power supply before charger leads are connected or disconnected. Battery terminals should be shielded, since a battery contains energy and a spark can be caused by any conductor which touches its terminals or exposed connecting straps.

When internal combustion engines are operated inside buildings, the exhaust fumes must be properly discharged to the open air. Petroleum spirit or mixture must be contained in metal cans which should be kept in a store. In any area where battery charging or the testing of fuel injection systems is carried out there must be good ventilation, and no sources of ignition. Inspection pits often present serious hazards. They should be of adequate length to allow safe access and exit while a car is in position. If there is an inspection pit, petrol may enter it. Since petrol vapour is heavier than air it will remain there and be a hazard if there is any source of ignition. All sources of ignition must therefore be excluded.

## Work with plastics

Work with plastic materials brings additional hazards into workshops. Many of the materials used (polymers, resins, adhesives and materials acting as catalysts and accelerators) readily produce very dangerous situations in the form of poisonous fumes, skin irritants, risk of fire and explosions. Do not allow resin or 2-pack

adhesive hardener, or that supplied with filler or 2-pack stopper to come into contact with skin or eyes. Read carefully the safety notes supplied on the tin, tube or packaging.

## Jacks and axle stands

Special care should be taken when any type of lifting equipment is used. NEVER even consider working under your car using only a jack to support the weight of it. Lifting jacks are for raising vehicles not supporting them, and must be replaced by adequate supports before any work is begun on the vehicle. Axle stands are available from many discount stores, and all auto parts stores. These stands are absolutely essential if you plan to work under your car. Simple triangular stands (fixed or adjustable) will suit almost all of your working situations. Drive-on ramps are very limiting because of their design and size.

When jacking the car from the front, leave the gearbox in neutral and the brake off until you have placed the axle stands under the frame. Make sure that the car is on level ground first! Then put the car into gear and/or engage the handbrake and lower the jack. Obviously, DO NOT put the car in gear if you plan to turn over the engine! Leaving the brake on, or leaving the car in gear while jacking the front of the car will necessarily cause the jack to tip (unless a good quality trolley jack with wheels is being used). This is unavoidable when jacking the car on one side, and the use of the handbrake in this case is recommended. If the car is older and if it shows signs of weakening at the jack tubes while using the factory jack, it is best to purchase a good scissors jack or hydraulic jack – preferably trolley-type (depending on your budget).

## Workshop safety – summary

1 Always have a fire extinguisher at arm's length whenever welding or when working on the fuel system – under the car, or under the bonnet.
2 NEVER use a naked flame near the petrol tank.
3 Keep your inspection lamp FAR AWAY from any source of dripping petrol (gasoline); for example, while removing the fuel pump.
4 NEVER use petrol (gasoline) to clean parts. Use paraffin (kerosene) or white (mineral) spirit.
5 NO SMOKING!

**If you do have a fire, DON'T PANIC. Use the extinguisher effectively by directing it at the base of the fire.**

## Paint spraying

NEVER use 2-pack, isocyanate-based paints in the home environment or home workshop. Ask your supplier if you are not sure which is which. If you have use of a professional booth, wear an air-fed mask. Wear a charcoal face mask when spraying other paints, and maintain ventilation to the spray area. Concentrated fumes are dangerous!

Spray fumes, thinners and paint are highly inflammable. Keep away from naked flames or sparks.

Paint spraying safety is too large a subject for this book. See Lindsay Porter's *The Car Bodywork Repair Manual* (Haynes) for further information.

## Fluoroelastomers – *Most Important! Please Read This Section!*

Many synthetic rubber-like

materials used in motor cars contain substances known as fluoroelastomers (containing fluorine). These are commonly used for oil seals, wiring and cabling, bearing surfaces, gaskets, diaphragms, hoses and 'O' rings. If they are subjected to temperatures greater than 315°C, they will decompose and can be potentially hazardous. Fluoroelastomer materials will show physical signs of decomposition under such conditions in the form of charring of black sticky masses. Some decomposition may occur at temperatures above 200°C, and it is obvious that when a car has been in a fire or has been dismantled with the assistance of a cutting torch or blow torch, the fluoroelastomers can decompose in the manner indicated above.

In the presence of any water or humidity, including atmospheric moisture, the by-products caused by fluoroelastomers being heated can be extremely dangerous.

According to the Health and Safety Executive, 'Skin contact with this liquid or decomposition residues can cause painful and penetrating burns. Permanent irreversible skin and tissue damage can occur.' Damage can also be caused to eyes or by the inhalation of fumes created as fluoroelastomers are burned or heated.

If you are in the vicinity of a vehicle fire or a place where a vehicle is being cut up with cutting equipment, the Health and Safety Executive recommend the following action:

1   Assume, unless you know otherwise that seals, gaskets and 'O' rings, hoses, wiring and cabling, bearing surfaces and diaphragms are fluoroelastomers.
2   Inform firefighters of the presence of fluoroelastomers and toxic and corrosive fume hazards when they arrive.
3   All personnel not wearing breathing apparatus must leave the immediate area of a fire.

After fires or exposure to high temperatures:
1   Do not touch blackened or charred seals or equipment.
2   Allow all burnt or decomposed fluoroelastomer materials to cool down before inspection, investigation, tear-down or removal.
3   Preferably, don't handle parts containing decomposed fluoroelastomers, but if you must, wear goggles and PVC (polyvinyl chloride) or neoprene protective gloves whilst doing so. Never handle such parts unless they are completely cool.
4   Contaminated parts, residues, materials and clothing, including protective clothing and gloves, should be disposed of by an approved contractor to landfill, or by incineration according to national or local regulations. Original seals, gaskets and 'O' rings, along with contaminated material, must not be burned locally.

Symptoms and clinical findings of exposures:
A   Skin/eye contact:
Symptoms may be apparent immediately after contact, or there may be considerable delay following exposure. Do not assume that a lack of immediate symptoms means there has been no damage; delays of minutes in treatment can have severe consequences:

1   Dull throbbing ache.
2   Severe and persistent pain.
3   Black discoloration under nails (skin contact).
4   Severe, persistent and penetrating burns.
5   Skin swelling and redness.
6   Blistering.
7   Sometimes pain without visible change.
B   Inhalation (breathing) – immediate:
1   Coughing.
2   Choking.
3   Chills lasting one or two hours after exposure.
4   Irritation.
C   Inhalation (breathing) – delays of one to two days or more:
1   Fever.
2   Cough.
3   Chest tightness.
4   Pulmonary oedema (congestion).
5   Bronchial pneumonia.

*FIRST AID*
A   Skin contact:
1   Remove contaminated clothing immediately.
2   Irrigate affected skin with copious amounts of cold water   or lime water (saturated calcium hydroxide solution) for 15   to 60 minutes. Obtain medical assistance urgently.
B   Inhalation:
Remove to fresh air and obtain medical supportive treatment immediately. Treat for pulmonary oedema.
C   Eye contact:
Wash/irrigate eyes immediately with water followed by normal saline for 30 to 60 minutes. Obtain immediate medical attention.

# 2 Tools & Working Facilities

## Introduction

A selection of good tools is a fundamental requirement for anyone contemplating the maintenance and repair of a motor vehicle. For the owner who does not possess any, their purchase will prove a considerable expense, offsetting some of the savings made by doing-it-yourself. However, provided that the tools purchased are of good quality, they will last for many years and prove an extremely worthwhile investment.

To help the average owner to decide which tools are needed to carry out the various tasks detailed in this manual, we have compiled three lists of tools under the following headings: Maintenance and minor repair, Repair and overhaul, and Special. The newcomer to practical mechanics should start off with the 'Maintenance and minor repair' tool kit and confine himself to the simpler jobs around the vehicle.

Then, as his confidence and experience grows, he can undertake more difficult tasks, buying extra tools as, and when, they are needed. In this way a 'Maintenance and minor repair' tool kit can be built up into a 'Repair and overhaul' tool kit over a considerable period of time without any major cash outlays. The experienced do-it-yourselfer will have a tool kit good enough for most repairs and overhaul procedures and will add tools from the 'Special' category when he feels the expense is justified by the amount of use these tools will be put to.

## Maintenance and minor repair tool kit

The tools given in this list should be considered as a minimum requirement if routine maintenance, servicing and minor repair operations are to be undertaken.

We recommend the purchase of combination spanners (ring one end, open-ended the other); although more expensive than open-ended ones, they do give the advantage of both types of spanner.

> *Combination spanners — $7/16$.*
> *$1/2$, $9/16$, $5/8$, $11/16$, $3/4$, $13/16$, $15/16$ in.*
> *AF*
> *Combination spanners — 5, 6, 8, 10 and 12 mm*
> *Adjustable spanner — 9 inch*
> *Engine sump/gearbox/rear axle drain plug key (where applicable)*
> *Spark plug spanner (with rubber insert)*
> *Spark plug gap adjustment tool*
> *Set of feeler gauges*
> *Brake adjuster spanner (where applicable)*
> *Brake bleed nipple spanner*
> *Screwdriver — 4 in. long × ¼ in. dia. (plain)*
> *Screwdriver — 4 in. long × ¼ in. dia. (crosshead)*
> *Combination pliers — 6 inch*
> *Hacksaw, junior*
> *Tyre pump*

Tyre pressure gauge
Grease gun (where applicable)
Oil can
Fine emery cloth (1 sheet)
Wire brush (small)
Funnel (medium size)

## Repair and overhaul tool kit

These tools are virtually essential for anyone undertaking any major repairs to a motor vehicle, and are additional to those given in the Basic list. Included in this list is a comprehensive set of sockets. Although these are expensive they will be found invaluable as they are so versatile — particularly if various drives are included in the set. We recommend the ½ square-drive type, as this can be used with most proprietary torque wrenches. If you cannot afford a socket set, even bought piecemeal, then inexpensive tubular box spanners are a useful alternative.

The tools in this list will occasionally need to be supplemented by tools from the Special list.

Sockets (or box spanners) to cover range in previous list
Reversible ratchet drive (for use with sockets)
Extension piece, 10 inch (for use with sockets)
Universal joint (for use with sockets)
Torque wrench (for use with sockets)
'Mole' wrench — 8 inch
Ball pein hammer
Soft-faced hammer, plastic or rubber
Screwdriver — 6 in. long × ⁵/₁₆ in. dia. (plain)
Screwdriver — 2 in. long × ⁵/₁₆ in. square (plain)
Screwdriver — 1½ in. long × ¼ in. dia. (crosshead)
Screwdriver — 3 in. long × ⅛ in. dia. (electrician's)
Pliers — electrician's side cutters

Pliers — needle noses
Pliers — circlip (internal and external)
Cold chisel — ½ inch
Scriber (this can be made by grinding the end of a broken hacksaw blade)
Scraper (this can be made by flattening and sharpening one end of a piece of copper pipe)
Centre punch
Pin punch
Hacksaw
Valve grinding tool
Steel rule/straightedge
Allen keys
Selection of files
Wire brush (large)
Axle stands
Jack (strong scissor or hydraulic type)

## Special tools

The tools in this list are those which are not used regularly, are expensive to buy, or which need to be used in accordance with their manufacturer's instructions. Unless relatively difficult mechanical jobs are undertaken frequently, it will not be economic to buy many of these tools. Where this is the case, you could consider clubbing together with friends (or a motorists' club) to make a joint purchase, or borrowing the tools against a deposit from a local garage or tool hire specialist.

The following list contains only those tools and instruments freely available to the public, and not those special tools produced by the vehicle manufacturer specially for its dealer network.

Valve spring compressor
Piston ring compressor
Ball joint separator
Universal hub/bearing puller
Impact screwdriver
Micrometer and/or vernier gauge
Carburettor flow balancing device (where applicable)
Dial gauge
Stroboscopic timing light

Dwell angle meter/tachometer
Universal electrical multi-meter
Cylinder compression gauge
Lifting tackle
Trolley jack
Light with extension lead

## Buying tools

For practically all tools, a tool factor is the best source since he will have a very comprehensive range compared with the average garage or accessory shop. Having said that, accessory shops often offer excellent quality tools at discount prices, so it pays to shop around.

Remember, you don't have to buy the most expensive items on the shelf, but it is always advisable to steer clear of the very cheap tools. There are plenty of good tools around, at reasonable prices, so ask the proprietor or manager of the shop for advice before making a purchase.

## Care and maintenance of tools

Having purchased a reasonable tool kit, it is necessary to keep the tools in a clean and serviceable condition. After use, always wipe off any dirt, grease and metal particles using a clean, dry cloth, before putting the tools away. Never leave them lying around after they have been used. A simple tool rack on the garage or workshop wall, for items such as screwdrivers and pliers is a good idea. Store all normal spanners and sockets in a metal box. Any measuring instruments, gauges, meters etc., must be carefully stored where they cannot be damaged or become rusty.

Take a little care when the tools are used. Hammer heads inevitably become marked and screwdrivers lose the keen edge on their blades from time-to-time. A little timely

attention with emery cloth or a file will soon restore items like this to a good serviceable finish.

## Working facilities

Not to be forgotten when discussing tools, is the workshop itself. If anything more than routine maintenance is to be carried out, some form of suitable working area becomes essential.

It is appreciated that many an owner mechanic is forced by circumstance to remove an engine or similar item, without the benefit of a garage or workshop. Having done this, any repairs should always be done under the cover of a roof.

Wherever possible, any dismantling should be done on a clean flat workbench or table at a suitable working height.

Any workbench needs a vice: one with a jaw opening of 4 in. (100 mm) is suitable for most jobs. As mentioned previously, some clean, dry storage space is also required for tools, as well as the lubricants, cleaning fluids, touch-up paints and so on which soon become necessary.

Another item which may be required, and which has a much more general useage, is an electric drill with a chuck capacity of at least 5/16 in. (8 mm). This, together with a good range of twist drills, is virtually essential for fitting accessories such as wing mirrors and reversing lights.

Last, but not least, always keep a supply of old newspapers and clean, lint-free rags available, and try to keep any working areas as clean as possible.

## Spanner jaw gap comparison table

| Jaw gap (in.) | Spanner size |
|---|---|
| 0.250 | ¼ in. AF |
| 0.275 | 7 mm AF |
| 0.312 | 5/16 in. AF |
| 0.315 | 8 mm AF |
| 0.340 | 11/32 in. AF/ ⅛ in. Whitworth |
| 0.354 | 9 mm AF |
| 0.375 | ⅜ in. AF |
| 0.393 | 10 mm AF |
| 0.433 | 11 mm AF |
| 0.437 | 7/16 in. AF |
| 0.445 | 3/16 in. Whitworth/ ¼ in. BSF |
| 0.472 | 12 mm AF |
| 0.500 | ½ in. AF |
| 0.512 | 13 mm AF |
| 0.525 | ¼ in. Whitworth/5/16 in. BSF |
| 0.551 | 14 mm AF |
| 0.562 | 9/16 in. AF |
| 0.590 | 15 mm AF |
| 0.600 | 5/16 in. Whitworth/ ⅜ in. BSF |
| 0.625 | ⅝ in. AF |
| 0.629 | 16 mm AF |
| 0.669 | 17 mm AF |
| 0.687 | 11/16 in. AF |
| 0.708 | 18 mm AF |
| 0.710 | ⅜ in. Whitworth/7/16 in. BSF |
| 0.748 | 19 mm AF |
| 0.750 | ¾ in. AF |
| 0.812 | 13/16 in. AF |
| 0.820 | 7/16 in. Whitworth/ ½ in. BSF |
| 0.866 | 22 mm AF |
| 0.875 | ⅞ in. AF |
| 0.920 | ½ in. Whitworth/9/16 in. BSF |
| 0.937 | 15/16 in. AF |
| 0.944 | 24 mm AF |
| 1.000 | 1 in. AF |
| 1.010 | 9/16 in. Whitworth/ ⅝ in. BSF |
| 1.023 | 26 mm AF |
| 1.062 | 1 1/16 in. AF/27 mm AF |
| 1.100 | ⅝ in. Whitworth/11/16 in. BSF |
| 1.125 | 1 ⅛ in. AF |
| 1.181 | 30 mm AF |
| 1.200 | 11/16 in. Whitworth/ ¾ in. BSF |
| 1.250 | 1 ¼ in. AF |
| 1.259 | 32 mm AF |
| 1.300 | ¾ in. Whitworth/ ⅞ in. BSF |
| 1.312 | 1 5/16 in. AF |
| 1.390 | 13/16 in. Whitworth/15/16 in. BSF |
| 1.417 | 36 mm AF |
| 1.437 | 1 7/16 in. AF |
| 1.480 | ⅞ in. Whitworth/1 in. BSF |
| 1.500 | 1 ½ in. AF |
| 1.574 | 40 mm AF/15/16 in. Whitworth |
| 1.614 | 41 mm AF |
| 1.625 | 1 ⅝ in. AF |
| 1.670 | 1 in. Whitworth/1 ⅛ in. BSF |
| 1.687 | 1 11/16 in. AF |
| 1.811 | 46 mm AF |
| 1.812 | 1 13/16 in. AF |
| 1.860 | 1 ⅛ in. Whitworth/1 ¼ in. BSF |
| 1.875 | 1 ⅞ in. AF |
| 1.968 | 50 mm AF |
| 2.000 | 2 in. AF |
| 2.050 | 1 ¼ in. Whitworth/1 ⅜ in. BSF |
| 2.165 | 55 mm AF |
| 2.362 | 60 mm AF |

# ③ **Specifications**

## *Austin Healey Sprite MkI ('Frogeye')*

| | |
|---|---|
| **Type designation** | Austin-Healey Sprite developed under Austin Drawing Office number A.D.O.13. Later known as Austin-Healey Sprite MkI. |
| **Built** | Abingdon, England from March 31, 1958 to 1961. Also built from knock-down ktis in Sydney, Australia unti mid-1962. |
| **Engine** | BMC A-series unit as used in Morris Minor/Austin A35 except for twin HSI (1⅛ in)SU carburettors set at a slight angle from the horizontal and with individual 'pancake' type air filters, special valve springs. Stellited exhaust valve seats and copper-lead main and big-end bearings. Cast iron block and head, pressed steel sump, 4-cylinder in-line, overhead valve with pushrods, camshaft in block. Capacity 948cc (57.87 cu.in) Bore & Stroke 62.9 x 76.2mm (2.48 x 30in).<br>Maximum power: 43bhp (net) at 5000 rpm.<br>Maximum torque (net): 52lb/ft at 3300rpm.<br>Maximum bmep (net): 136lb/sq.in at 3000rpm.<br>Fuel pump: A.C. mechanical type, mounted in side of block and driven by camshafter.<br>Sump capacity: 6⅞ Imp pints (3.34 litres) |
| **Transmission** | Rear wheel drive from front mounted engine. Four speed gearbox bolted to rear engine plate.<br>Synchromesh available on top three ratios.<br>Overall gear ratios: Top, 4.22; 3rd, 5.96; 2nd, 10.02; 1st, 15.31. Final drive, 4.22 to 1.<br>Reverse 19.68 Hypoid bevel rear axle. Clutch of Borg and Beck manufacture, 6¼ in diameter, hydraulic operation. |

| | |
|---|---|
| **Chassis frame and bodywork** | 2-door, 2-seater convertible of all-steel unitary (chassisless) construction. Floorpan presses and constructed at John Thompson Motor Pressings Ltd in Wolverhampton, England with sills of 0.048in (1.22mm) thickness. A substantial front scuttle receives front end loadings and comprises a central, vertical box running almost from scuttle top to floor into which the gearbox body protrudes and each side of which are driver's and passenger's footwells. The battery and heater shelf forms the top face of the box as seen from inside the engine compartment. Protruding forward from the scuttle are 'chassis' legs, tied together at their forward end by a box-section crossmember. The one-piece floor (the propellor shaft runs above it, inside the transmission tunnel) proceeds back from a floor-level crossmember parallel with the scuttle/dashboard top to a shallow rear bulkhead and is supported by the deep transmission tunnel, 2-piece sills and a box section running front-to-rear in line with the rear springs and mounted on top of the floor. Rear spring loadings are taken forward into a hollow rear bulkhead of triangular section and the floor/box section already described. Other body panels, including the stressed rear panel, were produced and fitted at the Pressed Steel Company, Swindon. Bodyshell rust inhibited, and painted, at the Morris works at Cowley. Wheelbase: 6ft 8in (203cm). Track: front 3ft 9¾in (116cm).         rear: 3ft 8¾in (114cm). Overall length: (without front bumper) 11ft 0⅝in (337cm), (with front bumper) 11ft 5¼in (349cm). Overall width: 4ft 5in (135cm). Overall height: 4ft 1¾in (126cm) but 3ft 8⅛in (112 cm) with hood down. Ground clearance: 5in (13cm). Turning circle: right: 31ft 2½in (9.5cm).         left: 32ft 1½in (9.8cm). Kerb weight: 1328lb (602kg). Weight distribution: 55% front/45% rear. Fuel tank capacity: 6 Imp gallons/27.3 litres/7.2 U.S.gallons. |
| **Suspension** | Front: Standard Austin A35 coil spring and wishbone components in conjunction with Armstrong lever-type shock absorbers which also act as upper arms of the wishbone assembly. Rear: Quarter-elliptic 15-leaf springs with 16 inch free length between mounting bracket and axle. Upper torque links fabricated from channel pressings run above, and parallel to, the springs. Rubber bump stops and canvas rebound straps. |
| **Steering** | Morris Minor-type steering rack giving 2½ turns from lock-to-lock. |
| **Brakes** | Conventional Lockheed hydraulic system with M.G.-type shared brake and clutch master cylinder. Front: 7in drum with twin leading 1³/₁₆in wide shoes. Rear: 7in drum with leading-and-trailing 1³/₁₆in wide shoes. Handbrake operated by cable and rod, with its compensating gear attached to the axle casing. |
| **Wheels and Tyres** | Ventilated pressed steel disc wheels, 4 studs 13 × 3½in. 5.20 × 13in tubeless tyres. Tyre pressures: 18psi front: 20psi rear. |
| **Electrical system** | 12 volt 43 amp hour battery mounted ahead of the scuttle. Positive earth Lucas dynamo (with integral mechanical tachometer drive mounted at its rear) and Lucas voltage regulator. Lucas coil ignition and wiring harness made up to standard Lucas colour coding scheme. 2 fuses, non-cancelling direction indicators (white front, amber rear), self-parking windscreen wipers. |

| Performance | Maximum speed 81mph |
|---|---|
| | Speed in gears: 3rd gear 65mph, 2nd gear 38mph, 1st gear 23mph |
| | Acceleration: 0-50mph, 13.4 secs; 0-60mph, 20.5 secs |
| | Standing quarter-mile: 21.2 secs |
| | Acceleration in gears: |
| | Top: 20-40mph, 12.6 secs; 40-60mph, 14.5 secs |
| | Third: 20-40mph, 7.8 secs; 40-60mph 14.5 secs |
| | Fuel consumption: Driven hard, 33 miles per Imperial gallon. Touring, 44 miles per Imperial gallon. |

## MG Midget Mk I and Austin-Healey Sprite Mk II

*Please note that the specifications in this section relate to the M.G. Midget MkI and Austin-Healey Sprite MkII on introduction. For production specification changes see following appendix.*

| Type designation | M.G. Midget MkI and Austin-Healey Sprite MkII. |
|---|---|
| **Built** | Abingdon, England, 1961-71 (Sprite), 1961-79 (Midget). |
| **Engine** | Cast iron block and head, pressed steel sump, 4-cylinders in-line, overhead valve, camshaft in block.<br>Capacity 948cc<br>Bore & Stroke 62.94 × 76.2mm<br>Maximum power: 46bhp (net) at 5500 rpm with 9:1 CR.<br>Maximum torque: 52.8lb/ft at 3000rpm.<br>2 SU HS2 1¼ inch carburettors |
| **Transmission** | Rear wheel drive from front mounted engine.<br>Four speed gearbox with synchromesh on top three ratios, bolted to rear engine plate. Ratios: 3.2:1, 1.916:1, 1.357:1, 1.0:1, reverse 4.114:1, final drive ratio 4.22:1 |
| **Body** | 2-door, 2-seater convertible of unitary construction. Loadings fed into floorpan structure constructed of pressed steel components at John Thompson Motor Pressings, Wolverhampton. Dimensions: Overall height 4ft 1¾ inches, length 11ft 5⅞ inches, wheelbase 6ft 8 inches, ground clearance 5 inches, width 4ft 5 inches, front track 3ft 9¾ inches, rear track 3ft 8¾ inches, fuel capacity 6 Imperial gallons. |
| **Suspension** | Front: independent, coil springs.<br>Rear: quarter-elliptic springs. |
| **Steering** | Morris Minor rack and pinion, 2¼ turns lock-to-lock. |
| **Brakes** | 7 inch Lockheed drums front and rear, hydraulically operated. |
| **Wheels & tyres** | 13 inch ventilated pressed steel disc wheels, 5.20 × 13 tubeless tyres. |
| **Electrical system** | 12 volt 43 amp hour battery. Positive earth Lucas dynamo with tachometer drive to rear. Lucas voltage regulator, coil ignition and wiring harness made up to standard Lucas colour coding scheme. |
| **Performance** | Maximum speed 87mph<br>Speed in gears: 3rd gear 68mph, 2nd gear 46mph, 1st gear 28mph.<br>Accelerations (0-60): 19.6 seconds.<br>Standing ¼ mile: 21.8 seconds.<br>Acceleration in gears: Top: 20-40mph, 14.4 sec; 50-70mph, 19.4 sec;<br>Third: 20-40mph, 8.8 sec; 40-60mph 11.3 sec.<br>Fuel consumption: 32-38mpg. |

# Production Modifications

## Sprite MkI ('Frogeye')

The **Chassis Number** (or **Car Number**) is stamped on a plate secured to the left-hand inner wheel arch valance under the bonnet. The **Engine Number** is stamped on a plate secured to the right-hand side of the cylinder block above the dynamo.

The Chassis, or Car Number consists of a code which presents the following information:

**1st character** indicates make (H = Healey)
**2nd character** indicates engine type (A = A-series engine)
**3rd character** indicates the factory code for body type (N = 2-seater tourer)
**4th number** indicates series (the Sprite was the fifth in the Austin-Healey series, from the factory's point of view).

### Production modifications

Chassis numbers quoted here are what manufacturers know as 'pure' chassis numbers (i.e. *all* cars built after the number shown are fitted with those parts which relate to the chassis number change point). However, it may well be that, because of production line supply techniques, some cars which appear before the given change point will be fitted with 'later' parts.

The Sprite MkI is notable for having had an exceptionally small number of production modifications. Many of those shown here are minor in nature and nearly all took place within the first six months of the model's life.

**Chassis No. AN5 501:** March 31st, 1958, production began. May 20th, 1958, Austin-Healey Sprite announced.
Options: UK May 1958: heater £20.16s.3d; radio £25.0s.0d;

tachometer £4.10s.0d; front bumper and over-riders £6.0s.0d; screenwasher £2.5s.0d; 6-ply tyres £7.2s.6d; laminated windscreen £4.2s.6d; fresh air unit £6.0s.0d; tonneau cover £6.0s.0d. (NB: tachometer and heater were probably 'theoretical' options in that they were fitted before delivery except in the case of export cars intended for warmer countries where heaters were more often not fitted. In this way, it is surmised, advertised prices could be kept as low as possible.)

**AN5 946:** Gearbox synchro assembly improved.
**AN5 1073:** Thermostat type changed.
**AN5 1397:** Inlet and exhaust valves – modified type fitted.
**AN5 1551:** Carb fuel chamber lids modified.
**AN5 1606:** Sidescreen mounting brackets, fixing screws and door top finishers modified.

**AN5 3444**: Tachometer cable improved.

**AN5 3689**: Speedometer cable improved.

**AN5 4333**: Rear axle case slightly modified in conjunction with altered radius arm mounting bracket, incorporating shock absorber mounting points for extra location. Shock absorber assembly modified accordingly.

**AN5 4695**: Under-bonnet air intake shape modified.

**AN5 4800**: Steering arm fixing bolts reduced in number from two to one per side.

**AN5 4996**: Clutch pedal modified.

**AN5 5321**: Ferrule-blanking tool hole in rear crossmember fitted.

**AN5 5477**: October 16th, 1958, nine-stud hood-to-screen top fixing changed to slot-in type of screen fixing.

**AN5 10344**: Door handles (interior) shortened and chrome plated knobs added at their ends and the latches improved. Rear wheel arch chassis rails strengthened and reinforced. Windscreen side stanchions and hood front panel modified at same time.

**Late 1959/Early 1960**: Hardtop model introduced with Warwick-designed glass reinforced plastic hardtop as standard and with modified sidescreens built by Weathershields Ltd in place of one-piece lightweight sidescreens. Weathershields' sidescreens incorporate two-piece Perspex (Plexiglas) panels, the rear of which slide open. (*NB:* It is suspected these improved sidescreens became another 'theoretical' optional extra in that they were listed as such but were probably fitted to the cars prior to delivery.)

**AN5 34558**: March 1960, sliding sidescreens were catalogued as standard.

**AN5 50116**: Very early 1961, production ended.

## Sprite MkII on/ Midget MkI on

**May 1961; A-H Sprite MkII. Chassis numbers H-AN6 101 to H-AN6 24731.**
More powerful 948cc engine now giving 52bhp (SAE) from modified camshaft, larger valves, different (higher compression ratio) pistons, SU HS2 (1¼ inch) carbs replacing earlier 1⅛ inch type. HS2 carburettors now with plastic dashpot top screws in place of earlier brass type and with modified choke linkage. Different inlet and exhaust manifolds now fitted, the exhaust manifold being one piece in place of the earlier type with top blanking plate.

Gearbox still with smooth casing (later types have a ribbed casing) but with higher ratio gears identical to those in the optional high ratio gearbox offered to MkI Sprite owners.

Trim identical to Frogeye Sprite except for changes of switch position, lever switches fitted in place of push-pull type, barrel type lighting switch (surrounding ignition switch) replaced by flick switch, and relative position of headlamp and ignition warning lights, mounted in tachometer and speedometer dials, reversed.

Extensive bodywork changes as described in text and hood and tonneau modified to suit new rear bodywork. Single piece hood frame replaced by split type and storage bag provided.

**June 1961; M.G. Midget MkI. Chassis numbers G-AN1 101 to G-AN1 16183.**
Similar to Sprite in most respects although price was £20 higher plus Purchase Tax in the U.K. Detail changes to justify price increment and change of marque name: waist rail chrome strips on bodywork, centre chrome finishing strip on bonnet, plain chrome hub caps (Sprite hub caps had a pressed ''AH'' motif), grille with vertical slats and a central 'MG' badge,

different seat patterns (while MkII Sprite used MkI seats, MkI Midget seats had a horizontal bar across the top of the squab and front of the cushion and the piping was in a contrasting colour). Hardtop cars and those fitted with the optional sidescreens had a sliding rear as well as front section to the 'Windshields' sidescreens.

**October 1962; A-H Sprite 'MkII½'. Chassis numbers H-AN7 24732 to H-AN7 38828. October 1962 M.G. Midget 'Mk1½'. Chassis numbers G-AN2 16184 to G-AN2 25767.**
A larger engine of 1098cc capacity fitted giving 56bhp at 5500rpm. Crank journal diameters were the same as those of the 948cc engine although their length was increased. Compression ratio was marginally lower at 8.9:1 and similar carburettors were fitted with appropriately different jets. Improved type gearbox fitted with much stronger baulk ring synchromesh replacing earlier cone type (externally identifiable by ribbed alloy casing).

Disc brakes were fitted with a wire wheel option, the stub axle and bottom kingpin bush being modified to suit.

Morris Minor type rear wheel cylinders incorporating handbrake mechanism abandoned for units with separate handbrake operation. Brake shoes adjusted by MGB/Mini type of backplate adjuster and consequently brake drums no longer fitted with adjustment hole. Disc wheels no longer with ventilation holes.

Front suspension wishbones now reinforced with strengthening gusset.

Sealed beam headlamps fitted.

External bodywork modifications: none.

Number of trim modifications carried out involving: revised seats and dashboard, padded crash rail at top and bottom of dash, door casings padded and door tops padded to match dash crash rail, carpets fitted instead of mats, leathercloth inside doors to match door casings instead of rubber trim,

simulated onyx steering wheel and grab handle no longer fitted. Smiths instruments used in place of Jaeger and a badge fitted to the middle of the the boot (trunk) lid similar to that of the MGB.

Similar M.G. Midget changes were made concurrently with those to the Sprite.

## March 1964; A-H Sprite MkIII. Chassis numbers H-AN8 38829 to H-AN8 64755.

New 1098cc engine, very similar to previous unit but substantially redesigned. Now with 2" main bearing engine to alleviate 'crank whip' problem suffered by its predecessor. Mechanical fuel pump replaced by SU electric type situated beneath driver's side (in UK) rear wheelarch. Mechanical fuel pump 'mounting' now a solid casting and the camshaft, with wider lobes, no longer with fuel pump cam. Improved inlet manifold and larger bore exhaust fitted. Gearbox essentially unchanged but subtle changes took place to the internal specifications of the 'ribbed-casing' gearbox throughout its production life (1961-74).

Rear suspension extensively redesigned. Now with half-elliptic rear springing. Different type of rear spring hangers fitted at the front end of the springs while at the rear of the springs, new spring hangers pick up at existing chassis rails with no extra reinforcement necessary. Rear axle essentially unchanged but with different spring attachment points. Rear dampers fitted with larger chambers.

Doors substantially altered. Wind-up windows instead of sidescreens mean that door pocket space and some elbow room is lost. External door handles and door locks now fitted and opening quarter-lights incorporated. Door shapes slightly altered around the A-post area to accommodate a modified bulkhead top panel which in turn was altered to suit a new wrap-around windscreen which replaced the previous almost flat screen. Hoot attached to screen by MGB-type toggle fasteners and the hood shape and hood sticks were

modified. Hood tension supplied by the fold-open action of the hood sticks rather than the spring loading found on earlier hoods.

New dashboard with completely revised layout but with same switch and dial functions except key start instead of pull starter switch. Indicator switch now steering column mounted instead of left-right toggle switch mounted on dash. Steering wheel now similar to MGB-style but with only two spokes. Horn push mounted in steering wheel centre embellished with 'Austin' crest instead of the earlier Sprite flash logo.

Trim unchanged from the 'MkII ½' except that trim colours include blue and red as well as black while red hoods were fitted to red cars. (NB: These were the only Sprites not to be fitted with black hoods as standard.)

## March 1964; M.G. Midget MkII. Chassis numbers G-AN3 25788 to 52411.

Identical to contemporary Sprite except price which was £20.00 more in the UK and 170 dollars more in the USA. "M.G." badge mounted in centre of vertically slatted grille. Centre chrome bonnet strips and chrome waist line strips fitted; plain hub caps; "M.G." octagon and the word "Midget" on the boot lid; horn push has "M.G." logo in the centre. Winged "M.G." logo mounted in middle of dash.

## October 1966 to late 1969; A-H Sprite MkIV. Chassis numbers H-AN9 64756 to 79236.

Completely redesigned engine (still A-series) of 1275cc with 'pocketed' block (i.e. tappet covers no longer fitted). Timing chain now has double link with two rows of teeth on the sprockets, there is a damper on the front of the crankshaft nose to reduce vibration, the cylinder head is longer and is fitted with larger valves and the radiator and heater outlets are at different angles.
From engines 12CD/Da/H1745 (US-market) and 12 CE/Da/H874 (UK-market) the water pump impellers and inlet pipe are enlarged

and of greater capacity. Ignition types changed several times during the engine's production run and export cars were often modified to suit local regulations, particularly in the case of US cars. All 1275cc engines have a larger bore but a shorter stroke than their predecessors and have a higher rev limit of 6300rpm compared with 6000 of the 1098cc engine. Both the car's gearbox and rear axle were unchanged although the rear springs were uprated.

Bodywork changes were based on the rear cockpit area which was enlarged at the expense of the rear bulkhead top panel which became narrower. Small alterations were made to the rear wing tops to accommodate this change. The hood was restyled and fixed to the rear deck and gained an integral folding mechanism replacing the previously fitted fold-up and pack-away type.

Trim was basically unchanged and all cars were fitted with black trim, except for the first few cars which had optional red trim.

**Early 1968**: Reversing lights fitted as standard. Remote control gearbox turret included reversing light switch. Electrics converted to negative earth but still dynamo generated.

Black plastic 'corporate' B.L. window winder handles fitted and winder mechanism spindle altered to suit. Internal door lock lever broadened and quarter-light catch changed from curved type to flatter, chubbier style. Internal door handle now black plastic.

Eared wheel spinners discontinued on wire wheeled cars and US-style hexagonal spinners fitted.

**Late 1968**: Revised door casing with different type of material used. Seat upholstery modified; white edge piping replaced by black and seats upholstered with a significantly coarser grained material. Petrol sender unit no longer aluminium top with 6-screw fastening. Now plastic float, pressed steel top flush with top of tank. 3.9:1 differential replaced 4.2:1 unit together with changed speedometer gearing. Oil pressure/water temperature gauge changed from externally illuminated/°F to internally illuminated/°C. Fuel gauge also internally illuminated and with altered graphics. Crossflow radiator fitted with expansion bottle and different hoses and thermostat housing. This led to relocation of the washer bottle.

**October 1966 to late 1969; M.G. Midget MkIII. Chassis numbers G-AN4 52412 to 67637.**
As for contemporary Sprite MkIV, except Midget loses central bonnet trim.

**October 1969 to late 1970; A-H Sprite MkIV continues. Chassis numbers H-AN10 85287 to 86766. October 1969 to late 1971 M.G. Midget MkIII continues. Chassis numbers G-AN5 74886 to 105500.**
Rostyle (mag-style) wheels replace plainer disc wheels. Revised recessed black grille. Black sills with chrome strips. Black anodised windscreen surrounds (deleted again after only a couple of months). Slimmer bumpers fitted front and rear with new over-riders. Rear bumper split with number plate situated between bumper halves, number plate lights situated in bumper. Front side lamps lowered to equalise the gap between headlamps and new thinner bumpers. Round plastic boot badge in place of chrome. Front badge now in grille. Winged badge on bonnet deleted. Revised rear lights, 1 piece, squarer pattern, commonised with MGB.

Quieter twin silencer exhaust system with rear box mounted visibly in line with and beneath rear bumper.

Redesigned seats now recliners as standard, not as option. Headrest facility incorporated. Covers of welded vinyl (instead of stitched as previously) with embossed pattern. Revised trim, especially door casings which now have embossed panels. Tan trim with certain body colours. New 3-spoke steering wheels with round holes in spokes. Sprite steering wheels with blank

centre, Midget with ''M.G.'' badge. Oil pressure/Water temperature gauge no longer in degrees but marked ''Cold-Normal-Hot''. Metal gearlever turret with grommet deleted. Replaced by rubber turret completely covered by leathercloth gaiter. Indicator switch incorporating dip switch and horn push. Header rail toggle clips now painted grey instead of chrome and dipping interior mirror windscreen bracket modified for safety reasons.

**Early 1970**: Courtesy light switches on inner door pillars with light under dashboard. Boot courtesy light fitted. Bonnet and boot fitted with telescopic stays. Uprated heater and integral heater box: heater, motor and blower all in one casing.

**January 1971; Austin Sprite MkIV continues. Chassis numbers A-AN10 86802 to 87824.**
''Healey'' name deleted from Sprite. Front and rear badges modified accordingly. Revised steering wheel with horn push back in centre instead of on stalk. Column locking/ignition key instead of dash mounted. (First modified cars fitted with chrome blanking plug in dash where ignition key was situated. Later dashes modified.)

Sprite discontinued in June 1971.

**January 1972 to 1974 M.G. Midget MkIII continues. Chassis numbers G-AN5 105501 to G-AN5 153920.**
Rear wheel arches modified to rounded shape, similar to original Sprite. 'MkII' Rostyle wheels fitted.

Tumble switches on dash replaced by rocker switches.

Yellow ochre interior trim fitted to certain specific body colours. Better quality carpets fitted. Interior door pull handles now corporate — BL MGB/Marina non-swivelling

type. BL gear knob fitted. Steering wheel now with long slots presses through in place of round holes.

Deeper petrol tank now of 7 gallon (Imp.) capacity. Sender unit now located by internal circlip bayonet ring. Altered steering rack fitted (of Vitesse/Herald/Spitfire type) with appropriately altered track-rod ends and longer steering arms giving lower geared steering.

1275cc model discontinued in September 1974.

**October 1974 to November 1979 M.G. Midget 1500. Chassis numbers G-AN6 154101 to G-AN6 229526.**
**October 1974**: Triumph 1500 engine (specially tuned) and Marina-type all-synchromesh gearbox fitted. Black energy-absorbing bumpers fitted with a return to squarer style of rear wheel arch. Hazard warning lights, door mirrors, anti-roll bar, tonneau cover and rail now standard.
**January 1977**: Headrests supplied as standard.
**April 1977**: Inertia reel seat belts fitted as standard.
**April 1978**: Radio console speaker/radio aerial fitted. 2-speed wipers, cigar lighter and handbrake failure warning light added.
**September 1977**: Door mirror fitted to driver's side. Rear axle ratio raised from 3.9:1 to 3.72:1. New fascia panel with ''M.G.'' badge deleted. New instruments — commonised with Spitfire. Steering wheel motif now silver on black. New washer jets fitted.
**October 1978**: Dual line braking system fitted.
**November 1979**: Last M.G. Midget built.

# 5 Identify Your Car

The following guide gives an at-a-glance picture of where any particular Midget or Sprite fits into the scheme of things. (Courtesy of Spridgebits Ltd).

1. **Chassis numbers:** Only the prefix of the chassis number is shown (e.g. GAN-3, HAN-8). The serial number following this is sometimes referred to in the text of the catalogue.

2. **Engines and engine numbers:** Cars are often re-engined; if there is doubt about your car's original specification, refer to other identifying features.

3. **Specific terminology:**
*"Early hood"* – Early Frogeyes have a different windscreen and hood. The windscreen has a chrome-plated steel frame; the hood secures onto nine lift-the-dot fasteners. Later windscreen frames are aluminium with a channel for the later bar-fitting hood.
*"First facelift"* – The 1275 models in late 1969 had a major facelift. This included: split rear quarter-bumpers in place of the large one-piece bumper; black sills with the badge "SPRITE" or "MIDGET" and a chrome trim strip; black grille with centre badge; 'early' rostyle wheels with square slots; reclining seats with headrest slots.
*"Second facelift"* – In early 1972 the Midget models (Sprites had been discontinued) had a revised rear bodyshell with cutaway round rear wheel arches ("round wheel arch" in text of catalogue). Other changes included: later rostyle wheels (Ford-type); rocker-switch dashboard; 7-gallon petrol tank.

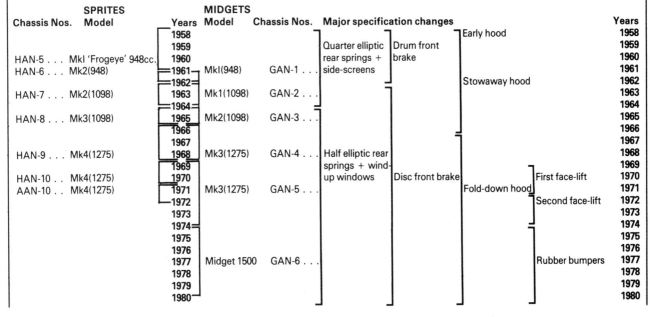

| SPRITES Chassis Nos. | Model | Years | MIDGETS Model | Chassis Nos. | Major specification changes | | Years |
|---|---|---|---|---|---|---|---|
| | | 1958 | | | | Early hood | 1958 |
| | | 1959 | | | | | 1959 |
| HAN-5 . . . | MkI 'Frogeye' 948cc. | 1960 | | | Quarter elliptic rear springs + side-screens | Drum front brake | 1960 |
| HAN-6 . . . | Mk2(948) | 1961 | MkI(948) | GAN-1 . . . | | | 1961 |
| | | 1962 | | | | Stowaway hood | 1962 |
| HAN-7 . . . | Mk2(1098) | 1963 | Mk1(1098) | GAN-2 . . . | | | 1963 |
| | | 1964 | | | | | 1964 |
| HAN-8 . . . | Mk3(1098) | 1965 | Mk2(1098) | GAN-3 . . . | | | 1965 |
| | | 1966 | | | | | 1966 |
| | | 1967 | | | | | 1967 |
| HAN-9 . . . | Mk4(1275) | 1968 | Mk3(1275) | GAN-4 . . . | Half elliptic rear springs + wind-up windows | | 1968 |
| | | 1969 | | | | | 1969 |
| HAN-10 . . | Mk4(1275) | 1970 | | | | Disc front brake | First face-lift | 1970 |
| AAN-10 . . | Mk4(1275) | 1971 | Mk3(1275) | GAN-5 . . . | | Fold-down hood | 1971 |
| | | 1972 | | | | Second face-lift | 1972 |
| | | 1973 | | | | | 1973 |
| | | 1974 | | | | | 1974 |
| | | 1975 | | | | | 1975 |
| | | 1976 | | | | | 1976 |
| | | 1977 | Midget 1500 | GAN-6 . . . | | Rubber bumpers | 1977 |
| | | 1978 | | | | | 1978 |
| | | 1979 | | | | | 1979 |
| | | 1980 | | | | | 1980 |

# ⑥ Colour Schemes

Before purchasing paint for your car, have your supplier check with a paint sample (or 'colour chip') against the original colour to ensure that you are purchasing the colour that you require.

| Colour | Factory code | Aftermarket codes (U.S.) | Model | Year |
|---|---|---|---|---|
| Black | BK1 | DITZ 9000 | Midget | 1961-79 |
| | BLVC122 | DUP 99 | MGL | 1963-80 |
| | | | MG100 | 1963-67 |
| | | | MGC | 1967-69 |
| Old English White | WT3 | RM BM149 (1) | Midget | 1961-67 |
| | | RM BM150 (2) | MGB | 1963-67 |
| | | DITZ 8177 | MG1100 | 1963-67 |
| | | DUP 8207 | MGC | 1967 |
| Snowberry White | WT4 | RM BM151 | Midget | 1968-69 |
| | | | MGB | 1968-69 |
| Glacier White | BLVC 59 | RM BM155 | Midget | 1970-77 |
| | | DITZ 8845 (9) | MGB | 1970-77 |
| | | DITZ 90074 (10) | | |
| | | DUP 8579 | | |
| Leyland White | BLVC 243 | DITZ 90106 | Midget | 1978-79 |
| | | DUP H7896 | MGB | 1978-80 |
| Farina Gray | GR11 | RM BM016 | Midget | 1961-62 |
| Grampian Gray | GR12 | RM BM018 | MGB/GT | 1967-69 |
| | | | MGC/GT | 1967-69 |
| Chelsea Gray | GR15 | RM BM008 | MGB-Roadster | 1963-65 |
| | | DITZ 31733 | only | |
| | | DUP 8198 | | |
| Dove Gray | GR26 | RM BM013 | Midget | 1962-65 |
| | | DITZ 32085 | | |
| Dark Silver | GR36 | | MG1100 | |
| Dover Gray | GR34 | RM BM014 | MG1100 | |

| Colour | Factory code | Aftermarket codes (U.S.) | Model | Year |
|---|---|---|---|---|
| Mirage | BLVC 11 | RM BM176 | Midget | 1974 |
| | | DITZ 33135 | MGB | 1974 |
| | | DUP 43277 | | |
| Sandy Beige | BG15 | RM BM146 | MGB/GT | 1965-68 |
| | | DITZ 22213 | MG1100 | 1963-67 |
| | | | MGC/GT | 1967-68 |
| Golden Beige | BG 19 | RM BM140 | MGB/GT | 1967-68 |
| | | | MGC | 1967-68 |
| Bedouin | BLVC 4 | RM BM163 | Midget | 1971 |
| | | | MGB | 1971 |
| Antelope | BLVC 7 | RM 156 | | |
| | | DITZ 32890 | MGB | 1970 |
| | | DUP 8578 | | |
| Russet Brown | BLVC 205 | DITZ 24378 | Midget | 1978-79 |
| | | DUP 44848 | MGB | 1978-80 |
| Pale Primrose | YL 12 | RM BM131 | Midget | 1965-70 |
| | | DITZ 81499 | MGB | 1965-70 |
| | | | MGC | 1967-69 |
| Bronze Yellow | BLVC 15 | RM BM157 | Midget | 1972-75 |
| | | DITZ 81827 | MGB | 1972-75 |
| | | DUP 8581 | | |
| Harvest Gold | BLVC 19 | RM BM170 | Midget | 1972-75 |
| | | DITZ 82018 | MGB | 1972-75 |
| | | DUP 30013 | | |
| Sand Glow | BLVC 63 | DITZ 24300 | Midget | 1976-77 |
| | | DUP 44565 | MGB | 1976-77 |
| Bracken | BLVC 93 | RM BM187 | Midget | 1974-76 |
| | | DITZ 60760 | MGB | 1974-76 |
| | | DUP 43275 | | |
| Chartreuse | BLVC 167 | DITZ 45189 | Midget | 1976-77 |
| | | DUP 44629 | MGB | 1976-77 |
| Inca Yellow | BLVC 207 | DITZ 83209 | Midget | 1978-79 |
| | | DUP 44880 | MGB | 1978-79 |
| Snap Dragon Yellow | BLVC 235 | DITZ 82462 | MGB | 1980 |
| | | DUP 45475 | | |
| Damask Red | RD 5 | RM BM112R | | |
| | BLVC 99 | DITZ 71064 (3) | Midget | 1973-77 |
| | | DITZ 72261 (4) | MGB | 1973-77 |
| | | DUP 8819 | | |
| Tartan Red | RD 9 | RM BM124R | Midget | 1961-69 |
| | | DITZ 71062 (5) | MGB | 1963-69 |
| | | DITZ 71416 (6) | MG1100 | 1963-67 |
| | | DUP 8204 | MGC | 1967-69 |
| Blaze Red | BLVC 16 | RM BM162 | Midget | 1971-75 |
| | | DITZ 60637 | MGB | 1971-75 |
| | | DUP 30007 | | |
| Black Tulip | BLVC 23 | RM BM 168M | Midget | 1973 |
| | | DITZ 14417 | MGB | 1973 |
| | | DUP 43274 | | |
| Flame Red | BLVC 61 | RM BM160R | | |
| | | DITZ 71861 (7) | Midget | 1970-72 |
| | | DITZ 72066 (8) | MGB | 1970-72 |
| | | DUP 8571 | | |
| Aconite | BLVC 95 | RM BM181D | Midget | 1974-75 |
| | | DITZ 14728 | MGB | 1974-75 |
| | | DUP 43274 | | |

| Colour | Factory code | Aftermarket codes (U.S.) | Model | Year |
|---|---|---|---|---|
| Vermilion Red | BLVC 118 | DITZ 60932 | Midget | 1978-79 |
| | | DUP 45471 | MGB | 1978-80 |
| Flamenco Red | BLVC 133 | DITZ 72144 | Midget | 1975-77 |
| | | DUP 43661 | MGB | 1975-77 |
| Carmine Red | BLVC 209 | DITZ 72065 | Midget | 1978-79 |
| | | DUP 43019 | MGB | 1978-80 |
| Connaught Green | GN 18 | RM BM080 | MG1100 | 1963-67 |
| | | DITZ 32252 | | |
| British Racing Green | GN 25 | RM BM079 | Midget | 1964-70 |
| | | DITZ 43342 | MGB | 1964-70 |
| British Racing Green | GN 29 | RM BM078 | Midget | 1964-70 |
| | | DUP 8194 | MGB | 1964-70 |
| | | | MGC | 1967-69 |
| Almond Green | GN 37 | RM BM076 | Midget | 1961-62 |
| Green Mallard | BLVC 22 | RM BM169D | Midget | 1972-73 |
| | | DITZ 44638 | MGB | 1972-73 |
| | | DUP 30014 | | |
| Wild Moss | BLVC 24 | RM BM165 | | |
| | | DITZ 44447 | | |
| | | DUP 30008 | | |
| New Racing Green | BLVC 25 | RM 167 | Midget | 1971 |
| | | DITZ 44446 | MGB | 1971 |
| | | DUP 30012 | | |
| Aqua | BLVC 60 | RM BM159 | Midget | 1972 |
| | | DITZ 14075 | MGB | 1972 |
| | | DUP 8821 | | |
| Lime Flower | BLVC 20 | RM BM166 | Midget | 1973 |
| | | DITZ 44448 | MGB | 1973 |
| | | DUP 30010 | | |
| Citron | BLVC 73 | RM BM177 | Midget | 1974-76 |
| | | DITZ 44947 | MGB | 1974-76 |
| | | DUP 43276 | | |
| Tundra | BLVC 94 | RM BM 178 | Midget | 1974-76 |
| | | DITZ 44978 | MGB | 1974-76 |
| | | DUP 43278 | | |
| Brooklands Green | BLVC 169 | DITZ 45190 | Midget | 1976-79 |
| | | DUP 44630 | MGB | 1976-80 |
| Mineral Blue | BU 9 | RM BM 060 | Midget | 1965-69 |
| | | DITZ 12115 | MGB | 1965-69 |
| | | DUP 8182 | MGC | 1967-69 |
| Basilica Blue | BU 11 | RM BM037 | Midget | 1965-69 |
| Iris Blue | BU 12 | RM BM054 | MGB-Roadster | 1963-65 |
| | | DITZ 12235 | only | |
| | | DUP 8184 | | |
| Clipper Blue | BU 14 | RM BM042 | Midget | 1961 |
| | | DITZ 12297 | | |
| Smoke Gray | BU 15 | RM BM028 | MG1100 | 1963-67 |
| | | DITZ 32040 | | |
| Ice Blue | BU 18 | RM BM052 | Midget | 1962-64 |
| | | DITZ 12631 | | |
| Blue Royale | BU 38 | RM BM039 | Midget | 1970 |
| | | DITZ 12635 | MGB | 1970 |
| Bermuda Blue | BU 40 | RM BM158 | | |
| | | DITZ 12630 | MGB | 1970 |
| | | DUP 8582 | | |
| Riviera Blue | BU 44 | RM BM065 | Midget | 1965- |
| | | DITZ 13123 | MGB | 1965-68 |

| Colour | Factory code | Aftermarket codes (U.S.) | Model | Year |
|---|---|---|---|---|
| Riviera Silver Blue | BU 47 | | MGC | 1968 |
| Midnight Blue | BLVC 12 | RM BM171D | Midget | 1972-73 |
| | | DITZ 14245 | MGB | 1972-73 |
| | | DUP 30011 | | |
| Teal Blue | BLVC 18 | RM BM164 | Midget | 1971-74 |
| | | DITZ 14244 | MGB | 1971-74 |
| | | DUP 30006 | | |
| Tahiti Blue | BLVC 65 | DITZ 14866 (11) | Midget | 1975-77 |
| | | DITZ 15096 (12) | MGB | 1975-77 |
| | | DUP 43907 | | |
| Pageant Blue | BLVC 224 | DITZ 15231 | Midget | 1978-79 |
| | | DUP 45473AH | MGB | 1978-80 |

## *Mk I ('Frogeye') Sprite Colour Schemes*

| Colour | Interior trim colours |
|---|---|
| Speedwell Blue/Iris Blue (same colour: different names) | Dark Blue seats/Light Blue piping. Dark Blue trim. Black rubber mats. |
| Leaf Green | Dark Green/Dark Green piping. Green trim. Green mats. |
| Old English White | EITHER Red seats/White piping. Red trim. Red mats. OR Black seats/White piping. Black trim. Black mats. |
| Cherry Red | Red seats/White piping. Red Trim. Red mats. |
| Primrose | Black seats/Primrose piping. Black mats. Black Trim. |
| Whitehall Beige/Nevada (same colour: different names) | Cherry Red seats/White piping. Red Trim. Red mats |
| Dark Green | Green seats/Green piping. Green Trim. Green mats. |

N.B. There is some dispute as to whether the Dark Green colour combinations, as shown in BMC Body Service Parts List, ever actually existed. It could also be that Black seats with Black piping were used with Old English White bodywork.

291

# 7 Clubs & Specialists

**The following addresses and telephone numbers were believed to be correct at the time of going to press. However, as these are subject to change, particularly telephone area codes, no guarantee can be given for their continued accuracy.**

Of course, a good deal of the Midget's and Sprite's attractiveness comes from the pleasure they give to the person sitting in the driver's seat. But the lone pleasures of owning, maintaining, restoring and driving a Spridget are multiplied several times over when those pleasures and the experiences of them can be shared with others and when a little more can be learned about the car. The best way of meeting like-minded enthusiasts is by joining the appropriate one-make club which provides meetings, competitions and shows for the enthusiast to attend and which is the best source for all practical, down to earth information on running the car. And not only will there be social and practical benefits from joining the club, there will probably be financial ones too, saving the membership fee several times over.

Clubs and services are detailed in the following list with,

after each one, a brief résumé of what it has to offer. There are, of course, others, but the ones shown below are those which are most well known and which, in the author's opinion, have most to offer the Midget and Sprite owner.

## Clubs

**Midget and Sprite Club:**
They say, "What makes our club tick? This simple answer is the enthusiasm of our members towards their cars. MASC is a club run by enthusiasts for enthusiasts; no professionals or business interests. We all put something into the club and we all get something out in return."
Address: Midget and Sprite Club, General Secretary – Nigel Williams, 15 Foxcote, Kingswood,

Bristol BS15 2TX. To join the **Austin Healey Club** send an s.a.e. to Mrs C. Holmes, 4 Saxby Street, Leicester LE2 0ND.

**MG Owners' Club:**
Generally accepted as *the* British club for Midget owners. Social activities through semi-autonomous Area Centres. Special offers on spares and tools. Points system indicating members' rating of main specialist suppliers. National and "Mini-National" meetings. Professional, colour monthly magazine and annual Year Books. Goes Midget racing too. Address: MG Owners' Club, Membership Secretary, Octagon House, Swavesey, Cambridgeshire CR4 1BR.

**MG Car Club:** Direct descendent of original, factory supported club. Excellent for racing connections. Monthly magazine with good historical and technical

content. Secretaries for "Areas" and for most models of MG Not commercially minded. Address: MG Car Club, s.a.e. to Kimber House, PO Box 251, Abingdon, Oxon OX14 1FF.

*Other Clubs*
There are many area centres in both the UK, USA and other countries, such as Australia. Their contact addresses are varied and prone to change. Please contact one of the major British clubs, such as the MG Owners' Club, who will undoubtedly be pleased to assist.

## Specialists

**British Motor Industry Heritage Trust:** Among many other things, the Trust offers the Production Record Trace Service which enables owners of Sprites, Midgets and most other Rover Group makes and models to verify the original colour, trim, hood, equipment, manufacturing date and special features, if any, relating to their cars and recorded when the car was produced. Write to BMIHT at Heritage Motor Centre, Banbury Road, Gaydon, War, CV35 0BJ. Tel: 01926 641188. www.heritage-motor-centre.co.uk

**MG Enthusiast Ltd,** Hothouse Publishing, 5 North Street, Titchmarsh, Northants NN14 3DH. Tel: 01733 246500 www.mgenthusiast.com The only magazine devoted exclusively to the MG marque.

**Moss Europe Ltd:** Formerly Sprite and Midget Centre but now part of the international Moss organisation. Everything you could imagine and more for Sprites and Midgets including their own clearly illustrated Parts Manual. Find them at www.moss-europe.co.uk Tel: Head office: 0208 867 2020

**Moss Motors Ltd:** The parent company in the United States can be found at 440 Rutherford Street, Goleta, CA 93117. Tel: 001 805 968 1041.

**Spares and Restoration:** Spridgebits, who are featured throughout the book and who supplied most of the parts for use in it, have ceased trading.

The best way of finding a reputable specialist is to join a club, go to meetings and find out from others who is (and who is not) recommended.

**SIP (Industrial Products) Ltd:** Comprehensive range of quality workshop equipment: MIG welders, spot and arc welders, spray guns and compressors in all shapes and sizes. Keen prices! SIP (Industrial Products) Ltd., Gelders Hall Road, Shepshed, Loughborough, Leicestershire LE12 9NH. Tel: 01509 500300. www.sip-group.com

# ⑧ British & American Thread Systems

The Spridget 1958-1980 uses Unified National Fine (UNF) in almost all applications, which is completely compatible with American Fine (AF) or SAE threads. A few applications use a Unified National Coarse (UNC) compatible with American coarse threads (some studs into the block and gearcase). There are only a few applications of BSF (British Standard Fine) or BSW (British Standard Whitworth – coarse). The dampers (shock absorbers) use a BSF thread for their filler screws. All Lucas electrics use Whitworth until around 1969 when the change was made to metric.

### Threads per Inch

|  | BSW | UNC | BSF | UNF |
|---|---|---|---|---|
| ⅛ (.125) | 40 | (US) No. 5-40 |  |  |
| ³⁄₁₆ (.1875) | 24 | (US) No. 10-24 | 32 | (US) No. 10-32 (.190 dia) |
| ¼ (.250) | 20 | 20 (190 dia) | 26 | 28 |
| ⁵⁄₁₆ (.3125) | 18 | 18 | 22 | 24 |
| ⅜ (.375) | 16 | 16 | 20 | 24 |
| ⁷⁄₁₆ (.4375) | 14 | 14 | 18 | 20 |
| ½ (.500) | 12 | 13 | 16 | 20 |

**Note**: Although the BSW and UNC threads per inch are the same in popular sizes, the angle of the thread differs, and they are incompatible. The BSF and UNF are not compatible either, as the tpi are different for each dia.

Screws used in the MG are almost all crosshead. Slotted-head screws are simply not acceptable for a good restoration. A popular screw size in the MG is 2BA (British Association), but that size is fully compatible with the American No. 10-32 screw.

|  | Diameter | Threads/inch |  |
|---|---|---|---|
| **2BA** | .185 | 31.358 | (the BA screws use a metric pitch) |
| **No. 10-32** | .190 | 32 |  |
| **4BA** | .1417 | 38.5 | These screws are not as compatible as the 2BA or 10-32, but are infrequently used. |
| **No. 6-40** | .1372 | 40 |  |

Except for the interior panels and a very few applications in other places, all the screws are "machine thread" NOT self tapping.

## British Standard Pipe

In the applications listed below, BSP threads are used. These ARE NOT compatible with any American threading system, and the proper BSP screws and fittings MUST be used.

| Size | Diameter | Threads/inch |
|---|---|---|
| 1/8 | .3830 | 28 |
| 1/4 | .5180 | 19 |
| 3/8 | .6560 | 19 |
| 1/2 | .8250 | 14 |

## Uses of B.S.P. on Sprites and Midgets

| | | |
|---|---|---|
| Radiator drain hole (if fitted) | | ¼ BSP |
| Oil Cooler and fittings | | ½ BSP |
| Engine Block: | Sump drain plug | ¼ BSP |
| | Water drain plug | ¼ BSP |
| | Oil hole plug (left side) | ⅜ BSP |
| | Oil pressure relief valve | ½ BSP |
| | Oil outlet (right rear) | ½ BSP |
| Fuel tank: | drain (if fitted) | ¼ or ⅛ |
| | fuel line | ¼ BSP |
| Fuel pump: | banjo bolts | ⅜ BSP |
| Fuel line: | at bulkhead | ¼ BSP |

Most of these BSP applications require the use of BSF/BSW wrenches.

# British & American Technical Terms

*As this book has been written in England, it uses the appropriate English component names, phrases, and spelling. Some of these differ from those used in America. Normally, these cause no difficulty, but to make sure, a glossary is printed below. In ordering spare parts remember the parts list will probably use these words:*

| English | American | English | American |
|---------|----------|---------|----------|
| Aerial | Antenna | Layshaft (of gearbox) | Countershaft |
| Accelerator | Gas pedal | Leading shoe (of brake) | Primary shoe |
| Alternator | Generator (AC) | Locks | Latches |
| Anti-roll bar | Stabiliser or sway bar | Motorway | Freeway, turnpike etc. |
| Battery | Energizer | Number plate | License plate |
| Bodywork | Sheet metal | Paraffin | Kerosene |
| Bonnet (engine cover) | Hood | Petrol | Gasoline |
| Boot lid | Trunk lid | Petrol tank | Gas tank |
| Boot (luggage compartment) | Trunk | Pinking | Pinging |
| Bottom gear | 1st gear | Propellor shaft | Driveshaft |
| Bulkhead | Firewall | Quarter light | Quarter window |
| Cam follower or tappet | Valve lifter or tapper | Retread | Recap |
| Carburettor | Carburetor | Reverse | Back-up |
| Catch | Latch | Rocker cover | Valve cover |
| Choke/venturi | Barrel | Roof rack | Car-top carrier |
| Circlip | Snap-ring | Saloon | Sedan |
| Clearance | Lash | Seized | Frozen |
| Crownwheel | Ring gear (of differential) | Side indicator lights | Side marker lights |
| Disc (brake) | Rotor/disk | Side light | Parking light |
| Drop arm | Pitman arm | Silencer | Muffler |
| Drop head coupe | Convertible | Spanner | Wrench |
| Dynamo | Generator (DC) | Sill panel (beneath doors) | Rocker panel |
| Earth (electrical) | Ground | Split cotter (for valve spring cap) | Lock (for valve spring retainer) |
| Engineer's blue | Prussian blue | Split pin | Cotter pin |
| Estate car | Station wagon | Steering arm | Spindle arm |
| Exhaust manifold | Header | Sump | Oil pan |
| Fast back (Coupe) | Hard top | Tab washer | Tang; lock |
| Fault finding/diagnosis | Trouble shooting | Tailgate | Liftgate |
| Float chamber | Float bowl | Tappet | Valve lifter |
| Free-play | Lash | Thrust bearing | Throw-out bearing |
| Freewheel | Coast | Top gear | High |
| Gudgeon pin | Piston pin or wrist pin | Trackrod (of steering) | Tie-rod (or connecting rod) |
| Gearchange | Shift | Trailing shoe (of brake) | Secondary shoe |
| Gearbox | Transmission | Transmission | Whole drive line |
| Halfshaft | Axleshaft | Tyre | Tire |
| Handbrake | Parking brake | Van | Panel wagon/van |
| Hood | Soft top | Vice | Vise |
| Hot spot | Heat riser | Wheel nut | Lug nut |
| Indicator | Turn signal | Windscreen | Windshield |
| Interior light | Dome lamp | Wing/mudguard | Fender |

## Miscellaneous points

An oil seal is fitted to components lubricated by grease!

A 'damper' is a shock absorber, it damps out bouncing and absorbs shocks of bump impact. Both names are correct, and both are used haphazardly.

Note that British drum brakes are different from the Bendix type that is common in America, so different descriptive names result. The shoe end furthest from the hydraulic wheel cylinder is on a pivot; interconnection between the shoes as on Bendix brakes is most uncommon. Therefore the phrase 'Primary' or 'Secondary' shoe does not apply. A shoe is said to be 'Leading' or 'Trailing'. A 'Leading' shoe is one on which a point on the drum, as it rotates forward, reaches the shoe at the end worked by the hydraulic cylinder before the anchor end. The opposite is a 'Trailing' shoe and this one has no self-servo from the wrapping effect of the rotating drum.

# Haynes
# Restoration
# Manuals

**Haynes**
**Restoration Manual**
MGB (2nd Edition)

History    Mechanics
Buying     Interior
Specification  Electrics
Bodywork  Modifications

Lindsay Porter

**For more information on books please contact:** Customer Services,
**Haynes Publishing**, Sparkford, Yeovil, Somerset BA22 7JJ, UK
Tel. **01963 442030** Fax: **01963 440001**
Int. tel: **+44 1963 442030** Fax: **+44 1963 440001**
E-mail: **sales@haynes.co.uk** Website: **www.haynes.co.uk**